Realtime Web Apps

With HTML5 WebSocket, PHP, and jQuery

Jason Lengstorf
Phil Leggetter

Realtime Web Apps: With HTML5 WebSocket, PHP, and jQuery

ISBN 978-1-4302-4620-6

ISBN 978-1-4302-4621-3 (eBook)

Trademarked names, logos, and images may appear in this book. Rather than use a trademark symbol with every occurrence of a trademarked name, logo, or image we use the names, logos, and images only in an editorial fashion and to the benefit of the trademark owner, with no intention of infringement of the trademark.

The use in this publication of trade names, trademarks, service marks, and similar terms, even if they are not identified as such, is not to be taken as an expression of opinion as to whether or not they are subject to proprietary rights.

While the advice and information in this book are believed to be true and accurate at the date of publication, neither the authors nor the editors nor the publisher can accept any legal responsibility for any errors or omissions that may be made. The publisher makes no warranty, express or implied, with respect to the material contained herein.

President and Publisher: Paul Manning
Lead Editor: Ben Renow-Clarke
Technical Reviewer: Phil Leggetter
Editorial Board: Steve Anglin, Mark Beckner, Ewan Buckingham, Gary Cornell, Louise Corrigan,
    Morgan Ertel, Jonathan Gennick, Jonathan Hassell, Robert Hutchinson, Michelle Lowman, James Markham,
    Matthew Moodie, Jeff Olson, Jeffrey Pepper, Douglas Pundick, Ben Renow-Clarke, Dominic Shakeshaft,
    Gwenan Spearing, Matt Wade, Tom Welsh
Coordinating Editor: Anamika Panchoo
Copy Editor: Nancy Sixsmith
Compositor: SPi Global
Indexer: SPi Global
Artist: SPi Global
Cover Designer: Anna Ishchenko

Distributed to the book trade worldwide by Springer Science+Business Media New York, 233 Spring Street, 6th Floor, New York, NY 10013. Phone 1-800-SPRINGER, fax (201) 348-4505, e-mail orders-ny@springer-sbm.com, or visit www.springeronline.com. Apress Media, LLC is a California LLC and the sole member (owner) is Springer Science + Business Media Finance Inc (SSBM Finance Inc). SSBM Finance Inc is a Delaware corporation.

For information on translations, please e-mail rights@apress.com, or visit www.apress.com.

Apress and friends of ED books may be purchased in bulk for academic, corporate, or promotional use. eBook versions and licenses are also available for most titles. For more information, reference our Special Bulk Sales–eBook Licensing web page at www.apress.com/bulk-sales.

Any source code or other supplementary materials referenced by the author in this text is available to readers at www.apress.com. For detailed information about how to locate your book's source code, go to www.apress.com/source-code/.

For Tim the cat.

—Jason Lengstorf

Contents at a Glance

Contents

About the Authors

Jason Lengstorf is a 20-something from Portland, Oregon who has spent the last decade or so learning how to make a living without wearing pants. Along the way, he started Copter Labs, wrote a few books, drew a few pictures, and spoke to a few like-minded geeks. He's a music nerd, a foodie, a shameless coffee snob, and a big fan of wandering the globe.

Phil Leggetter is a Developer Evangelist at Pusher and has been developing and using real-time web technologies for more than 10 years. His focus is to help people use these technologies to build the next generation of interactive and engaging real-time web applications. He does this through writing articles; creating sample open-source applications; running workshops; and speaking at universities, companies, and conferences.

Acknowledgments

This book owes its very life to Phil Leggetter, who was able to keep things moving along. He added tons of background information about the technologies and did a great job of adding clear explanations and examples. Without his help, we'd probably still be stuck on the first half of the book.

To Ben and Ana, your patience was hugely appreciated.

To Alison, thank you for not leaving me when I stayed up all night writing.

To Nate, thanks for providing friendly competition and reminding me that there's always a next step once I've accomplished a goal.

To my dad, thanks for always being an inspiration. To my mom, thanks for putting up with me and Dad for all these years.

To Drew, thanks for coming on board at Copter Labs so I could clear time to work on this project. To Alex, Anne, Jason, Kevin, Rob, Roger, and Wes, thanks for being part of the Copter team.

To Richelle, Troy, Taunja, Chris, and all the other friends who help prevent me from becoming an unwashed hermit, thanks for continuing to invite me to do things.

—Jason Lengstorf

Introduction

A couple of years back, I went to a conference called "Keeping It Realtime." It was a collection of presenters who were deep in the trenches of the realtime world, solving problems that most of the rest of the world had never even heard about.

The power of this technology was staggering, and the number of places that it was already being used was pretty surprising. I wanted to know more, start using it *right then*. How could I start using this wonderful, magical new idea in my own applications?

I sat down in the audience for one of the hands-on sessions and was immediately lost. A small, shy dude with a beard was at the podium with his laptop, mumbling into the microphone and coding in Vim at *incredible* speeds. By the time I was able to figure out that he was initializing socket.io, he'd already gotten halfway through the meat of the app.

My spirits sank, and I started to wonder whether this kind of awesome technology was reserved only for that elite shadow group of secret ninja developers. If I can't keep up with a guy who is *teaching* this stuff, how am I ever supposed to build anything on my own?

If you've ever asked a really smart developer how to do something, you might know the feeling: when someone hits a certain level of smart, they can sometimes forget how to talk to the rest of us who haven't used that tech before. This puts us in a situation in which we can either dig through tons of complex code and specifications and rough documentation, or we can just give up.

This book is intended to help demystify realtime coding and make it accessible to any developer with medium PHP and JavaScript chops. If you want to use this stuff in real projects *right now*, and don't need to know how to build a Flash polyfill or maintain Node.js, this book is right up your alley.

We believe that while theory is fun and necessary, the real exciting part of development is in putting it to use and seeing it come to life. To that end, the technologies used in this book are simple to set up and don't require you to learn a new programming language or framework; the book is based on the same web technologies used in some of the most popular apps, websites, and content management systems out there today.

Realtime should belong to the caffeinated masses, so grab your coffee (or tea) and let's get started. You'll be up and running with realtime before it gets cold.

■ ■ ■

PART I

Getting Familiar with the Required Technologies

Building a web application isn't a one-dimensional exercise. Modern web developers will be required to leverage a number of technologies to build apps that meet the needs of their users.

In this part of the book, you'll become familiar with the technologies you'll use to build your first realtime web application. Since this project is leveraging some of the more common web technologies in use at the time of writing, much of this part of the book should be familiar to you and can be skipped if you feel comfortable without a review.

CHAPTER 1

■ ■ ■

What Is Realtime?

If you've been keeping up with trends in web development over the last year or two, no doubt you've seen the term *realtime* tossed around. But what *is* realtime? How is it different from current web technologies, and why should we bother using it?

To better understand what realtime means and how it's changing the Internet as we know it, let's look at the history of the problem it attempts to solve: how can we affect the state of our web apps on the client side without requiring any action on the user's part?

The Evolution of Media

Let's be honest: when it comes to information, we have a desire to hear the news first. This desire can be attributed to a natural thirst for knowledge, the perceived opportunity that being the first to know might give us, or simply because it means we can be the ones with all the gossip. In some cases, we may even value being the first to get the news more than we care what the news is about. (That, coincidentally, is the *entire* reason why hipsters exist.) We want to know first, and that means we want to know *the instant* this information becomes available.

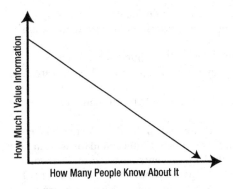

Figure 1-1. Perceived value of certain types of information tends to dwindle as it becomes commonplace

This relentless pursuit of staying current has driven us to where we are today: we weren't satisfied with cave paintings or handwritten tomes; the printing press gave us books and fliers, but we still wanted more; newspapers and other periodicals gave us updates as quickly as every morning, but that stuff all happened *yesterday*; and radio and television could only get us information in hours, or—on a good day—minutes.

The Internet gave us the ability to share information with global audiences. But it could still take a long time for the information to be discovered, and we relied on things like email and forums to spread the word. Google changed all that by making data much more discoverable. Even so, the speed of its page indexing meant that we would still need to wait for our data to be discoverable via search. The invention of "live blogging" meant that we could receive frequent updates if we knew where to look, and those destinations were frequently well known media brands.

Social media upped the ante and created a global network in which news could be shared as it occurred, by anybody. Services like Twitter were our primary sources of information during events such as the revolution in Egypt in 2011.[1] The first realtime web game-changer, however, was that for the first time, the instant that new information was posted it was also discoverable through search. This started to demonstrate the value of instant access to new information on the Internet, increased user expectation for "live content," and even lead to the well-known technology commentator Robert Scoble asking if "the real-time web was a threat to Google."[2]

Social media platforms were turning into realtime communication platforms. No sooner would you post a status update, than you would get a reply from one or more users. This fast, interactive feedback was very new to the majority of us who, outside of those of us that played Flash-based games, were used to Internet applications offering only relatively static single-user experiences. This new multiuser interactive functionality leads to a much more compelling and engaging user experience.

Media had evolved from offering delayed and static content to having the potential to be richer, live, and interactive. Users saw these experiences and the expectations they now have of their Internet application has dramatically increased.

Even with all this instant gratification, demonstrated by the Internet and social media, many sources still aren't giving us our news as live content or offering us interactive and engaging experiences. Why not?

Web Sites, Not Web Apps

The Internet has traditionally been used to share static content. A web site was simply a structure of static entities belonging to a single collection. The primary focus of a web site was to display its content, and the idea that "Content is King"[3] hasn't changed for many. Even when we came up with technologies to create "dynamic content," what we actually meant was that our server could now dynamically generate static content based on a differing, but defined, set of parameters and values.

The application we used to view the entities on the Internet, the Web Browser, naturally focused on ensuring that it met the needs of the day: downloading and rendering HTML and images, and understanding how to following links—and that was initially enough.

In the same way that forms of media were driven to evolve, so were our web sites. We wanted our web sites to look much nicer, so we introduced CSS. We wanted them to be more reactive to user input (can you believe you used to be able to charge for DHTML libraries? e.g., drop-down menus), so along came JavaScript (let's forget VBScript ever existed). These technologies enhanced the capabilities of the Web Browser, but focused on letting us enhance *pages* on our web site.

A few pioneers saw beyond static web sites and started thinking about dynamic web applications. With web apps, the focus shifts away from the server to the client. The client has to do much more work; it retrieves and loads content dynamically, it changes the user interface (UI) based on user feedback, and the UI is presented in a way that we would be traditionally associated with a desktop application. There's much less focus on pages reloading and the concept of a page in general. Content also becomes much less text-based, and we start to achieve much more visually appealing and interactive representations of data within a web application.

---

[1]http://en.wikipedia.org/wiki/2011_Egyptian_revolution

[2]http://scobleizer.com/2009/02/09/is-the-real-time-web-a-threat-to-google-search/

[3]http://en.wikipedia.org/wiki/Web_content#Content_is_king

HTTP Hacks

As more of us (we developers are the pioneers) started to build web applications, the demands on the web browser increased. Performance became a problem; not just the web browser application but also the machines that the browsers were running on. Those really pushing the boundaries of web technologies and web applications also hit a big stumbling block: HTTP.[4]

HTTP was designed to be a protocol in which a client makes a request for data and receives a response. However, some web applications began to require that information be sent from the server to the client. So we had to start hacking! Hacking can result in nonstandardized and complex solutions. Throw the state of feature support across web browsers into the mix, and you can imagine the complexity of some of the solutions to this problem (we'll cover some of them later).

It has taken solutions like Twitter and Facebook, with their enormous popularity, to demonstrate the benefit and need for experiences powered by realtime web technologies. This has lead to a vast improvement and availability of realtime web technologies, driven by demand.

But First: What Does "Realtime" Actually Mean?

The term *realtime* refers to the timely nature between an event's occurrence and our being made aware of it. The measurement in time between an event occurring and the delivery of that event really depends on the event. If the event is applying your foot to a car brake, then the time between your foot going down and the brakes being applied has to be absolutely minimal. However, if the event is sending a chat message in a soccer forum and it is displayed to other users, a few seconds is unlikely to make a big difference. Ultimately, the event needs to be delivered in a short enough amount of time for that event to still be relevant; to still have meaning within the context it applies. Imagine getting slapped in the face: there is no delay between the impact of the slap and the registration of pain. This is realtime. If there were a delay, it would be awfully confusing.

However, the ability to add any kind of realtime experience wasn't initially all that easy. But developers are not easily defeated and have come up with clever workarounds and "hacks" to solve the communication breakdown between the server and the client.

■ **Note** Some of the earliest methods of creating two-way communication with the server have been omitted here because they're not often used.

AJAX

As JavaScript started to become more prevalent, developers started to leverage the XMLHttpRequest object[5] to send HTTP requests *asynchronously*, or without requiring a reload of the current page. This is called *AJAX*, or Asynchronous JavaScript and XML.

This method is great for adding user triggered functionality to a web app, so still typically relied on an event in the browser, such as a click, and therefore didn't really solve any problems in the quest to keep content up-to-the-minute.

Polling

After AJAX took hold, it was a short jump to try and take the browser event out of the equation and to automate the process of getting new information. Developers set up a refresh interval using something like the JavaScript `setInterval()` function to check for updates every *n* seconds.

---

[4]en.wikipedia.org/wiki/Hypertext_Transfer_Protocol
[5]www.w3.org/TR/XMLHttpRequest/

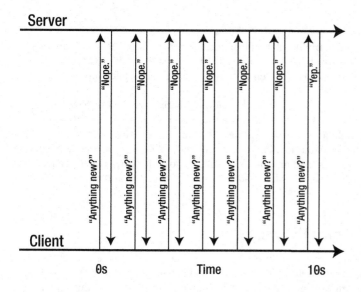

Figure 1-2. *Polling sends HTTP requests frequently to check for new information*

To better understand just how wasteful this can be, you can think of this communication as a conversation between the client and server:

```
CLIENT: Hi! Can I have some data?
SERVER: Sure. Here you go!
[time passes]
CLIENT: Do you have any new data for me?
SERVER: No.
[time passes]
CLIENT: Do you have any new data for me?
SERVER: No.
[time passes]
CLIENT: Do you have any new data for me?
SERVER: No.
[time passes]
CLIENT: Do you have any new data for me?
SERVER: I do! Here you go!
```

Just like real life, conversations like these between the client and server are both annoying and not very productive.

Although this polling solution is definitely a start, it has its shortcomings. Most notably, it creates a lot of empty requests, which create a lot of unnecessary overhead for an app. That overhead can prevent an app from scaling well: if an app polls once a second for new data, and 100,000 users are all using the app simultaneously, that's 6,000,000 requests per minute.

If you take into account the overhead of each HTTP request—in a test by Peter Lubbers, each request/response totaled 871 bytes[6]—there's a lot of extra information being sent back and forth just to find out that nothing new has happened on the server.

---

[6]http://soa.sys-con.com/node/1315473

HTTP Long-Polling

The next step in the realtime evolutionary chain is HTTP *long-polling*, which is the practice of opening an HTTP request for a set period of time to listen for a server response. If there is new data, the server will send it and close the request; otherwise, the request is closed after the interval limit is reached and a new one will be opened.

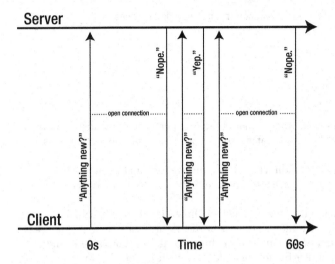

Figure 1-3. *HTTP long-polling keeps an HTTP request open for a period of time to check for updates*

Compared with standard polling, this is much more efficient. It saves on overhead and reduces the number of requests sent by the app. The client and server conversation then becomes the following:

```
CLIENT: Hi! Can I have some data?
SERVER: Sure. Here you go!
CLIENT: Thanks! I'm ready for more, if it comes in.
[time passes]
SERVER: I have new data for you! Here you go!
CLIENT: Thanks! I'm ready for more, if it comes in.
```

Much better. This approach provides a mechanism by which the server can alert the client about new data *without requiring any action on the part of the client*.

One of the main problems with HTTP long-polling can be seen if there is a requirement for client/server bidirectional communication. Once the long-polling HTTP connection is open, the only way for the client to communicate with the server is to make another HTTP request. This can result in double the resources being used: one for server-to-client messages and another for client-to-server messages. The exact impact of this really depends on how much bidirectional communication is occurring; the more chatty the client and server are with each other, the greater the resource drain.

Another problem with this approach is that between long-polling requests there is a short period where it's possible for the data on the client to be out of sync with the data on the server. Only when the connection has been re-established can the client check to see if there is any new data available. The negative impact of this really depends on the data, but if the data is highly time-sensitive, it's definitely not a good thing.

HTTP Streaming

HTTP *streaming* is very similar to HTTP long-polling, except the connection isn't closed when new data is available or at a given interval. Instead, new data is pushed over the existing connection which remains open.

The conversation between client and server now becomes the following:

```
CLIENT: Hi! Can I have some data? And please let me know whenever any new data comes along.
SERVER: Sure. Here you go!
[time passes]
SERVER: I have new data for you! Here you go!
[time passes]
SERVER: I have more new data for you! Here you go!
```

The benefit of this solution is that the connection between the client and server is persisted so the instant new data is available it can be sent to the client, and any new data after that is also sent over the same connection. This ensures that the server and client are kept in sync.

HTTP streaming does still suffer from an inability to offer bidirectional communication and therefore the potential resource implications associated with the necessity to use a second connection for client-to-server communication.

One big problem with the HTTP streaming approach is the inconsistencies of how it is achieved within different web browsers. In Gecko-based browsers, it is possible to use multipart replace headers which indicate to the browser to replace the older content that was last received with newer content. In other browsers this isn't possible, so the response buffer keeps on growing until there is no other choice but to close and reopen the connection to the server.

Additional Problems with HTTP-based Solutions in Web Browsers

The requirement to use multiple connections for bidirectional communication and cross-browser implementation differences isn't the only problem with HTTP-based solutions. Browsers also restricted the destination of HTTP requests from a web page and the number of connections that could be established.

The capability for JavaScript running in a web page to make a request to the server has long been restricted to only allowing a request to the same domain.[7] For example, if the web page is www.example.com/index.html, JavaScript could only make a request to a resource on www.example.com or by manipulating the value of document.domain in JavaScript, it is possible to make a request to any example.com subdomain such as sub.example.com. This restriction was put in place by browser vendors for security reasons but, as with a number of security restrictions, it blocked the legitimate use cases for making a request to other domains. The need to make these requests has now been addressed with cross-origin resource sharing (CORS).[8] CORS has good browser support,[9] but there are obvious older browser considerations.

The restriction on the number of connections that could be made was enforced per-domain e.g. requests to www.example.com. In earlier browsers, this meant as few as two connections could only be made to the same domain. For HTTP-based solutions, this meant that you could only have one page of a web app or site open which was using HTTP long-polling or streaming. If you tried to open a second page the connections would fail. The workaround for this was to have lots of subdomains that mapped back to the same server. Connection restrictions are still enforced in modern browsers, but the number of connections allowed is now much more reasonable.[10]

---

[7] http://en.wikipedia.org/wiki/Same_origin_policy
[8] http://en.wikipedia.org/wiki/Cross-origin_resource_sharing
[9] http://caniuse.com/#search=cors
[10] www.browserscope.org/?category=network

A NOTE ON THE TERMINOLOGY

There are a number of different terms that have been used to describe the HTTP-based realtime web solutions. Most of these are umbrella terms that encompass the various methods developers use to achieve a server to client communication over HTTP.

These terms include Comet, HTTP Server Push, and AJAX Push, among a slew of others. The problem is that although some of these terms have very specific definitions and techniques—especially Comet—they tend to hold different meanings for different people.

The position held in this book is that *Comet* is a term used to define a paradigm within an application structure: namely that of simulating bidirectional communication between the server and the client using two HTTP connections.

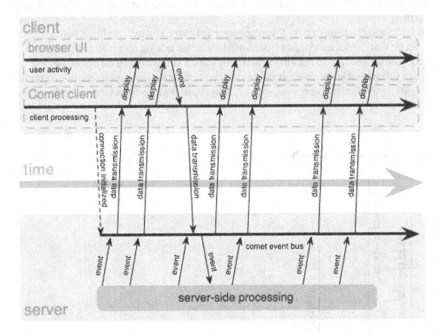

Figure 1-4. *The Comet paradigm means two-way communication between client and server*[11]

> Comet applications can deliver data to the client at any time, not only in response to user input. The data is delivered over a single, previously-opened connection.
>
> —Alex Russell

There have even been arguments that newer technologies such as HTML5 WebSockets are *part* of the Comet paradigm and not a replacement for it. However, Alex Russell (who coined the term) has now confirmed that we should consider *Comet* as an umbrella term for old HTTP-based hacks and look to the future with a new technology called WebSockets.[12]

---

[11]Diagram and quote source: http://infrequently.org/2006/03/comet-low-latency-data-for-the-browser/
[12]http://j.mp/websockets-comet

*Are Web Sockets a form of Comet? Or is Comet just the HTTP hacks? I'm gonna go for the latter definition.
The phrase and the hacks should probably ride off into the sunset together. I, for one, welcome our non-
HTTP realtime overlords. To the extent that we can forget about old browsers, we can all get on board
with "Web Sockets" and the need for any particular umbrella goes away.*

—Alex Russell

The Solution: WebSockets

No doubt you've heard people talking about HTML5 and all its neat new features. Two of these new features directly apply to realtime web technologies and client server communication—a fantastic result demonstrating that the web standards organizations and browser vendors really do listen to our feedback.

Server-Sent Events and the EventSource API[13] are a formalization of the HTTP streaming solution but there is one more solution that's even more exciting.

You may have heard the term *WebSockets* a time or two. If you've never really looked into realtime before, WebSockets may not have shown up on your radar except as a buzzword in articles talking about all the great new features of HTML5. The reason why WebSockets are so exciting is that they offer a standardized way of achieving what we've been trying to do through Comet hacks for years. It means we can now achieve *client server bidirectional realtime communication over a single connection*. It also comes with built-in *support for communication to be made cross-domain*.

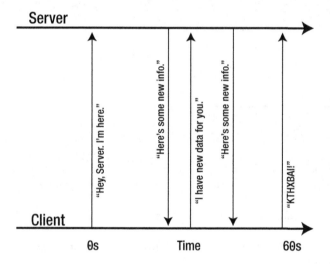

Figure 1-5. *Websockets open a full-duplex connection, allowing bidirectional client server communication*

The WebSocket specification is part of HTML5, which means that web developers can use the WebSocket protocol in modern browsers.[14]

---

[13]www.w3.org/TR/eventsource/

[14]http://caniuse.com/#feat=websockets

According to the WHATWG,[15] the WebSocket protocol defines a standardized way to add realtime communication in web applications:

The WebSocket protocol enables two-way communication between a user agent running untrusted code running in a controlled environment to a remote host that has opted-in to communications from that code. The security model used for this is the Origin-based security model commonly used by Web browsers. The protocol consists of an initial handshake followed by basic message framing, layered over TCP. The goal of this technology is to provide a mechanism for browser-based applications that need two-way communication with servers that does not rely on opening multiple HTTP connections (e.g. using XMLHttpRequest or <iframe>s and long polling).[16]

One of the most beneficial implications of widespread WebSocket support is in scalability: because WebSockets use a single TCP connection for communication between the server and client instead of multiple, separate HTTP requests, the overhead is dramatically reduced.

The WebSocket Protocol

Because full-duplex communication cannot be achieved using HTTP, WebSocket actually defines a whole new *protocol*, or method of connecting to a server from a client.

This is accomplished by opening an HTTP request and then asking the server to "upgrade" the connection to the WebSocket protocol by sending the following headers:[17]

```
GET /chat HTTP/1.1
Host: server.example.com
Upgrade: websocket
Connection: Upgrade
Sec-WebSocket-Key: dGhlIHNhbXBsZSBub25jZQ==
Origin: http://example.com
Sec-WebSocket-Protocol: chat, superchat
Sec-WebSocket-Version: 13
```

If the request is successful, the server will return headers that look like these:

```
HTTP/1.1 101 Switching Protocols
Upgrade: websocket
Connection: Upgrade
Sec-WebSocket-Accept: s3pPLMBiTxaQ9kYGzzhZRbK+xOo=
Sec-WebSocket-Protocol: chat
```

This exchange is called a *handshake*, and it's required to establish a WebSocket connection. Once a successful handshake occurs between the server and the client, a two-way communication channel is established, and both the client and server can send data to each other independently.

Data sent after the handshake is enclosed in *frames*, which are essentially chunks of information. Each frame starts with a 0x00 byte and ends with a 0xFF byte, meaning that every message sent has only two bytes of overhead in addition to the message's size.

---

[15]http://wiki.whatwg.org/wiki/FAQ#The_WHATWG
[16]www.whatwg.org/specs/web-socket-protocol/
[17]These example headers were borrowed from http://tools.ietf.org/html/rfc6455

So we've made it very clear that this is great news for web developers. But it's not all unicorns and ice cream cones, unfortunately: as ever, we'll be waiting for a minority of users and companies to upgrade to modern browsers. We're also going to be waiting for some parts of the Internet infrastructure to catch up. For instance, some proxies and firewalls block legitimate WebSocket connections. This doesn't mean we can't start using them in our applications, however.

Why Bother Learning about Realtime Web Technologies?

You might be wondering why it's worth learning any of this; this technology may initially seem complicated, hard to support, difficult to learn, and it's too new to matter.

The truth is that realtime technology is already changing the way we interact with the web: as mentioned earlier, social networks such as Facebook are using realtime components now; Spike TV worked with the company Loyalize to allow viewers of the season finale of *Deadliest Warrior* to participate in a number of live polls that altered the course of the television program;[18] Google has added realtime functionality into several of its projects, including Google Docs and Google Analytics.

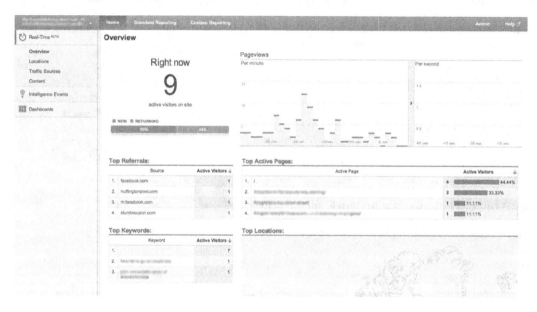

Figure 1-6. *Google Analytics uses realtime technology to display analytics data*

If we hope to stay current as web developers, we need to embrace realtime technology sooner rather than later. Fortunately for us, there are whole companies dedicated to making the move from the boring old pull-powered web to the spankin' new holymolyawesome realtime-powered web. All we have to do is think of something cool to build with it.

---

[18]www.adweek.com/news/technology/deadliest-warrior-finale-close-social-tv-feedback-loop-134782

Using Realtime Web Technologies in Your Apps Now

Although you may not be able to start relying entirely on WebSocket technology for your new web app, there are a growing number of companies and projects aiming to give you access to realtime web functionality *today*. Their approaches vary from using (gasp!) Flash[19], which has actually had socket support for years, as a fallback when WebSockets are not natively available to focusing on the HTTP-based solutions we mentioned earlier.

Some of the options include Socket.io,[20] Faye,[21] SignalR,[22] PubNub,[23] Realtime.co,[24] and Pusher[25] (for a more comprehensive list of solutions see the Realtime Web Technologies Guide).[26]

We'll be focusing on using Pusher in this book.

Summary

Realtime is what's happening now. Using this functionality, we can let the client know that new data is available without incurring a ton of overhead, which allows us to create apps that give our users live content experiences with updated information *as it becomes available* instead of after they request updates. More importantly, it lets us build interactive functionality that provides a much more engaging experience for the users of our applications. This keeps them coming back for more.

Now that you've seen where realtime comes from, what it means, how it works, and the benefits it provides, you can start choosing the tools to build your first realtime web application. In the next chapter, we'll discuss all the component technologies and programming languages you'll be using to build the app.

---

[19]https://github.com/gimite/web-socket-js
[20]http://socket.io/
[21]http://faye.jcoglan.com/
[22]http://signalr.net/
[23]http://www.pubnub.com/
[24]http://www.realtime.co/
[25]http://pusher.com/
[26]http://www.leggetter.co.uk/real-time-web-technologies-guide

CHAPTER 2

■ ■ ■

The Tools

In this chapter, you'll get a rough idea of the app you'll be building in order to learn how to use realtime web technologies. You'll be using that rough idea to determine the tools needed to build the app, as well as doing a quick once-over of the role and function of each.

By the end of this chapter, you should be refreshed on the technologies you already know, and ready to start learning the new bits.

What Are We Building?

Before we do anything else, it's probably a good idea to take a look at what we're trying to build. This should give us a rough outline of what the app needs to do, which allows us to create a list of tools that we'll need to make it all happen.

Our goal over the course of this book is to create a question and answer app. This app will allow a presenter to create a "room" that attendees can then join.

Attendees will be able to ask a question that will be immediately displayed on the presenter's device—anything with a browser, such as a laptop, tablet, or smartphone—to be answered. If another attendee has already asked the question, attendees will be able to vote for the answer to give the presenter an indication of which questions are most pressing.

The presenter will be able to mark a question as answered and will also be able to close a room when the presentation is over. The result of these actions will instantly be shown to all attendees.

What Does That Mean Development-Wise?

Now that we know the basic capabilities of the app, we need to break it into the various layers, which will also help us separate the app into technologies.

First, we need a user interface so that the users have **an easy way to interact with our application**. Without a great user interface, it doesn't matter how cool or useful our app is; it simply won't get used if it's difficult or confusing.

Second, we need to **process user requests and handle the various actions** they perform during the course of interaction with the app. For the app to be useful, it will need to do stuff.

Third, we need to **store user-supplied application data** so that rooms can be archived, settings stored, and various other pieces of data can persist throughout the app.

Fourth, the **updates need to be instant**. If users have to constantly refresh to get data, there's a much higher probability for overlap of questions and missed information. The usefulness of this app depends almost entirely on the realtime nature of information delivery.

Finally, we need to ensure that it's **easy and painless to authenticate** and start using the site. Users will likely be using this app for the first time right as a presentation is starting, so they won't have a lot of time to fill out personal details or check for confirmation e-mails; we need to get them up and running with the app as close to instantly as possible.

Choosing Our Tools

Now that we have a rough idea of the various pieces of the app, we can choose technologies to meet the needs of each piece. Let's take a look at the various technologies you'll be using to build this application and dig into the role each one will play.

HTML5

HTML5 is one of those technologies that created a huge stir in the development world, so its meaning has been heavily diluted by marketers, bloggers, and the general geek media.

While the release of HTML5 meant a lot of changes and improvements to the way we develop websites, we're focusing on a few key pieces that will help you make the app possible.

■ **Tip** If you want a full overview of HTML5, the additions and improvements it has made from the previous specification, there is an excellent walkthrough at `http://diveintohtml5.info/`

Why Do We Need It?

HTML5 will provide several things that we will need to make our app work in the manner we want, namely these:

- **Markup to create our app's user interface:** Without a markup language, it would be difficult to present the application data to the user in a way that is easy to understand. Nearly every website and web application on the Internet uses some form of HTML to present its data, and ours is no different.

- **WebSockets to allow realtime interactions between the presenter and the attendees:** We'll go into more detail on this later in the chapter.

- **Cleaner, easier syntax than the previous HTML specification:**[1] The new elements in HTML5—such as `<header>` and `<section>`—make markup much easier to scan and debug, which reduces maintenance headaches and speeds up our initial development.

- **The data attribute, which allows us to include extra data easily:** This on its own is not particularly useful, but when we pair it with jQuery it provides a really simple and valid syntax for handling special effects and events. You'll learn more about this later on, when you start using jQuery.

- **More robust form elements to improve the user interface:** Originally, HTML only supported a pitiful few input types, which meant that developers had to shoehorn most data into an `<input>` with `type="text"` and rely on client- and server-side validation scripts to make sure that the proper information was provided. While HTML5 hasn't fully solved the problem of validation yet, it *has* provided us with many more useful input types—including `e-mail`, `number`, and URL—which improve the user experience on some modern browsers.

What Role Does it Play?

In our application, HTML5 will play the role of the app's skeleton. It will provide a structure into which data and effects will fit.

---

[1] This is 100% the opinion of the authors.

How Does it Work?

HTML5 is interpreted by the browser, which reads the HTML tags and assigns presentational styles. These can be modified with CSS, which we'll cover next.

■ **Note** Because this book assumes a working knowledge of HTML, only the new features of HTML5 that will be used in this book are going to be explained. If you need more information on HTML or HTML5, check out *Beginning HTML5 and CSS3*,[2] by Christopher Murphy, Richard Clark, Oli Studholme, and Divya Manian.

EXERCISE 2-1: CREATE AN HTML FILE USING HTML5 TAGS

Here's a basic example of HTML5 markup using some of the new tags:

```
<!doctype html>
<html lang="en">

    <head>
        <meta charset="utf-8" />
        <title>Realtime Web Apps &ndash; Exercise 02-01</title>
    </head>

    <body>

        <header>
            <h1><em>Realtime Web Apps</em> &ndash; Exercise 02-01</h1>
            <p>
                Published on
                <time datetime="2012-05-28T20:26:00-07:00">May 28, 2012</time>.
            </p>
        </header>

        <section>
            <p>
                This is an example HTML file to demonstrate really basic
                HTML5 markup.
            </p>
            <p>
                We're using several of the new HTML5 elements, including
                the <code>&lt;section&gt;</code> and
                <code>&lt;time&gt;</code> elements.
            </p>
        </section>
```

---

[2]http://www.apress.com/9781430228745

```
    <footer>
        <p>All content &copy; 2012 Jason Lengstorf &amp; Phil Leggetter</p>
    </footer>

</body>

</html>
```

This code, when loaded in a browser, will be rendered similar to Figure 2-1.

Figure 2-1. *The browser output generated by our HTML5 markup*

CSS3

Similar to HTML5, CSS3 has been over-hyped and watered down. At its core, the adoption of the CSS3 spec was a step toward removing our dependence on hacky techniques and tons of images to create cool effects on our websites. It introduced support for visual effects—drop shadows, rounded edges, gradients, and more—and gave developers a way to use nonstandard fonts without Flash or JavaScript hacks. It provided new ways to select elements and gave us a way to animate elements on a page without using Flash or JavaScript.

Why Do We Need It?

CSS3 gives us tools to do some pretty cool effects that will improve our app. These include:

- **Visual effects to make the user interface look good:** We're visual creatures, and we tend to be drawn to things that are visually appealing. You'll use CSS3 to give the app a little flair using things like drop shadows and gradients.

- **Non-essential animations to improve the user experience:** Since they're not fully supported yet, we can't rely on CSS3 transitions for essential animations, but we can definitely use them to add some extra pizzazz for users on modern browsers.

- **Style rules to tell the browser how to display the markup:** In order to give our app its basic look and feel, we need to create a stylesheet with rules to tell the browser what each element on the page looks like. This is the overarching purpose of CSS.

What Role Does It Play?

For our purposes, CSS3 will act as the visual layer. It will give the app its "skin" and provide that polished aesthetic we're after and create small, non-essential effects to enhance the user experience for those who are using browsers that support them.

How Does It Work?

CSS is linked into the HTML document via a `link` tag in the document's `head`. It is then parsed by the browser to apply style rules to the elements contained in the markup. This book assumes basic knowledge of CSS, so we'll be covering only the new features of CSS3 that you'll be using in the application.

EXERCISE 2-2: ADD CSS TO THE PAGE

Let's continue with our code from Exercise 2-1 and add some CSS to the page. Start by creating a new folder called `styles` in the same folder as the HTML file, and create a new file in `styles` called `02.css`.

Next, add a `<link>` tag to the HTML file we created in Exercise 02-01 in the `<head>` section. This will load our CSS file:

```
<head>
    <meta charset="utf-8" />
    <title>Realtime Web Apps &ndash; Exercise 02-01</title>
    <link rel="stylesheet" href="styles/02.css" />
</head>
```

The CSS file is empty right now, so let's add a few rules to give our HTML some style. We'll include some CSS3 for extra flair as well:

```
/*
 * Exercise 02-02, Realtime Web Apps
 *
 * @author Jason Lengstorf <jason@copterlabs.com>
 * @author Phil Leggetter <phil@leggetter.co.uk>
 */

html { background: #efefdc; }

body {
    width: 660px;
    margin: 40px auto;
    background: #def;
    border: 2px solid #779;

    /* Creates two shadow effects: outer and inner */
    -webkit-box-shadow: 0 1px 6px #88a, inset 0 -1px 10px white;
    -moz-box-shadow: 0 1px 6px #88a, inset 0 -1px 10px white;
    -o-box-shadow: 0 1px 6px #88a, inset 0 -1px 10px white;
```

```
    -ms-box-shadow: 0 1px 6px #88a, inset 0 -1px 10px white;
    box-shadow: 0 1px 6px #88a, inset 0 -1px 10px white;
}

section {
    margin: 20px 30px 10px;
    padding: 20px 20px 10px;
    overflow: hidden;
    background: white;
    border: 1px solid #dfdfef;

    /* Creates two shadow effects: outer and inner */
    -webkit-box-shadow: inset 0 1px 4px #88a, 0 1px 10px white;
    -moz-box-shadow: inset 0 1px 4px #88a, 0 1px 10px white;
    -o-box-shadow: inset 0 1px 4px #88a, 0 1px 10px white;
    -ms-box-shadow: inset 0 1px 4px #88a, 0 1px 10px white;
    box-shadow: inset 0 1px 4px #88a, 0 1px 10px white;
}

body,section {
    /* Sets a border radius for every element that needs it */
    -webkit-border-radius: 15px;
    -moz-border-radius: 15px;
    -o-border-radius: 15px;
    -ms-border-radius: 15px;
    border-radius: 15px;
}

footer { margin: 0 0 10px; }

h1 {
    margin: 20px 30px 10px;
    color: #446;
    font: bold 30px/40px georgia, serif;
}

p {
    margin: 0 0 10px;
    font: 15px/20px sans-serif;
    color: #557;
}

h1,p { text-shadow: 1px 1px 1px #88a; }

header p {
    margin: 0;
    padding: 2px 40px;
    border-top: 1px solid #779;
    border-bottom: 1px solid #779;
    color: white;
    font-size: 12px;
```

```
    font-style: italic;
    line-height: 20px;
    text-shadow: 1px 1px 1px #779;

    /* Adds a gradient fade */
    background: #889;
    background-image: -webkit-linear-gradient(top, #aac 0%, #88a 100%);
    background-image: -moz-linear-gradient(top, #aac 0%, #88a 100%);
    background-image: -o-linear-gradient(top, #aac 0%, #88a 100%);
    background-image: -ms-linear-gradient(top, #aac 0%, #88a 100%);
    background-image: linear-gradient(top, #aac 0%, #88a 100%);
    background-image: -webkit-gradient(
                        linear,
                        left top,
                        left bottom,
                        color-stop(0, #aac),
                        color-stop(1, #88a)
                      );
}

footer p {
    margin: 0;
    color: #889;
    font: italic 12px/1.67em sans-serif;
    text-align: center;
    text-shadow: 1px 1px 1px white;
}
```

Save these rules in 02.css; then save and refresh the HTML file to see the rules take effect (see Figure 2-2). For best results, use an up-to-date browser that supports CSS3 effects, but the stylesheet will work in any browser because only non-essential effects were added with CSS3.

Figure 2-2. *The (slightly updated) HTML file with a CSS stylesheet applied*

■ **Note** You may have noticed that there are a few rules that are declared multiple times with a vendor prefix (the `-webkit-`, `-moz-`, and such) that might look a little confusing. Because CSS3 isn't 100 percent finalized yet, each browser handles the new rules just a little differently.

This could cause issues for developers if there was no way to compensate between browsers, so vendor prefixes were added to allow for different rules to be applied to each browser in kind. The hope is that someday soon there will be one unified syntax for each of the new CSS3 rules, but while things are still in flux, this is a necessary evil.

JavaScript and jQuery

JavaScript is a client-side scripting language, which means that it is executed on the user's computer. This makes it ideal for tasks such as animating the elements on a page, doing calculations on-the-fly, and various other actions that would otherwise be extremely inconvenient if they required a page refresh.

JavaScript also allows for certain server-side actions to be performed by calling scripts asynchronously. This technique is commonly referred to as AJAX: Asynchronous JavaScript and XML. The *XML* part of this term came about because the request would commonly return XML data. Although this isn't the common use case anymore, the name has stuck. What AJAX allows, in essence, is for a different page to be loaded and its contents returned to the current page using JavaScript. The page that is loaded can receive data from the AJAX request, process it, store it, retrieve new data, and return that data to the script that requested it. (We talked about this a little earlier in Chapter 1).

For all its capabilities, however, JavaScript has long been a troublesome animal due to its less-than-exemplary documentation, sometimes confusing syntax, and inconsistent implementation on other browsers. Thus the learning curve for JavaScript had been steep and it required a serious time investment from any developer hoping to use it in a project.

In response to this frustration, several groups and individuals set out to simplify JavaScript and make it accessible to everyone. They created frameworks that handled common tasks, overcame cross-browser troubles, and provided good documentation and support communities for new developers.

There were dozens of these frameworks at first, including MooTools, YUI, Dojo, Prototype, and jQuery. Each had advantages and disadvantages, but the one that seemed to bolster the most community support was jQuery, largely for its great documentation and wonderfully simple syntax.

Why Do We Need It?

Improved JavaScript documentation, a general uptake in the use of the technology, and language standardization has lead to a much better development experience for developers using the language. However, there are still cases in which a library can be very useful. jQuery will deal with any outstanding cross-browser inconsistencies and also give us the tools we need to perform tasks such as these:

- **Creating animations to indicate what's happening in the app:** Showing the user what's happening by animating various actions is a great way to enhance the user interface and it adds to that overall polish that we're shooting for.

- **Handling user events:** When the user interacts with the app—whether it's a click, a tap, or a swipe—the browser fires an event that jQuery can detect and perform a task based on the user's action.

- **Displaying the results of realtime events:** When certain actions are performed by users, the app will need to display the result of the action to all the users currently interacting with it. You'll be using WebSocket technology and Pusher to handle sending the data—we'll cover this shortly—but information received over the WebSocket connection will trigger an event, just like a click or any other user interaction. We'll use jQuery to handle those events and perform tasks based on what's happening in the app.

What Role Does It Play?

jQuery will play the part of half the brains of the app. It will notice anything that changes in the app based on a user interaction or realtime events and handle that change appropriately, either by animating something, or updating the user when a change is made somewhere else (as on another user's device).

How Does It Work?

JavaScript is loaded into the HTML markup using a `<script>` tag, which is parsed by the browser. This book assumes a basic knowledge of jQuery, so a lot of the basics will be skipped for brevity.

■ **Note**   If you want to study up on the basics of jQuery, grab a copy of *Pro PHP and jQuery*[3] by Jason Lengstorf.

> ## EXERCISE 2-3: ADD A SIMPLE JQUERY EFFECT

To experiment with jQuery, let's add a small script to the HTML file that will do the following:

1. Bind to hover events on all `<code>` elements.

2. When a hover occurs, it will then take the text from the tag that the user has hovered their mouse over and use the text contents of that element to identify other elements on the page; for example, `<code>&lt;time&gt;</code>` identifies other `<time>` elements.

3. The background of the other elements will then be set to yellow.

The first step is to create a new folder called `scripts` in the same directory as your HTML file and create a new file called `03.js` inside it.

Next, load jQuery and `03.js` into the HTML file using the `<script>` tag, inserting them just above the closing `</body>` tag:

```
</footer>

<script src="http://code.jquery.com/jquery-1.7.2.min.js"></script>
<script src="scripts/03.js"></script>

</body>
```

---

[3]http://www.apress.com/9781430228479

Now we need to add our code into 03.js. Going into more detail about the code, the steps it will follow are as follows:

- Bind two functions to the hover event for each <code> tag: one for when the mouse enters the hover state, and one for when it exits the hover.

- Detect the tag name inside the <code> element using jQuery's .text() method; use a simple regular expression to remove any characters that are not alphanumeric (to remove the opening and closing brackets); and cast the matched string as a String to prevent a bug.

- On hover, find matching elements, store the original background color on each element using .data(); then change the background color to yellow using .css().

- When the hover ends, retrieve the original background color with .data(); then restore it using .css().

```
/*
 * Exercise 02-03, Realtime Web Apps
 *
 * @author Jason Lengstorf <jason@copterlabs.com>
 * @author Phil Leggetter <phil@leggetter.co.uk>
 */

(function($) {

    // Highlights the element contained in the <code> tag
    $('code').hover(
        function() {
            var elem = $(getElementName(this)),
                bg   = elem.css("background");
            elem.data('bg-orig', bg).css({ "background": "yellow" });
        },
        function() {
            var elem = $(getElementName(this)),
                bg   = elem.data('bg-orig');
            $(elem).css({ "background": bg });
        }
    );

    /**
     * Retrieves the element name contained within a code tag
     */
    function getElementName(element) {
        return String($(element).text().match(/\w+/));
    }

})(jQuery);
```

Save your code; then reload the HTML and mouse over one of the <code> tags to see the results (shown in Figure 2-3).

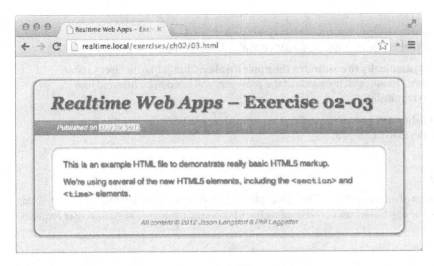

Figure 2-3. *A simple jQuery effect highlights HTML5 tags when their names are hovered. The <time> element is highlighted when the user hovers over the <time> text*

PHP

PHP is a server-side scripting language that provides powerful tools for processing data. It was created to give developers a way to build dynamic content in their HTML markup, and has since grown into one of the most widely used server-side scripting languages on the Internet.

PHP isn't the only language we could use because there are many languages that let us build web applications. Many languages also let us use realtime web technologies, but some do it better than others. Node.js is heavily associated with realtime web technologies, mainly due to its evented nature and socket.io,[4] which is probably the most well known of realtime web frameworks; Ruby has a number of solutions with the most popular being FAYE;[5] .NET has a reasonably new Microsoft-backed solution called SignalR;[6] Python has a number of solutions based on the Tornado framework;[7] and so on.

Interestingly enough, PHP applications, which most commonly run on Apache, don't tend to be all that well suited to realtime web technologies because they have been built with HTTP and the request response paradigm in mind. They haven't been built to handle maintaining large numbers of persistent connections or even high volume polling. This actually gives us a great reason to use Pusher, which, as a hosted service, takes away the potential pain of maintaining our realtime web technology infrastructure.

---

[4] http://socket.io
[5] http://faye.jcoglan.com
[6] http://signalr.net/
[7] http://www.tornadoweb.org/

Why Do We Need It?

Your app will be leveraging several of PHP's features to add functionality into the app, such as these:

- **Generating output dynamically to customize the app's display:** Things like the user's name, the name of the current "room," and the name of the presenter will need to be inserted into the HTML markup dynamically.

- **Hooking into the Pusher API to enable realtime communication:** We'll go over this later in this chapter, and in detail in Chapter 3.

What Role Does It Play?

If JavaScript/jQuery is half the brain of our app, PHP will be playing the role of the other half. It will do the heavy lifting as far as processing the data sent to the app by our users and sending back processed responses to various user requests.

How Does It Work?

PHP is a *preprocessor*, which means that it does its calculations and data manipulation prior to the page being rendered. This means that PHP code is embedded into the markup, and the server reads the PHP and replaces it with the proper output before it delivers the markup to the browser.

■ **Note** This book assumes a working knowledge of PHP, so basic concepts and syntax will not be covered. If you want to brush up on your PHP chops, get your hands on *PHP for Absolute Beginners*,[8] by Jason Lengstorf.

EXERCISE 2-4: USE PHP TO INSERT DYNAMIC CONTENT

Let's experiment with PHP by inserting the current date into our markup dynamically. To do this, we need to save a new copy of our HTML as a PHP file, which we'll name 04.php.

Next, let's insert some PHP at the very top of the file, just above the `<!doctype>` declaration:

```php
<?php

    // Set the timezone and generate two formatted date strings
    date_default_timezone_set('US/Pacific');
    $datetime = date('c');
    $date_fmt = date('F d, Y');

?>
<!doctype html>
```

As the comment indicates, this code sets the time zone to the Pacific time zone and then stores two formatted date strings in variables.

---

[8]http://www.apress.com/9781430224730

Now that we have our variables, let's insert them into the `<time>` tag by inserting the following in our markup:

```
<header>
    <h1><em>Realtime Web Apps</em> &ndash; Exercise 02-04</h1>
    <p>
        Published on
        <time datetime="<?php echo $datetime; ?>">
            <?php echo $date_fmt; ?>
        </time>.
    </p>
</header>
```

Save this file; then load it in your browser to see the current date displayed (see Figure 2-4).

Figure 2-4. Using PHP, the current date is output in the markup

MySQL

MySQL is a database management system—a *relational database management system* (RDBMS) to be precise—that is the most widely used on the planet. It provides an easy-to-read syntax for storing and retrieving data from tables, and that allows developers to create applications that can store data such as user settings and, in the case of our app, room names and questions.

Why Do We Need It?

Certain pieces of data—such as the names of rooms and the questions that have been asked—will need to be stored in a database for later retrieval:

- **The details of a room:** Details such as room name and session information so the presenter can come back to the room at a later date for reference.

- **The questions asked in each room:** This allows a new attendee to join late and not miss anything.

What Role Does It Play?

MySQL will play the role of our app's memory. It will remember details about various rooms and questions, and have them ready should they be needed in the future.

How Does It Work?

MySQL is installed on the server and works by creating a database, tables within the database, and rows within the tables.

Each row is a particular piece of data. For instance, if the table were called *rooms*, each row would contain a room's information such as its name, unique identifier, and other related data.

■ **Note**   MySQL is also covered in the aforementioned *PHP for Absolute Beginners*.

EXERCISE 2-5: FUN WITH MYSQL

Because integrating MySQL with our HTML markup would require a little too much setup, let's get geeky and play with MySQL on the command line instead. You will, of course, need MySQL installed and configured on your system. Open up a terminal and connect to MySQL replacing *your_username* with your MySQL username:

```
mysql -uyour_username -p
```

You should be prompted for your password and then you'll be connected to your MySQL server. You can also use a desktop client or phpMyAdmin for this exercise—on Mac we recommend SequelPro,[9] and on Windows we've heard good things about Navicat.[10]

Once you're connected to the server, create a database to play with and ensure things are working as expected. Let's call it awesome_test_db:

```
CREATE DATABASE awesome_test_db;
```

This should give you the following output:

```
Query OK, 1 row affected (0.00 sec)
```

Now let's select the database we will execute queries against:

```
USE awesome_test_db;
```

This should tell you that the database was changed, which means we can now create a table:

```
CREATE TABLE awesome_things (
    id       INT PRIMARY KEY AUTO_INCREMENT,
    name     VARCHAR(64),
    percent TINYINT
);
```

---

[9]http://www.sequelpro.com/
[10]http://www.navicat.com/en/

With a table ready, we can insert a few rows; each row has the name of a thing and a percentage that indicates how awesome it is. Remember that this is just for fun and to demonstrate MySQL is working:

```
INSERT INTO awesome_things (name, percent)
VALUES
    ('Wooden sunglasses', 72),
    ('Pabst Blue Ribbon', 85),
    ('Bands no one has heard of', 100),
    ('Vintage clothing', 67);
```

This should give you the following output:

```
Query OK, 4 rows affected (0.00 sec)
Records: 4  Duplicates: 0  Warnings: 0
```

Now that we know what's awesome, let's make sure we know all of the things that are more than 75 percent awesome:

```
SELECT CONCAT(name, ': ', percent, '% awesome, which means I'm onboard.')
FROM awesome_things
WHERE percent>75
ORDER BY percent DESC;
```

Using CONCAT() allows us to combine the output into a sentence rather than just looking at raw data. Using the WHERE clause, we can filter results so that we only see rows that are more than 75 percent awesome, and because we want to see the most awesome things first, we order by the percent in *descending order*, or high-to-low. When executed, you will see the following:

```
+----------------------------------------------------------------------+
| CONCAT(name, ': ', percent, '% awesome, which means I'm onboard.') |
+----------------------------------------------------------------------+
| Bands no one has heard of: 100% awesome, which means I'm onboard.   |
| Pabst Blue Ribbon: 85% awesome, which means I'm onboard.           |
+----------------------------------------------------------------------+
2 rows in set (0.00 sec)
```

Now that you know what's awesome, you may want to destroy the evidence by dropping the database altogether:

```
DROP DATABASE awesome_test_db;
```

This removes the database altogether so that your MySQL server isn't cluttered with test data.

HTML5 WebSocket Technology and Pusher

We already talked a bit about WebSocket and realtime, but let's recap: HTML5 WebSocket allows applications to push data to the client rather than requiring the client to constantly ask for new data.

EXERCISE 2-6: TRYING OUT THE WEBSOCKET API

Let's have a look at the native WebSocket API to get an idea of how it can be used. Create an HTML file with the following content. This file contains JavaScript that connects to a WebSocket echo test service. This means that you can test connecting, sending, and receiving messages.

```
<!doctype html>
<html lang="en">

    <head>
        <meta charset="utf-8" />
        <title>Trying out the WebSocket API 02-06</title>
    </head>

    <body>

        <script>
            var ws = new WebSocket( 'ws://echo.websocket.org' );

            ws.onopen = function() {
              console.log( 'connected' );
              console.log( '> hello' );
              ws.send( 'hello' );
            };
            ws.onmessage = function( ev ) { console.log( '< ' + ev.data ); };
            ws.onclose = function() { console.log( 'closed' ); };
            ws.onerror = function() { console.log( 'error' ); };
        </script>

    </body>

</html>
```

If you open up this page in a browser that supports WebSocket and open up the browser's JavaScript console, you'll see the following:

```
connected
> hello
< hello
```

The connected message is displayed when WebSocket has connected to the server, and the onopen function handler has been called. The code then logs > hello to indicate it's going to send hello over the WebSocket connection to the server using the WebSocket send function. Finally, when the server echoes back the message, the onmessage function handler is called, and < hello is logged to the console.

This demonstrates how to use the WebSocket API and gives you a glimpse of how useful it could be. But, as we covered in Chapter 1, the WebSocket API is not fully supported in all browsers just yet, and we need a fallback mechanism. As a result, implementing realtime apps can be cumbersome, tricky, and extremely time-consuming if we have to handle browser compatibility issues ourselves.

Fortunately for the rest of us, there are a number of services out there that have overcome these hurdles and created APIs that start by checking for WebSocket support; then regressively check for the next-best solution until they find one that works. The result is powerful realtime functionality without any of the headache of making it backward-compatible.

Among these companies offering realtime services, Pusher stands out for its extreme ease of implementation, free accounts for services that don't have large user bases, great documentation, and helpful support staff.

Pusher provides a JavaScript library[11] that not only handles fallbacks for older browsers but also offers functionality such as auto-reconnection and a Publish/Subscribe[12] messaging abstraction through its API, which can make it much easier to use than simply dealing with generic messages, as would be the case if we used the native WebSocket API.

Finally, because Pusher is a hosted service, it will handle maintaining the persistent connections over which data will be delivered and can deal with scaling to meet demand for us. Although this latter point might not be a big deal for our sample application, it's a valid consideration when you are building a production application.

For those reasons, we'll be using Pusher in this book to build our realtime.

Why Do We Need It?

Pusher will allow you to add realtime notifications and updates to the application, including the following:

- **Updating all users when a new question is added:** This means that when a user adds a new question, all users currently using the app in that room will receive the new question immediately.

- **Updating attendees when the presenter marks a question "answered":** When the presenter answers a question, marking it "answered" will instantly update all attendees' devices to prevent confusion.

- **Updating the presenter when more than one attendee wants the same question answered:** If more than one user is interested in having a question answered, they can upvote that question. The presenter will receive a visual indication to let them know that the question is pressing.

- **Updating all attendees when a room is closed:** When the presenter closes the room, attendees need to be updated so they know not to ask any questions that won't be answered.

What Role Does It Play?

Pusher will play the role of the app's nervous system: it will be informed when changes are made and relay that information to the brains of the app so that they can process the information.

---

[11]http://pusher.com/docs/client_libraries/javascript
[12]http://en.wikipedia.org/wiki/Publish%E2%80%93subscribe_pattern

How Does It Work?

In the simplest terms, Pusher provides a mechanism that lets the client "listen" for changes to the app. When something happens, Pusher sends a notification to all the clients who are listening so that they can react appropriately. This is the Publish Subscribe paradigm we mentioned earlier.

Chapter 3 is dedicated to the finer details, so we will skip the exercise in this section.

OAuth

Unlike the technologies discussed so far, OAuth is a protocol, not an actual programming language. It's a concept that was drafted in 2007 to address the issue presented by websites that provided services that overlap; think about how social networks can access your address book to look for friends or how a photo sharing site can tie into Twitter to let your followers know when you've posted a new photo.

The problem was this: when these services first started to work together, they required that users provided a username and password to access the service, which was potentially a huge risk. What was to stop a shady service from using that password for its own purposes, up to and including the possibility of changing your password and locking you out?

This was a big concern. OAuth devised a solution based on its study of a number of other attempts to solve the problem, using what it considered to be the best parts of each.

To paraphrase an excellent analogy from the OAuth website:[13]

> OAuth is like giving someone the valet keys to a luxury car. A valet key will only allow the car to drive a few miles; it doesn't allow access to the trunk; it prevents the use of any stored data in the cars onboard computers, such as address books. OAuth is similar to a valet key for your online services: you don't provide your password, and you're able to allow only certain privileges with the account without exposing all of your information.

For instance, Facebook uses OAuth for user authentication on third-party services. If you're already logged in to Facebook, you're presented with a dialog (on Facebook's domain), telling you which permissions are required and allowing you to accept or deny the request. Privileges are compartmentalized—reading someone's timeline is different from viewing their friends list, for example—to ensure that third-party services receive only the privileges they *need* to function.

This keeps users safe and reduces liability for web apps. It also provides a wonderful benefit for developers: we can allow a user to log in to our app with their Facebook, Twitter, or other credentials using a simple API.

Why Do We Need It?

We don't need it in the app that we're building, but it would be a neat feature so we've included it in Appendix A if you want to see how it could be included. In a nutshell, we would use OAuth to eliminate the need to build a user management system. This would also *hugely* reduce the time needed to sign up for an account without reducing the app's access to the information it needs to function.

Let's face it: most people have more accounts than they can remember on the Internet. The difference between someone using our app and not using our app could be something as simple as how many buttons he has to click to get started.

---

[13]http://oauth.net/about/

OAuth provides a great way to get everything we need:

- **Verify that the person is indeed real:** We can reasonably assume that anyone who is signed into a valid Facebook or Twitter account is a real person.

- **Collect necessary data about the user:** For this app, we would really only need a name and e-mail.

- **Reduce the barrier to entry:** By eliminating all the usual steps of creating an account, we could get the user into our app in seconds with just two clicks.

What Role Does It Play?

OAuth would be the gatekeeper for our app. It would use third-party services to verify the authenticity of a user and gather the necessary information for the app to function.

How Does It Work?

You'll find more details on the specifics of OAuth in Appendix A, but at its core, OAuth contacts the service through which we want to authenticate our user and sends a token identifying our app. The user is prompted to log in to the third party service if they're not already and then allow or deny the requested privileges from our app. If the user allows our app to access the requested data, the service sends back a token we can use to retrieve the necessary data and consider a user "logged in" to our app.

Summary

At this point, we have successfully defined a rough list of functionality and requirements for our app. We also used that information to flesh out a list of tools we will use to bring the app to life.

In the next chapter, you'll get familiar with Pusher and its underlying technologies, and you'll build your first realtime application.

CHAPTER 3

Pusher

Now that we've laid some foundation for the app and reviewed some of the programming languages we'll be using to build it, you can start getting familiar with the new technologies that will come into play.

First, let's get acquainted with Pusher, which will be responsible for the realtime interaction on our site. In this chapter, we'll explore the origins of Pusher, the underlying technology, some of the tools they provide to help development, and get our hands dirty by building a simple realtime activity tracking app.

A Brief History of Pusher

Pusher is part of a relatively new trend on the Internet known as *software as a service (SAAS)*. These companies provide a useful tool, utility, service, or other value to other developers for a fee. This allows us to use incredibly powerful new technologies without spending days—or weeks—trying to solve issues such as scalability and cross-browser support.

In early 2010, cofounders Max Williams and Damien Tanner were running one of the most successful Ruby On Rails shops in the UK. When they saw the need to synchronize data between their team members, they built a small tool to utilize the new HTML5 WebSocket API.

Once they realized how easy it was to create realtime applications using their infrastructure, they saw an opportunity that went beyond internal management tools.

Since then, Pusher has grown to become a dominant force in the realtime SaaS market, boasting an impressive client list that includes Groupon, MailChimp, and SlideShare.

Why Use Pusher?

One of the key reasons for using a hosted service like Pusher is that it speeds up the development process by making a previously complex goal much more achievable. One of the key parts of this is the speed at which that goal can be reached. But there are others, too. Since we are using the Pusher hosted service, it's worth highlighting some of the benefits of doing so.

Scalability

One of the first things a cloud-based SaaS offers is the promise of scalability, and Pusher is no different. It provides and scales realtime infrastructure so that we can focus on adding realtime interactive functionality to our application.

WebSocket, Fallback Support, and Auto-Reconnect

In Chapter 1 we demonstrated how great WebSocket technology is, but that there is still an unfortunate need to offer fallbacks for older browsers, or where tricky networks are involved. It should therefore come as a relief that Pusher also deals with fallbacks for older browsers. Its JavaScript library chooses the most appropriate connection method based on the browser runtime and the network conditions. The library also detects dropped connections and will automatically reconnect for you.

The library creates a connection between the user's browser and the Pusher service so that the instant new data is available it can be published and pushed to them. You can also publish information directly from the client. We'll dig deeper into the functionality that's available as we work our way through this chapter.

Other Client Libraries

Although the WebSocket specification now falls under the HTML5 umbrella, it's important to remember that it's a specification of a protocol. What this means is that any technology that can make a TCP connection can also make a WebSocket connection. Pusher takes advantage of this and also offers client libraries in a number of other technologies, including Objective-C for iOS development, Java for Android and desktop development, ActionScript for Flash, and C# for general .NET and Silverlight runtimes.

REST API

No hosted service is complete without a REST API, and Pusher is no different.[1] The REST API is primarily used for publishing data, but also offers functionality to query the state of your application within Pusher. Offering a REST API means that any technology that can make an HTTP request can use this API.

Server Libraries

Since the REST API requires authentication and has some potentially complex requirements, there have been a number of server libraries developed to make executing requests to the API easier. Since all you need to do to make a call to a REST API is make an HTTP request, it's no surprise that the number of libraries available is very long.[2] The most commonly used libraries include PHP, Ruby, .NET, Python, Node.js, and Java.

Developer Tools

Another increasingly useful feature of hosted services is some form of developer tooling that increases the ease at which development can take place. This is achieved by exposing the internal workings and logging information available to the service. In Pusher's case, this means exposing information such as connections and data flow related to the application that you are building. We'll use these tools as we build our application.

Documentation

Documentation is essential to any technology and even more so to a hosted service, which can be looked at as a black box—it's not like you can go digging around in the source code for all the components of a hosted service to find out what's going on—even if they do open source some of them or use existing open source ones.

---

[1]REST purists may argue that Pusher's REST API isn't strictly RESTful. We could have instead listed this as a Web or HTTP API.
[2]http://pusher.com/docs/server_libraries

So good documentation with lots of code examples can make the difference between deciding to use a service or not. Pusher's documentation[3] is a combination of user guide and reference, focusing on both exploring what is possible and letting you quickly find a way of achieving something.

Pusher Terminology

Before we get started with Pusher you should become familiar with some of the terminology.

A *connection* represents a persistent connection between a client, in our case a web browser, and the Pusher service. Messages are received via Pusher over this connection and we can also send messages to other users, via Pusher, over this connection.

Pusher uses the *publish-subscribe messaging pattern*[4] so uses the concept of a *channel* to identify something that the client application is interested in (e.g., "sports-news" or "apress-tweets"). A channel is represented simply by a name, and you register interest in a channel by *subscribing* to it.

Some have referred to the realtime web as the "evented web." This is because realtime web technologies are frequently used to communicate that some sort of event has occurred, and to deliver the data associated with that event to users or systems that are interested in knowing that it has occurred. For example, when somebody tweets, the system might inform all their followers about that tweet event and deliver the tweet data (twitter user, text, time of tweet, was it in reply to another tweet etc.) to them.

So, it may come as no surprise that Pusher also uses the concept of *events*. Events are used in conjunction with channels; when you subscribe to a channel you can then bind to events on that channel. For example, you could subscribe to the "apress-tweets" channel and bind to "new_tweet", "tweet_deleted", "tweet_favorited", and "retweeted" events. Events tie in really nicely with create, update, and destroy parts of CRUD (create, read, update, destroy) functionality; as well as user interface changes that reflect the result of an event.

In order to receive data, it has to be *published*. Data is published on a channel and associated with an event. To maintain the concept of the evented web, the act of publishing data on a channel is called *triggering* an event. As such, *trigger* and *publish* may be used interchangeably.

You'll see all these concepts in use as we develop our application, and this will demonstrate how you can easily use the same concepts in new or existing applications.

Getting Started with Pusher

The first thing you'll need to do before we start building an example application is sign up for a Pusher sandbox account. This is a free account that limits the number of simultaneous connections you can have open from your clients and the number of messsages you can send per day. This free account will be more than enough for all the applications presented in this book.

First, head over to the Pusher website at `http://www.pusher.com` and sign-up.

Once you've signed up, you'll be taken to your account home page, which has all the information you'll need to do a quick proof-of-concept for your account (see Figure 3-1.)

---

[3]`http://pusher.com/docs`
[4]`http://en.wikipedia.org/wiki/Publish%E2%80%93subscribe_pattern`

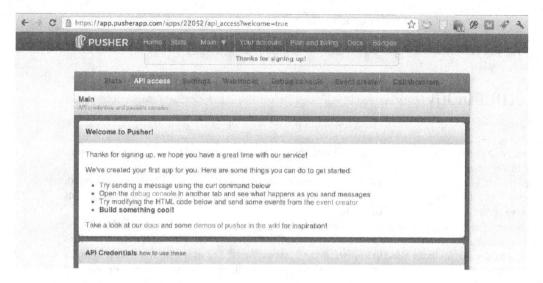

Figure 3-1. *The Pusher welcome screen*

For now, that's it. Seriously. Keep this page open, however, because you'll be using it in Exercise 3-1.

EXERCISE 3-1: A SIMPLE PUSHER TEST

To verify that your account is active and to demonstrate just how easy it is to get started with Pusher, let's put together an extremely simple HTML document and send a message to it.

First, create a simple HTML file. Inside, add the following markup:

```
<!doctype html>
<html lang="en">

    <head>
        <meta charset="utf-8" />
        <title>Realtime Web Apps &ndash; Exercise 3-2</title>
    </head>

    <body>

        <h1>Testing Pusher</h1>
        <p>
            This is a simple demo of how easy it is to integrate Pusher
            into an application.
        </p>

    </body>

</html>
```

Next, include the Pusher JavaScript library on the page by inserting this script tag just above the closing </body> tag:

```html
<!doctype html>
<html lang="en">

    <head>
        <meta charset="utf-8" />
        <title>Realtime Web Apps &ndash; Exercise 3-2</title>
    </head>

    <body>

        <h1>Testing Pusher</h1>
        <p>
            This is a simple demo of how easy it is to integrate Pusher
            into an application.
        </p>

        <script src="http://js.pusher.com/1.12/pusher.min.js"></script>

    </body>

</html>
```

The next thing to do is connect to Pusher. In the following code, replace the appKey variable value with the key listed in your Pusher application credentials.

```html
<!doctype html>
<html lang="en">

    <head>
        <meta charset="utf-8" />
        <title>Realtime Web Apps &ndash; Exercise 3-2</title>
    </head>

    <body>

        <h1>Testing Pusher</h1>
        <p>
            This is a simple demo of how easy it is to integrate Pusher
            into an application.
        </p>

        <script src="http://js.pusher.com/1.12/pusher.min.js"></script>
        <script type="text/javascript">
            var appKey =' 079be339124bac43c45c';
            var pusher = new Pusher(appKey);
        </script>

    </body>

</html>
```

When you create a new Pusher instance, a new connection will be established to the Pusher service.

The next thing to do is to check if you are connected. You can do this manually by using the Pusher Debug Console, one of the developer tools we mentioned earlier. To do this, go to the Pusher Dashboard for your application and click the Debug Console link. Now, in a different browser window, open up your new HTML document. If you take a look at the Pusher Debug Console, you'll see that a new Connection has been listed, as in Figure 3-2.

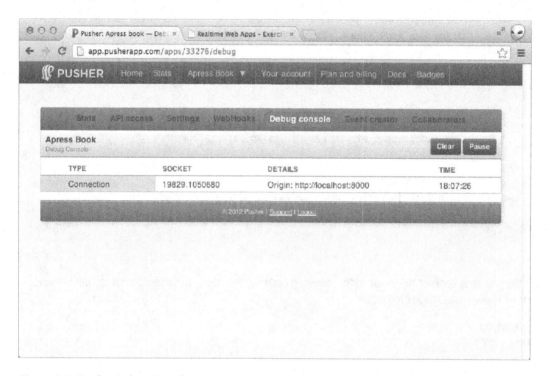

Figure 3-2. *Pusher Debug Console*

You can also check that a connection has been established within your code by binding to events on the `pusher.connection` object.[5] This can be useful if you want to give the user feedback about the connection status or if you need the application to act differently when a connection is not available—if the user is currently offline. As mentioned earlier, Pusher uses the concept of events, and this is also the case when monitoring connection state. In the code below we'll bind to the `state_change` event and display the current state in the page. The code changes required to achieve this are shown in bold:

```
<!doctype html>
<html lang="en">

  <head>
    <meta charset="utf-8" />
    <title>Realtime Web Apps &ndash; Exercise 3-2</title>
  </head>
```

---

[5]http://pusher.com/docs/connection_states

```
<body>

  <h1>Testing Pusher</h1>

  <div id="connection_state">&dash;</div>

  <p>
      This is a simple demo of how easy it is to integrate Pusher
      into an application.
  </p>

  <script src="http://js.pusher.com/1.12/pusher.min.js"></script>
  <script>
    var pusher = new Pusher( '079be339124bac43c45c' );
    pusher.connection.bind( 'state_change', function( change ) {
      document.getElementById( 'connection_state' ).innerHTML = change.current;
    } );
  </script>

</body>

</html>
```

For each connection state change, the function that is passed as the second parameter to the bind function is called. We can then update the page to show what the current connection state is.

Now that we know how to detect our connection state, we can look at subscribing to a channel. As mentioned earlier, channels are identified purely by a name: a string. You don't need to do anything to create a channel or provision it within Pusher. Simply by subscribing to it, it exists. You don't even need to worry about using up too many channels since they're actually just a way of routing data from a publisher (which we've yet to cover) to a subscriber. So, let's subscribe to a channel and bind to an event on it:

```
<!doctype html>
<html lang="en">

  <head>
    <meta charset="utf-8" />
    <title>Realtime Web Apps &ndash; Exercise 3-2</title>
  </head>

  <body>

  <h1>Testing Pusher</h1>

  <div id="connection_state">&dash;</div>

  <p>
      This is a simple demo of how easy it is to integrate Pusher
      into an application.
  </p>
```

```
<script src="http://js.pusher.com/1.12/pusher.min.js"></script>
<script>
  var pusher = new Pusher( '079be339124bac43c45c' );
  pusher.connection.bind( 'state_change', function( change ) {
    document.getElementById( 'connection_state' ).innerHTML = change.current;
  } );

  var channel = pusher.subscribe( 'test_channel' );
  channel.bind( 'my_event', function( data ) {
    alert( data );
  } );
</script>

</body>

</html>
```

As with handling connection events, the event handler is as simple as they come: when the event is triggered, the message being sent is displayed in an alert box.

Navigate to your HTML file in one browser window; within another, go to the Event Creator, which can be found within the Pusher Dashboard for your app. You'll be presented with the Event Creator form. Enter details that correspond to the JavaScript code we've just written; the channel name should be test_channel, and the event name should be my_event. Enter some text into the Event Data text area and click the Send Event button (see Figure 3-3).

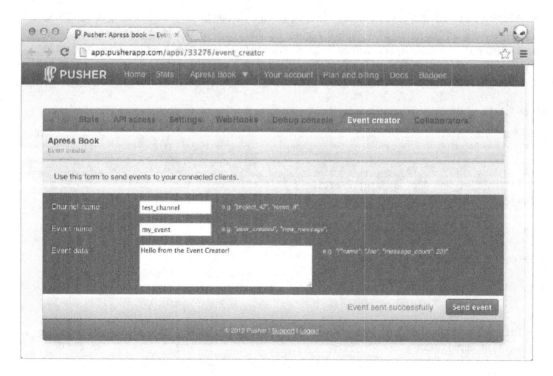

Figure 3-3. *Pusher Event Creator*

■ **Note** Pusher recommends that you send JSON as the event data and their libraries help you do this. For test purposes, and so that alert shows some human readable information, we'll just send text.

Upon pressing the Send Event button, you should receive an alert from your test script (two, if you still have the Pusher page open) that looks something like the one in Figure 3-4.

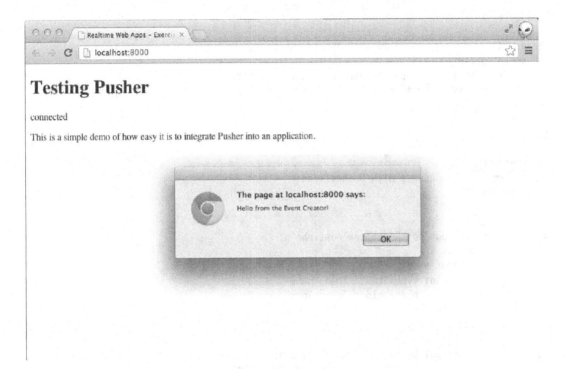

Figure 3-4. *Upon sending a test event from the Event Creator, an alert box appears*

In its simplest form, this is a working Pusher application. In the next exercise, you'll look at a more useful example.

Using Pusher to Send Events

Exercise 3-1 demonstrates how easy it is to receive events with Pusher, but what about sending them?

Thanks to its variety of API libraries, Pusher makes sending events just as easy as receiving them. We'll be using the PHP API library, which lives on GitHub at https://github.com/pusher/pusher-php-server.

EXERCISE 3-2: PUBLISHING & SUBSCRIBING WITH PUSHER

To get familiar with Pusher's server-side functionality, let's build a simple messaging system.

For the foundation, we'll reuse as much of the HTML and CSS that we wrote in the exercises in Chapter 2 as possible to save time. Create a new HTML file and enter the following code:

```html
<html lang="en">

    <head>
        <meta charset="utf-8" />
        <title>Realtime Web Apps &ndash; Exercise 3-2</title>
        <link rel="stylesheet" href="styles/layout.css" />
    </head>

    <body>

        <header>
            <h1>Send a Message with Pusher!</h1>
        </header>

        <section>
            <form method="post" action="post.php">
                <label>
                    Your Name
                    <input type="text" name="name"
                            placeholder="i.e. John" />
                </label>
                <label>
                    Your Message
                    <input type="text" name="message"
                            id="message" value="Hello world!" />
                </label>
                <input type="submit" class="input-submit" value="Send" />
            </form>
        </section>

        <aside>
            <h2>Received Messages</h2>
            <ul id="messages">
                <li class="no-messages">No messages yet...</li>
            </ul>
        </aside>

        <footer>
            <p>
                All content &copy; 2013 Jason Lengstorf &amp; Phil Leggetter
            </p>
        </footer>
```

```
            <script src="http://js.pusher.com/1.12/pusher.min.js"></script>
            <script
                src="http://code.jquery.com/jquery-1.7.2.min.js"></script>
            <script
                src="scripts/init.js"></script>

        </body>

</html>
```

This code creates a simple form that accepts a name and a message, as well as an unordered list to display any messages received.

Next, let's add some CSS. Create a folder called styles and add a new file to it named layout.css. This file is already linked to from the HTML we created previously. Add the following code to the new CSS file:

```
/*
 * Exercise 3-2, Realtime Web Apps
 *
 * @author Jason Lengstorf <jason@copterlabs.com>
 * @author Phil Leggetter <phil@leggetter.co.uk>
 */

html { background: #efefdc; }

body {
    width: 800px;
    margin: 40px auto;
    overflow: hidden;
    background: #def;
    border: 2px solid #779;

    /* Creates two shadow effects: outer and inner */
    -webkit-box-shadow: 0 1px 6px #88a, inset 0 -1px 10px white;
    -moz-box-shadow: 0 1px 6px #88a, inset 0 -1px 10px white;
    -o-box-shadow: 0 1px 6px #88a, inset 0 -1px 10px white;
    -ms-box-shadow: 0 1px 6px #88a, inset 0 -1px 10px white;
    box-shadow: 0 1px 6px #88a, inset 0 -1px 10px white;
}

section,aside {
    float: left;
    margin: 20px 30px 10px;
    padding: 20px 20px 10px;
    overflow: hidden;
    background: white;
    border: 1px solid #dfdfef;

    /* Creates two shadow effects: outer and inner */
    -webkit-box-shadow: inset 0 1px 4px #88a, 0 1px 10px white;
    -moz-box-shadow: inset 0 1px 4px #88a, 0 1px 10px white;
    -o-box-shadow: inset 0 1px 4px #88a, 0 1px 10px white;
```

45

```css
        -ms-box-shadow: inset 0 1px 4px #88a, 0 1px 10px white;
        box-shadow: inset 0 1px 4px #88a, 0 1px 10px white;
}

section {
    width: 400px;
}

aside {
    width: 226px;
    margin-left: 0;
}

body,section,aside,input {
    /* Sets a border radius for every element that needs it */
    -webkit-border-radius: 15px;
    -moz-border-radius: 15px;
    -o-border-radius: 15px;
    -ms-border-radius: 15px;
    border-radius: 15px;
}

footer { margin: 0 0 10px; }

h1,h2 {
    margin: 20px 30px 10px;
    color: #446;
    font-weight: bold;
    font-family: georgia, serif;
}

h1 {
    font-size: 30px;
    line-height: 40px;
}

h2 {
    font-size: 18px;
}

label,li {
    display: block;
    margin: 0 0 10px;
    font: 15px/20px sans-serif;
    color: #557;
}

h1,label,input,li { text-shadow: 1px 1px 1px #88a; }
```

```css
label input {
    display: block;
    width: 378px;
    border: 1px solid #dfdfef;
    padding: 4px 10px;
    font-size: 18px;
    line-height: 20px;

    /* Creates an inner shadow */
    -webkit-box-shadow: inset 0 1px 4px #88a;
    -moz-box-shadow: inset 0 1px 4px #88a;
    -o-box-shadow: inset 0 1px 4px #88a;
    -ms-box-shadow: inset 0 1px 4px #88a;
    box-shadow: inset 0 1px 4px #88a;
}

/* These MUST be separate rules to work */
input::-webkit-input-placeholder { color: #aac; text-shadow: none; }
input:-moz-placeholder { color: #aac; text-shadow: none; }
input:-ms-input-placeholder { color: #aac; text-shadow: none; }

input.input-submit {
    padding: 4px 30px 5px;
    background: #446;
    border: 1px solid #88a;
    color: #dfdfef;
    font: bold 18px/20px georgia,serif;
    text-transform: uppercase;

    /* Creates two shadow effects: outer and inner */
    -webkit-box-shadow: 0 1px 6px #88a, inset 0 -1px 10px white;
    -moz-box-shadow: 0 1px 6px #88a, inset 0 -1px 10px white;
    -o-box-shadow: 0 1px 6px #88a, inset 0 -1px 10px white;
    -ms-box-shadow: 0 1px 6px #88a, inset 0 -1px 10px white;
    box-shadow: 0 1px 6px #88a, inset 0 -1px 10px white;
}

aside h2,aside ul {
    margin: 0 0 10px;
}

aside ul {
    padding: 10px 0 0;
    border-top: 1px solid #dfdfef;
}

aside li {
    padding: 0 5px 10px;
    border-bottom: 1px solid #dfdfef;
}
```

```
footer {
    clear: both;
}

footer p {
    margin: 0;
    color: #889;
    font: italic 12px/1.67em sans-serif;
    text-align: center;
    text-shadow: 1px 1px 1px white;
}
```

Load your HTML file in a browser and you'll see your styled markup (see Figure 3-5).

Figure 3-5. *The styled page that will send and receive messages with Pusher*

Now that you have a page that has an area of the UI designated to both sending and receiving messages, we can start adding in realtime functionality by publishing and subscribing. Looking at the HTML, we know that the form will submit entries to a file called post.php; let's start by creating that file and including the Pusher PHP library.

Download the Pusher PHP library from https://github.com/pusher/pusher-php-server and copy the lib directory to the same folder where your HTML file is saved.

With that saved, we can create a new Pusher object and start sending data in just a few short lines of code to post.php:

```
<?php

ini_set('display_errors', 1);
error_reporting(E_ALL);

require_once 'lib/Pusher.php';
```

```
// Make sure you grab your own Pusher app credentials!
$key     = '1507a86011e47d3d00ad';
$secret  = 'badd14bcd1905e47b370';
$app_id  = '22052';
$pusher  = new Pusher($key, $secret, $app_id);

if (isset($_POST['name']) && isset($_POST['message']))
{
    $data = array(
            'name' => htmlentities(strip_tags($_POST['name'])),
            'msg'  => htmlentities(strip_tags($_POST['message'])),
    );

    $pusher->trigger('exercise-3-2', 'send-message', $data);
}
```

The first two lines turn on error reporting to make debugging easier (you would turn this off in a production site). Next, we include the Pusher PHP library, define app credentials (don't forget to plug in your own) and instantiate a new Pusher object, stored in $pusher.

Next, the script checks for the two required form values, name and message, and stores them in an array if they do exist. The array is then passed to Pusher using the trigger method, which triggers the send-message event on the channel we've named exercise-3-2. The event data passed to the trigger method will be sent as JSON, which the library handles for us.

At this point, submitting the form will cause Pusher to send an event, but before we can see the effect of this in our application, we need to add an event handler using JavaScript. But first, we can at least use the Pusher Debug Console to manually check that the event is being triggered (see Figure 3-6).

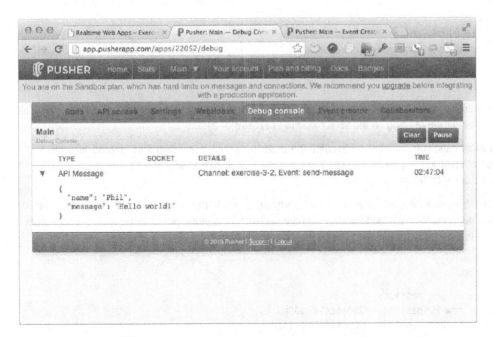

Figure 3-6. *The triggered event appearing as an API Message in the Pusher Debug Console*

In order to visualize this message in our application, we need to write the JavaScript to connect to Pusher, subscribe to a channel, and bind to an event.

Our HTML file included a script called `init.js`. So let's create that file in a directory called `scripts`. Inside, we'll add two code blocks: one will listen for events triggered by our server-side script, and one will capture form submissions and send them to `post.php` without refreshing the page. To start, let's add an event listener for custom Pusher events:

```
(function($){

    // Handles receiving messages
    var pusher  = new Pusher('1507a86011e47d3d00ad'),
        channel = pusher.subscribe('exercise-3-2);

    // Adds an event listener for the custom event triggered by Pusher
    channel
        .bind(
            'send-message',
            function(data) {
                var cont  = $('#messages');

                // Removes the placeholder LI if it's present
                cont.find('.no-messages').remove();

                // Adds the new message to the page
                $('<li>')
                    .html('<strong>'+data.name+':</strong> '+data.msg)
                    .appendTo(cont);
            }
        );

    // TODO: Handle form submission

})(jQuery);
```

This creates a new `Pusher` object using our app API key—(again, don't forget to use your own) and then subscribes to the channel we're using on the server side in Exercise 3-2).

Next we bind an event handler to the channel to catch the `send-message` event. When it's triggered, we grab the unordered list for message display, make sure to remove the placeholder message if it's present, and then append the new message to the bottom of the list.

To prevent the page from reloading, which would remove any messages from our application that had been added by JavaScript from our browser, we need to add a second code block to capture form submissions and post them via AJAX instead of using a page refresh. Add this by inserting the bold code:

```
(function($){

    // Handles receiving messages
    var pusher  = new Pusher('1507a86011e47d3d00ad'),
        channel = pusher.subscribe('exercise-3-2);
```

```
// Adds an event listener for the custom event triggered by Pusher
channel
    .bind(
        'send-message',
        function(data) {
            var cont  = $('#messages');

            // Removes the placeholder LI if it's present
            cont.find('.no-messages').remove();

            // Adds the new message to the page
            $('<li>')
                .html('<strong>'+data.name+':</strong> '+data.msg)
                .appendTo(cont);
        }
    );

// Handles form submission
$('form').submit(function(){
    // Posts the form data so it can be sent to other browsers
    $.post('post.php', $(this).serialize());

    // Empties the input
    $('#message').val('').focus();

    // Prevents the default form submission
    return false;
});

})(jQuery);
```

This code catches the submit event, sends the serialized form data to post.php, and empties the message input. It leaves the name input untouched to make repeated messages easier to send; to that end, it also puts focus back on the message input.

By returning false, the default form submission is prevented, which stops the page from reloading.

Now you're ready to test this app. Load your HTML file in a browser and send a message or two; the messages are shown in the list on the right side, as expected. But this isn't really the exciting part.

To see the power of realtime, load this test in two different browsers (or two windows in the same browser) and start sending some messages. With no polling and no page refreshes, you'll see that events in one window are affecting the display of the other (see Figure 3-7). This is realtime.

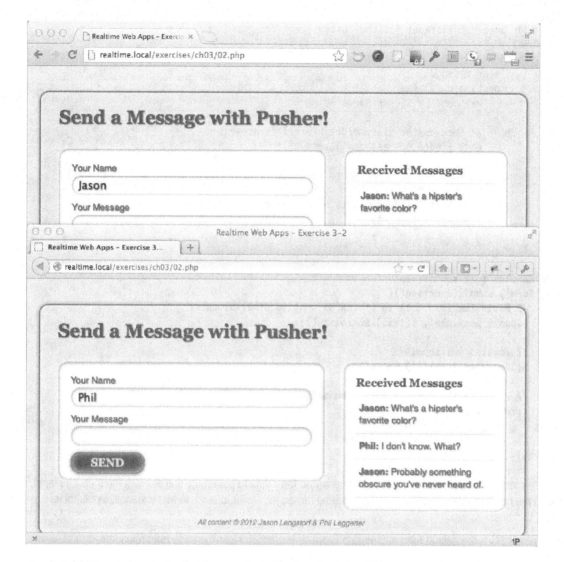

Figure 3-7. *Messages posted in one browser display in the other in realtime*

Debugging Your Pusher Application

As a developer, you'll know that things don't always go according to plan. When this happens, you need to start debugging your application to try and work out why what you are expecting to happen, isn't!

If you find yourself in this situation, developer tools are your best friends. And luckily all the major browser vendors now provide you with a good set of tools that give you access to a JavaScript console, execute code on the fly, debug running code, inspect elements within a web page, and much more. Hosted services are also exposing good developer tools that let you see what's going on within the service and perform some manual testing. We've seen this earlier with the Pusher Debug Console and Event Creator.

Whether you are using Pusher or any other realtime web technology, the browser developer tools are an essential part of your developer arsenal. Using the functionality we've discussed, such as using `console.log` to keep track of which parts of your code are being invoked, and checking variable values is a first simple step, breaking into executing code using either browser dev tool breakpoints or the debugger statement can also be very handy.

If you are using a third-party library, as we are here with the Pusher JavaScript library, it's essential that the library exposes a way of keeping track of what it's doing. The Pusher library does this by exposing a `Pusher.log` property as part of its API. As a final exercise, let's see how we use this—it may come in handy as you build your application.

EXERCISE 3-3: PUSHER LOGGING

As with most Pusher functionality, exposing the logging within the Pusher JavaScript library is very easy. All you need to do is assign a function to the `Pusher.log` property. Add the following code to the `init.js` file:

```
Pusher.log = function( msg ) {
    if( console && console.log ) {
        console.log( msg );
    }
};
```

If you now navigate to the HTML file in your browser and open your JavaScript console, you'll see the Pusher JavaScript library logging information that can be very useful during development (see Figure 3-8). As with most development logging, you should consider removing this logging functionality before you move your application into production.

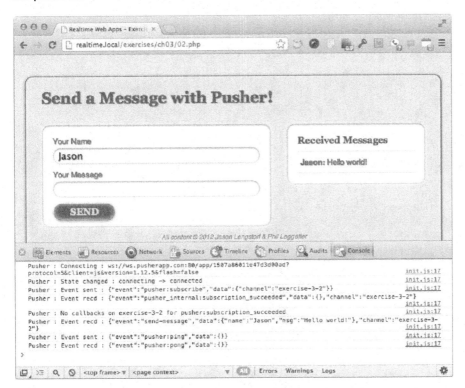

Figure 3-8. *Logging from the internal workings of the Pusher JavaScript library*

Summary

In about 60 lines of thoroughly commented code, you've just implemented a basic realtime layer into a web application. It really is that simple when you're using Pusher.

In the next chapter, we'll plan the application we're going to build in much more detail, starting with why we'll choose web over native.

PART II

Planning the App

Now that you're familiar with the technologies that will be used within this app, where they come from, and how they work, you can begin to plan the app.

This section of the book covers the planning of the app, starting with the decision to choose a web app over native apps, continuing with a definition of the app's functionality, and finally plotting the structure and architecture of the app's code. At the end of this part of the book, you should have the entire app planned, leaving only the actual build-out remaining.

■ ■ ■

CHAPTER 4

Choosing Web Apps Over Native Apps

For any developer with dreams of creating a new app, one of the first considerations that must be taken is the choice of platform: should this app be web-based with mobile considerations or should it be iPhone-only? Is there an audience to support a BlackBerry version of the app, or will most people use this app only on their laptops?

This chapter aims to cover some of the factors that you should consider when answering the "web or native app?" question. We'll then answer this question in the context of the question-and-answer app that will be built throughout the rest of this book.

Why Does It Matter?

At first glance, it might seem as if this decision is a trivial one that doesn't merit a lot of thought. This decision, however, will impact everything from how your app is coded (obviously) to how you monetize the app (less obviously), to how maintenance is handled.

Over the following pages, we'll explore the pros and cons of both web and native apps and then we'll apply the good and bad of both within the context of the app we're going to build, which should help us make an intelligent decision about which path is best for our situation.

■ **Note**   Every app is different, and most ideas have more than one effective method of execution. The decisions and opinions in this chapter are the result of the authors' cumulative experience, biases, and preferences, and—while they may not be exactly in line with your own ideas—are one way to create a simple and effective application.

Factors to Consider

Depending on what you are building, there will be a number of factors you'll need to consider when deciding whether your application should use native or web technologies. However, some factors can be applied generically to all applications. We'll cover some of those here.

Know Your User

If you are building an app, you really need to make sure that you are building it with your target users in mind. Knowing who your users are will give you a much better understanding of the platforms your application will need to run on, the type of features that a platform can expose, and the functionality you have the potential of offering your users. The type of user may also set a level of functional expectation, but we won't cover Personas[1] here.

For example, if your users are highly likely to have a new smartphone, you can start to think about accessing newer technology and using advanced features such as the accelerometer or camera on the device. It also means that you have the potential to build rich interactive web apps running in a modern mobile browser as well as native iOS and Android apps.

Conversely, knowing your user will also help you identify the things you really shouldn't be focusing on; if you know that all your users have a BlackBerry, there's no point in building an app for the iPhone (it really goes without saying, but we're saying it just to make the point).

It's also worth considering where your application may be used by a user. You may have plans for an innovative new control system in which a user interacts with the app through a series of star jumps monitored by the device's camera. But this is unlikely to be viable if your target users are likely to want to use the app on a train where space may be restricted. At the very least, they would receive a lot of strange looks from other passengers.

Similarly, if the user will be in a location where connectivity is restricted, an app shouldn't rely on retrieving data from a hosted API.

Marketing

There's no point building an awesome feature-rich application if nobody is going to use it. So, making potential customers aware of your application is vital to its success.

Using a **marketplace** represents a great opportunity for ensuring that your app—your product—is, at the very least, discoverable. There are more than half a million mobile apps on the App Store for iOS devices and Google Play for Android devices, which clearly proves that a marketplace is a great location for your app to be discovered. Microsoft has followed suit with the Windows Store. But you could, of course, argue that with so much competition it actually makes finding your application very difficult due to the vast selection of apps.

■ **Note** Apple redefined the meaning of *apps*: from simply representing a program that runs on some device to a whole concept with a flourishing ecosystem, including micropayments, when they created the concept of the App Store. A marketplace for the marketing, sales, and distribution of a product: the app. This is an amazing marketing achievement.

As well as being discoverable, a presence in a marketplace means your app has the opportunity to benefit from the in-marketplace review system. The theory is that if you build a great app, you'll receive great reviews and benefit by soaring up the app charts.

Marketplaces were initially created for native apps and have proven to be highly successful. The idea has been copied for web apps, but with much less success. There are efforts to change this, such as the Google Chrome Web Store,[2] Firefox Marketplace,[3] Facebook App Center,[4] and even the Apple "web apps" directory,[5] but the uptake is much slower than their native app counterparts.

---

[1]http://en.wikipedia.org/wiki/Persona_(user_experience)
[2]https://chrome.google.com/webstore
[3]https://marketplace.firefox.com/
[4]http://www.facebook.com/appcenter
[5]http://www.apple.com/webapps/

Established and controlled marketplaces can also come with a downside, however. Apple is notorious for its strange and sometimes outright dictatorial control over what can and can't be in the App Store, which can be a huge roadblock for app developers. One of the most famous cases of Apple's approval process causing a problem for app developers is Google Voice, which was denied[6] when submitting its iOS app to the App Store.

Fortunately for Google, web apps can circumvent Apple's approval process by allowing users to access them from any device with an HTML5–capable browser (which the iPhone has). Google made its Voice service into a web app, and Apple couldn't stop it from making the service available[7] to its users.

■ **Note**   Apple has since relented and now allows Google Voice to publish its app in the App Store.[8]

For a long time, one of the key factors of the success or failure of a product has been a strong online presence. Since Web Apps exist online, they naturally have that presence and can benefit from being discoverable via search engines, through natural search. In contrast, a native application has to have a whole new marketing website created, or simply rely on the marketplace web listing as an online representation and source of natural discovery.

Sales

Once your marketing has worked its magic, and the potential customer is about to convert into a real user, you need a mechanism for making a sale. Even if you are giving away your application, there is still a sales aspect; the user needs to commit to using your application in some way (e.g., signing up or downloading).

The first thing to consider here is trust. If you have created a native application that you are selling through a trusted marketplace—backed by a big brand such as Apple, Google, or Microsoft—users already have the peace of mind that the application has been vetted as part of the marketplace-submission process. In addition, any payments they make for the app go through the marketplace and not directly through the application or some other third–party payment system.

A web app doesn't benefit from the same inherited trust. It needs to create the trust by looking professional; residing on an encrypted (SSL) connection; and providing payment through a trusted, reliable, and professional mechanism. Consumers are hesitant to enter their credit card information on their phones, and that hesitation isn't unfounded: it's not easy to fill out a form on a touch screen, and harder still to pull out a credit card while doing it. Add to that the fact that someone using their phone is possibly in a public setting, entering financial information is even less appealing.

It therefore isn't surprising that third–party payment providers who handle the transaction and securely store payment details (such as PayPal, Square, Dwolla, GoCardless, and many more) are finding their services under increasing demand. Although integration with payment providers such as this is getting easier, it still requires additional developer effort.

Native apps, however, have a built-in commerce platform through their respective marketplaces, allowing for upfront pricing to buy the app, in-app purchases, paid upgrades, and more.

That's not to say that there aren't many other ways to monetize an app, both native and non-native, but that discussion is outside the scope of this book.

---

[6]http://arstechnica.com/tech-policy/2009/09/fcc-releases-confidential-details-of-google-voice-app-rejection/
[7]http://www.wired.com/business/2010/01/google-voice-web-app-circumvents-apples-blockade/
[8]http://itunes.apple.com/us/app/google-voice/id318698524?mt=8

Distribution

With the payment or free sign-up in place, the customer now needs to access your application in order to actually use it.

Native application marketplaces provide a tried-and-tested download mechanism, which also adds weight to the feeling of actually buying something. The app is downloaded, installed, and up and running very quickly.

But there's no denying that the Internet is becoming more and more available on all devices, and that trend isn't showing signs of stopping. As a result, there are more and more devices on the market (everything from iPhones and iPads; to Amazon Kindle Fire; to smartphones running Android, BlackBerry, Windows Phone, and so on) that have modern web browsers capable of doing most of what a desktop browser can do. This presents a unique opportunity for developers, who would otherwise need to create a number of native apps for ubiquitous support, to simply create one web app for all devices that is instantly available by navigating to a URL in the web browser.

Web apps provide a distinct advantage when it comes to applying updates. Rather than waiting for users to get around to updating to the latest version of your app with all the bells and whistles, you simply update the web app on your server, and users get the new version the next time they load your app while online. This is a huge benefit, especially for feeling out how users interact with a new app; as new features are rolled out and old bugs are squashed, the latest and greatest version of the app is instantly available to the user-base.

From a user's perspective, updates to native apps can be relatively easily applied by either paying for an upgrade or, via manual or automatic upgrade, through the marketplace's mechanism. However, a developer has to submit the update to the marketplace and wait for the verification process to complete. This can mean that simple or urgent app upgrades can take time to be distributed.

Look, Feel, and Performance

When developing a native application, the look and feel for that platform is often understood and well defined. Although there are web app user interface (UI) frameworks available, they won't exactly match the native feel for the platform they're running on. Also, for each platform the UI may be different, which means detecting this in the web app and maintaining a different skin for each. Even then, you can't control the browser chrome from within a web app so it will never exactly match the appearance of a native application.

But it's important to remember to try and embrace the web for the platform that it is, and to use web features to its advantage.

This is a blanket statement, and there are definitely exceptions to it, but because native apps are typically built based on the device's native languages, they generally tend to feel a little smoother.

Starting with the process of launching a native application: in a native app you find the app's icon, click it and it launches. For web, it's different and a bit more convoluted; first open the browser app, then either navigate to a URL or open a bookmark. If you are using multiple web apps then you also need to jump between tabs to switch application. This results in an user experience which isn't quite as smooth with a web app as it is with a native one.

Because web apps aren't running natively, there is a higher risk of jumps, stutters, stalls, tweaks, and other glitches that tend to downgrade the quality of the user experience. Not to say that you won't get this with native apps, but when running a web app within a browser app (which itself is running on the operating system), there is an additional layer that has the potential to cause problems.

Due to this, web apps are somewhat more limited in the amount of flashy additions that can be added without risking poor performance.

Some great strides have been made by browser vendors, HTML5 frameworks,[9] and startups[10] to combat this performance hit, and things will only improve. But, in some situations, such as intensive games, native will still be the best solution.

---

[9]http://www.sencha.com/blog/the-making-of-fastbook-an-html5-love-story
[10]http://gigaom.com/2012/11/25/famous/

Development

Although we've touched on some of the factors that impact developers, we should focus more on those that can impact development. So, let's dig a bit deeper into some of the things that really impact developing apps when thinking "web v native."

Language and Platform

HTML5 is becoming the cross-platform development technology of choice. Although not strictly a language, HTML5 includes HTML for view markup, CSS for view styling and animations, and JavaScript for application logic. And if you use one of these, you are highly likely to use all the others, too.

As already mentioned, web apps are available on any device with a web browser that supports the technologies used by that app. Most of today's smartphones have web browsers that support HTML5, CSS3, and JavaScript. On top of that, the percentage of "dumbphones" on the market is dwindling rapidly (and besides, a dumbphone doesn't tend to offer particularly interesting native apps, either, so they're sort of a moot point).

When developing a web app for mobile or tablet, instead of just desktop, the only added burden is consideration for the new screen sizes presented by mobile devices. Most common technologies for web design, such as HTML5 and CSS3, are supported by most mobile devices, meaning that it's likely going to be more difficult to get all the features of your app running on old versions of Internet Explorer than it will be to get it running on mobile browsers.

A very strong principle in software development is represented by the acronym *DRY*, which is short for Don't Repeat Yourself. Consolidating all supported platforms into one central codebase by focusing on building a single responsive web application is a huge step toward a DRY app.

There are platforms such as PhoneGap[11] and Trigger.io[12] that aim to make a web app into various platform-specific apps. The very existence of tools such as these is a testament to both the market for native applications and to the difficulty of learning how to code for different platforms. Microsoft has even created an application architecture called WinRT,[13] which allows apps to be developed in HTML5, enabling the possibility of using the same codebase for both native Windows 8 apps and a web app.

If you decide to focus on building native apps, chances are you'll be focusing on Objective-C for iOS devices, Java for Android, as well as a WinRT supported language for Windows devices. Learning a new programming language is a great thing, but it does add days, or even weeks, to a development schedule for a developer who doesn't know the language of choice for a given platform.

If your native app is developed for a platform that is superseded or replaced by another platform, you have no choice but to rebuild the app for the new system. For example, any apps developed for Symbian are quickly becoming irrelevant, and any Windows Phone 7 apps can't be upgraded to Windows Phone 8; they have to be rebuilt.

This introduces risk because a native app is heavily affected by the platform for which it is built. If by some freak occurrence, Apple were to suddenly shut down the App Store, developers would be left with no recourse or quick fix; they would simply have to start over and build their app for another platform, or call it quits and do something else altogether.

Maintenance

Maintaining one native app is probably about the same as maintaining one web app (or even a little easier, depending on the platform). The maintenance issue comes in when faced with multiplatform apps: one app becomes four if it needs to work on iOS, Android, BlackBerry, and Windows Phone. Suddenly, most maintenance is multiplied by four, and that doesn't even consider the strong possibility of a web–based companion tool or web app version of the app.

---

[11]http://phonegap.com/
[12]https://trigger.io/
[13]http://en.wikipedia.org/wiki/Windows_Runtime

On top of that, updates have to be downloaded by the user, so beyond a marketplace prompt, your encouragement, and notes in the support docs, there's nothing to guarantee that a user ever gets the latest version of the app.

With a web app, rather than rolling out fixes to the Android, iOS, BlackBerry, and Windows Phone versions of the app, only one version of the code—assuming the app is built to be responsive—needs to be updated to clean up issues on any device for which the app is designed.

Testing

When creating a web app, it's an effort to create a "one size fits all" app. Therefore, it requires diligent testing on all the devices it needs to support. Ideally, it should even be tested across different versions of each platform.

Native apps present similar issues to testing a website for cross-browser support: a fix for iPhone might introduce a new bug on Android, a change in one version of Android might have an unexpected side effect in a different version of Android, and there's always the possibility that a certain feature just can't work the same way on every device.

Feature Support

If your app needs to access the device's accelerometer or camera, the argument is over unless you know exactly what web browser your users will be using on their phone. For example, to access the webcam on a device from a browser, you use the getUserMedia API, which isn't supported by the latest versions of even the mainstream browsers;[14] as ever, Chrome, Firefox, and Opera are leading the way.

If you don't know whether all the users of your web application will have support for all the features it *requires*, your best choice is to create a native app.

Operating systems expose access to most hardware features to native apps. Browsers are slowly exposing access to these features, but again they're not available cross-browser. One such example is orientation control. In some applications, you may always want the user to be viewing in landscape mode—for example, a racing game—but although there are ways of detecting orientation initial state and changes, there isn't an API to control this in a web browser right now, so the only solutions are effectively hacks.[15]

Modern mobile web browsers are constantly evolving, and the number of browsers that do provide APIs that enable access to hardware and other operating system features are increasing all the time. But right now, native applications have the edge by providing complete control over the hardware and OS features that the application can access.

Connectivity

We live in an increasingly connected world, so it's no surprise that a lot of applications rely on connectivity.

To initially fetch our application, native or web, we need an Internet connection. A lot of the features offered by applications also require a connection, such as any piece of functionality that makes use of other Internet services or APIs (for example: public transport apps, features that synchronize your information across devices such as to-do or note-taking applications such as EverNote, or mapping applications that in no way could store all the information a user could potentially request).

Some of these applications, such as EverNote, can still provide useful functionality while offline. But others, such as Skype, can't offer any of its core functionality without a connection. They may as well refuse to open.

Once a native app is downloaded on your device, all the resources (in most cases, at least) are now stored on the device, meaning it should be possible to use it offline. But many applications assume connectivity leading to a very frustrating user experience.

---

[14]http://caniuse.com/#feat=stream
[15]http://stackoverflow.com/questions/5298467/prevent-orientation-change-in-ios-safari

There's no real reason for this to be the case, and the same goes with web applications. HTML5 has well-defined offline support,[16] including application file caching and local storage, so with developer care, it is possible to have a working offline web app in much the same way as a native application should function offline.

Choosing Based on Requirements

Given that both native apps and web apps have pros and cons, it's fairly evident that there's no clear right answer when it comes to choosing a platform for your app. Too many factors play into the decision for one or the other to simply be "better."

Instead, app developers should spend a reasonable amount of time considering their app, how it will be used, what it will do, and how they intend to monetize it. After they have the requirements figured out, they can run their app through the pros and cons listed previously, along with any additional considerations specific to their situation, and choose the approach that best benefits *their* application.

Choosing Web Apps Over Native Apps

For your app project, let's weigh the proposed features of the app against the previous pros and cons to make the best decision for this situation.

What Does this App Do?

Though we'll get significantly deeper into detail about this in the next chapter, at a glance this app provides a simple interface for an audience to ask questions of a presenter and for the presenter to receive those questions in realtime.

How Does this App Make Money?

For the purposes of this book, the app *doesn't* make money, but if it were going to be monetized, it's unlikely that someone would be willing to pay $0.99 to ask a question when they could simply raise their hand.

It would likely make more sense to charge presenters to create a room because the app serves to help them control the room and make sure that all questions are answered. Presenters would likely purchase the room just before setting it up, which is easiest to do on a desktop browser, so payment through a web interface might not be a deterrent.

How Will People Use this App?

Presumably, users will be in the physical space where the presenter is holding the event. This could be a classroom at a university, a meeting room at a convention, or the conference room at a large company's keynote.

Because it's likely that an attendee will not be at a desk, it's a safe assumption that she could be using a laptop, a tablet, or her phone to interact with the speaker, so the app should support as many devices as possible.

Does this App Need Access to Any Device Hardware?

The app doesn't need to access any of the user's phone hardware, such as the camera, so that's not something that you need to worry about for this project.

---

[16]http://www.w3.org/TR/offline-webapps/

The Final Decision: Let's Build a Web App

Given that this app doesn't need to access device hardware or charge a fee for accessing the app, given that the user base is not predictably using any particular device, and that there is an absolute requirement for Internet connectivity for audience-to-presenter communications, it makes the most sense for our app to be built as a web app.

Summary

In this chapter, you learned the benefits and pitfalls of building both native apps and web apps. Because there's no right or wrong answer, app developers need to consider each project individually to determine which approach will best benefit them.

In the next chapter, we'll get into the down and dirty details of the app to make sure we have all our ducks in a row before we start coding.

■ ■ ■

CHAPTER 5

Determining the App's Functionality and Structure

Now that we know we're building a web app and have our tools at the ready, we can start really planning the app's functionality. In this chapter, you will:

- Define what the app does
- Determine how users will interact with it (and what will differ based on a user's role)
- Come up with a plan for the site's back-end code and database
- Figure out a structure for the front end
- Create a simple wireframe for the app

By the end of this chapter, you should have a very clear idea of how the app will be built; this should eliminate wasted development hours and help keep the app on track.

What Does the App Do?

Before we can plan anything, you need a very clear and concise feature list. This will keep our feature list in check and help avoid any scope creep as you start designing and developing.

Give the App a Mission Statement

Let's start with a high-level overview of the app that should direct all the decisions you make regarding the app's functionality.

In one short paragraph, let's figure out how to describe the app:

This is a simple Q&A web app to allow attendees of a given event to ask questions of the presenter and confirm that a question by another attendee is relevant to them as well, all in real time. In addition, the presenter should have a list of questions and the number of people asking each, from which she can mark a question answered as she gives the answer to the group.

What Doesn't the App Do?

Equally important—if not more so—than the list of what the app does, is the list of what it *doesn't* do. This will inform decisions about whether or not a feature should be included in the app.

This app is intended to be a tool for presenters and attendees of an event that is occurring live and is most likely going to be used in the same physical space as the other attendees. Therefore, the app should *not*:

- Attempt to replace live discussion.

    - This means the app does not allow comments or answers within itself; it is solely there to present questions, not to answer or clarify them. Allowing discussion within the app could distract from the actual presentation.

- Provide any additional information about the session.

    - The app doesn't tell attendees what the session is about or provide any resources. That focus is still on the presenter because this app is not meant to take part in the presentation, only the Q&A.

- Provide any organizational tools for the presenter.

    - The presenter's dashboard is simply a list of questions, ranked by popularity, that can be marked as "answered." This is not a tool to help presenters get better at presenting; it's there to help them field questions from the room.

What Roles Will Users Play?

Now that we know what the app does—asks and answers questions—we can define the different types of users that will interact with it.

Because this is a pretty simple application, there are only two user roles: Presenter and Attendee.

Presenter

A presenter will create a room on the app's home view and then share that room with the people in attendance using a link that will be generated upon the room's creation. He will be provided with a button that ends the session, which closes it to further questions.

As questions are asked, they will show up on the presenter's screen in real time with one UI element that allows him to mark the question as answered.

Attendees

Attendees will join a room by either clicking the link provided by the presenter or by entering the room's ID, which will be the part of the URL that isn't the domain name (i.e., `http://example.com/`**1234**, where 1234 is the room's ID).

Upon joining the room, attendees will see questions that have been asked in this session previously (if any exist) with an option to vote up that question. Any new questions will appear on the screen in real time.

There will also be a form through which an attendee can ask her own question, which will be added to the list of questions already upvoted by her.

Finally, there will be a link to email the presenter directly if a question wasn't answered satisfactorily or if the question isn't appropriate for the whole group.

Front-End Planning

Your next step is to start fleshing out the approach you'll be taking with the app's front end, or the visual parts of the app with which users will interact.

In this section, you will organize your development approach for all the front-end technologies.

What Technologies Are We Using?

We've already discussed the tools we'll be using for this app, but to recap, you'll be building the front end of the site using the following:

- HTML5
- CSS3
- JavaScript
- jQuery
- The Pusher JavaScript library

You'll be using multiple aspects of each technology to craft a good-looking, easy-to-use, simple front-end for the app.

Using HTML5

As with pretty much all web apps, the front end will be built using HTML markup. For this app, you'll be taking advantage of some of the new elements and attributes introduced in HTML5.

You've probably already seen or used any of the new elements, such as the <article> and <footer> elements. In case you haven't, they're functionally identical to <div> elements, but they're better from a semantic standpoint because they're self-describing.

You will also be taking advantage of the new <input> types—namely the email type—to encourage touch screen devices to customize the keyboard to suit the data being entered.

Finally, you'll use the new data attribute to pass information to Cascading Style Sheets (CSS) and jQuery for various purposes. We'll get more into the how and why of that in the next chapter.

Going Minimalist with the HTML

■ **Caution**   The following is a borderline rant by the authors.

Good HTML markup is a relative term. Good how? Does being functional make it good? Well-formatted? Valid?

Like nearly everything in programming, most of what makes HTML markup "good" is entirely subjective. There is no globally recognized "right way" to write your markup, and that's probably a good thing because it allows developers to get creative with HTML elements to create really clever layouts.

However, there are *definitely* wrong ways to write markup. Things such as a different nested <div> for each applied CSS class is *wrong*; it's just sloppy programming. Using class names that are completely opaque is wrong. Throwing proper indentation and nesting to the wind is wrong.

For this app, we'll treat HTML like a dance floor: It needs to be clear of any debris and obstacles so the data being presented doesn't get tripped up.

Let's go over a few of the most common and detrimental markup practices and plan *not* to use any of them.

Abusing the <div> Element

The most obvious abuse of HTML markup is the application of new <div> elements for each new style to be applied. Not only does this add more elements to the Document Object Model (DOM) and make things like jQuery traversal less efficient and more complicated, but it makes later maintenance a nightmare, especially if someone else is going to have to deal with your code.

Using Completely Opaque Class Names

Another incredibly frustrating markup *faux pas* is the use of cryptic class names and IDs. In 99.999% of situations, the benefit of saving a few bytes by shortening the class name float-right to fl is completely negated by the headache it causes the people who have to attempt to understand and maintain that code later.

Completely Ignoring Indentation

Indentation is optional in HTML, and as a result it gets largely ignored by many developers. This doesn't necessarily hurt their quality of work, but it makes dealing with their markup more painful than necessary.

Given that the extra time required to at least *sort of* format markup is negligible, especially considering most modern integrated development environment (IDEs) indent code properly by default—it's just plain lazy not to take a moment to ensure people who have to deal with markup at a later date can read it by adding some white space.

AN EXAMPLE OF GOOD MARKUP VERSUS BAD MARKUP

To demonstrate the huge difference paying attention to your markup can make, let's look at a very small example that compares a snippet of bad markup with a rewritten snippet that accomplishes the same thing.

An Example with Bad Markup

First, let's look at the bad markup. In less than 3 seconds, can you figure out what this is and how you might fix an extra margin issue?

```
<td><div class="sb"><div class="im csh"><a
href="http://www.example.com/inventory/1234/"
title="Example Product"><img width="150" height="150"
src="http://www.example.com/images/1234.jpg" class="at"
alt="Example Product" title="Example Product" /></a></div></div></td>
```

This code is perfectly valid, but it's just awful. Where are all these <div>s coming from? What the hell does the class sb do? What about csh, im, or at? To fix the hypothetical margin issue, you would have to check every class referenced in this snippet before you could identify the offending styles.

On top of that, it's extremely difficult to tell what this snippet is without spending extra time really looking at it due to the complete lack of formatting. This will slow down future maintenance, especially if someone else is doing it.

The Same Example, but with Better Markup

Contrast the previous markup to this snippet:

```
<td class="show-badge">
    <a href="http://www.example.com/inventory/1234"
        class="image cushioned"
        title="Example Product">
        <img src="http://www.example.com/images/1234.jpg"
            class="product-thumbnail"
            alt="Example Product" />
    </a>
</td>
```

How long did it take you to figure out that this was an image thumbnail for a product? Not long, especially in comparison to the original snippet.

The extra `<div>`s have been eliminated because all those styles can be applied to the `<td>` or `<a>` elements. Class names have been expanded to be human-readable. (Our hypothetical margin issue probably comes from the `cushioned` class, at a guess.) Elements have been formatted to make scanning easy.

Making these small adjustments to your markup will take a few extra seconds but save *hours* of frustration down the road. So you should do it.

CSS3, Media Queries, and How That Affects the Design and HTML

To style the app, you'll be using CSS, including some of the new features of CSS3. Using features such as `box-shadow` and `border-radius` will allow you to give your app a layer of design polish without having to deal with tons of images.

Probably the most exciting new feature of CSS3 that you'll be implementing is adaptive layout using media queries. This will let you apply styles based on the browser's width, eliminating the need for browser sniffing, multiple versions of the app, or a layout that looks good only on a certain subset of devices.

However, using media queries brings up a few concerns that should be addressed in both the design and markup stages of the app. Because the layout will be changing to best fit on the screen on which it's displayed, there's a certain amount of flexibility in the layout that needs to be considered from the get-go.

One- and Two-Column Layouts

When looking at sites that implement adaptive layouts,[1] one of the most common techniques used is to change from multiple columns to a single column when the site is viewed on smaller screens.

At a glance, this doesn't seem like a big deal, but it can throw a wrench in your layout if content needs to flow in any way other than column one first, column two second, and so on (or vice versa). (For example, a site with advertisements in the sidebar would probably get into hot water with its advertisers if the ads were suddenly pushed off the screen below all the latest content.)

---

[1]For a gallery of adaptive layouts, see `http://mediaqueri.es`.

EXERCISE 5-1: PLAYING WITH A RESPONSIVE LAYOUT

In an effort to demonstrate the content reflow challenges that responsive layout can present, let's look at an example site.

For the purposes of this exercise, you've been charged with converting the design in Figure 5-1 to a responsive layout.

Figure 5-1. *A sample site that needs to be converted to a responsive layout*

This is a pretty standard layout: a header, a footer, a left-hand column with blog entries, and a right-hand column with standard "sidebar" content (ads and a newsletter capture).

Reflowing Content on Small Screens

Logically, when the site is rendered on a handheld device, it wouldn't make sense to show two columns side by side; the content would be far too cluttered and narrow. The natural solution is to switch to a single-column layout, which allows the content to be displayed in a more aesthetically pleasing manner.

However, the advertisers for this site won't stand for the ads to be buried beneath the blog entries—as more content is accumulated, there could be as many as eight entries displayed in the left column—so simply stacking the left column on top of the right one won't cut it.

To solve this problem, you need to somehow interleave the content from the left column with the content from the right. This requires a few adjustments to the markup to allow each section of the main content area to flow on its own.

Typically, a design like this might be marked up something like the following (simplified):

```
<header>...</header>

<section id="main-content">
    <article>...</article>
    <article>...</article>
</section>

<aside id="sidebar-content">
    <div id="ads">...</div>
    <div id="newsletter">...</div>
</aside>

<footer>...</footer>
```

This, however, puts the columns into "boxes" that don't allow you to reflow the content. To solve this, you'll need to make each piece of content its own box:

```
<header>...</header>

<article>...</article>
<aside id="ads">...</aside>
<article>...</article>
<aside id="newsletter">...</aside>

<footer>...</footer>
```

This markup resembles what a single-column layout should look like: Lead with an entry, then show ads, then show another entry, and then show the newsletter signup. In the future, additional entries will flow beneath the newsletter.

Now you can use media queries to arrange the content into two columns when the screen is wide enough, but stack content in an acceptable order when it's not.

Content Reflowing with Media Queries

To get the content to display properly, start with the smallest screen size. Nothing special about the markup; just some basic styles:

```
article {
    position: relative;
    margin: 0 0 2em;
    overflow: hidden;
}

aside {
    margin: 1.5em 0;
    padding: 1.5em 0;
    border-top: 1px dashed #955240;
    border-bottom: 1px dashed #955240;
}
```

Then, when the screen is wide enough, additional styles are applied to break the content into two columns. For this example, the media query that applies these rules is set to match any screen smaller than 768 pixels, which is a common tablet resolution.

The styles aren't anything too crazy: blog entries are floated left, and sidebar content is floated right, which arranges the content into two columns:

```
@media screen and (min-width: 768px) {

    article {
        position: relative;
        float: left;
        width: 55%;
        margin: 0 3% 2em 0;
    }

    aside {
        float: right;
        width: 42%;
        margin: 0 0 2%;
        padding: 0;
        border: none;
    }

}
```

▓ **Note**   The use of percentages allows the columns to grow or shrink depending on the screen size. When viewing this layout in a desktop browser, you can resize your window to see the content reflow to utilize available space.

Once the layout is completed, narrow screens will see a single-column layout with ads acceptably nestled below the first entry (Figure 5-2).

Figure 5-2. *Three screens showing the reflowed content from left to right*

■ **Note**   To see the layout in action and review the full source code of the above exercise, visit
`https://github.com/jlengstorf/responsive-design`.

Clickable Areas and Fat Fingers

Another difference when designing apps that will be used on mobile devices is the loss of precision when clicking (or tapping). If you've ever tried to use a website on your phone that was designed for full-sized browsers only, you may have experienced the frustration of trying to tap a link displayed in a list, but accidentally selecting the wrong one because your finger was too big to be precise.

For that reason, your user interface should feature big buttons and ensure that links have enough space around them to ensure users can click them easily, even with fat fingers.

Effects and Animations

To make the app feel like it is responding to user actions, you'll also be implementing effects and animations, including code to indicate which input or control a user has selected (including keyboard control) and simple animations to signify that a requested action has been performed.

Upvoting a Question

When an attendee taps the upvote button on a question, you'll want to add an effect to provide visual feedback. Simply highlighting the control and incrementing the vote count should be enough in this case.

Answering a Question

When a presenter answers a question, it should stay on the screen, but move somewhere less prominent. You'll need to implement effects to reorder the list of questions, moving the answered question below unanswered questions, as well as reducing its opacity to keep the focus on unanswered questions.

Feedback from UI Elements

Users can hover over or tab through the various UI elements in the app, so you'll want to be sure to add effects to let them know what's clickable or which form element has focus. This can be accomplished with CSS.

Other Effects

The site's back end will update the app with new data via Pusher whenever other users perform certain actions, so there has to be effects in place to handle manipulating the DOM to show the updates. We'll go into deeper detail on these effects in a later chapter.

Back-End Planning

The back end of the site is where all user actions need to be processed and stored. To make the app simple to maintain and quick to develop, let's run through how both the scripts and the database should be organized.

Model View Controller

The industry standard for software design in web applications is the *Model-View-Controller* (MVC) pattern. There are dozens of PHP frameworks available, and most of them are based on the MVC pattern.

Because of its widespread usage and the fact that it's generally considered the best approach for web applications, you'll be building this app using the MVC pattern.

A BRIEF INTRO TO THE MVC PROGRAMMING PATTERN

MVC sounds more complicated than it is. At its core, the concept of MVC is to separate any presentational elements (the view, which is commonly HTML markup) from data (the model, typically information stored in a database) from logic (the controller, which might be PHP code).

There are three pretty clear distinctions made in an app using the MVC pattern:

- **Controllers** Classes and code that manipulate data and interpret user input. This is what interprets user instructions (such as a page request), asks the model for the required data, manipulates it, and sends it to the view for output.

- **Models** Classes that read and write data. That's it. These classes don't do any manipulation to the data and they don't generate any output that would be shown to the end user.

- **Views** This is the code used to display information to the user. There is no logic of any kind done here; a view, in the web app context, should be as close to plain HTML as possible.

A typical request made to an MVC-based app should closely resemble these (see Figure 5-3).

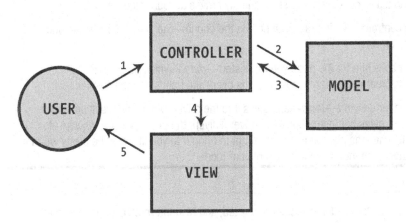

Figure 5-3. *A diagram showing the order of operations for a typical MVC request*

■ **Note** There's a lot of disagreement on how an MVC-based app should work, this is our take.

Let's take a walk through the steps shown in Figure 5-3 with the application we're building in mind.

1. The user interacts with the client application—the controller—by passing a command via the uniform resource indicator (URI). This could be a presentation attendee filling out and submitting the question form, or upvoting a question. Or it could be the presenter marking a question as answered. This results in a request being made from the client application to the server.

2. The controller processes that request, determines the action based on the request parameters. It then interacts with the appropriate model based on those inputs.

3. A model within MVC can also represent, or contain, the data access layer. In our application, this is the case. So when the model is interacted with as a result of a user submitting a question, it will result in the question being stored in the database. If it's a result of a question upvote, the fact that the question has been upvoted will also be persisted. After the model has handled the interaction, it returns the appropriate data to the controller.

4. The controller processes the response from the model and delivers it to the view.

5. The view updates according to the response from the controller. A question being submitted may result in the view changing to show all the questions for the presenter while highlighting the newly added question. Or in the case of an upvote, the question may change position in the view.

MVC Explained by a Silly Analogy

To understand MVC in its simplest form, think about ordering a pizza. You call the pizza parlor and speak to the cashier, who takes your order. When you complete your order, the cashier tells the cook what was ordered, and the cook sets about making the pizza. After the pizza is out of the oven, the cook gives it to the cashier, who packages the pizza for delivery and hands it to a delivery driver, who subsequently arrives at your home with the pizza.

In this example, the cashier is the controller. You interact with her via the phone—the *URI*—and give her your order—*instructions*—which she interprets.

The cook is the *model*. The cashier asks him for the pizza you requested—*data*—which he gives to the cashier. The cook takes the request, creates the pizza, cooks it in the oven, and hands it to the cashier.

The cashier then prepares the pizza for delivery—*logic*—and gives it to the driver, who is the resulting *view* from the interaction. After the cashier gives her instructions, the driver delivers the pizza to you—*display*—for your enjoyment. The driver never touches the pizza in any way except to bring it to you; it would be pretty weird if your pizza delivery driver had his hands on the raw ingredients of your food.

■ **Note** MVC dates back to 1979[2] and has been interpreted, reinterpreted, and re-reinterpreted by programmers across dozens of languages in the 30+ years since its conception. There is no absolute right way to implement MVC. It's a philosophical principle that guides development, and, as with all philosophies, it will vary in practice between camps. Don't stress about it.

Determining the Database Structure

In order to store information about the rooms and questions, you'll need a database. In this section, you'll come up with a list of data that needs to be stored and determine the structure for said data.

What Data Needs to Be Stored?

To start, let's make a list of everything that needs to be stored for the app to function properly. This includes both the room and question information:

- The room's name
- A unique identifier for the room
- Whether or not the room is active
- The presenter's name
- A unique identifier for the presenter
- The presenter's email
- The question

---

[2]http://heim.ifi.uio.no/~trygver/themes/mvc/mvc-index.html

- A unique identifier for the question
- Whether or not the question is answered
- The number of votes for the question

Database Normalization

In order to keep the database clutter-free and eliminate duplicate information, the database needs to be normalized.[3]

WHY DATABASE NORMALIZATION IS IMPORTANT

The easiest way to show why database normalization is important is to look at a simple example.

Imagine a database for a college that needs to track its professors and what classes each one is currently teaching. It needs to store the professor's name, email address, date of hire, and ID of the class they teach.

If the database is *not* normalized, it might look something like Table 5-1.

Table 5-1. *Table That Has Not Been Normalized*

Name	Email	Hire_date	Class
Jane Doe	jane.doe@example.org	2004-08-09	ECON-101
Tom Jones	tom.jones@example.org	2007-01-15	MATH-315

This may not look wrong at a glance, but when you start manipulating the data, things start to get a bit wonky.

For example, what happens when a new professor is hired, but doesn't have a class yet? There would be an empty column for that entry, which could cause issues for any applications that read this data.

Conversely, what if a teacher teaches two or more classes? There would be duplicate data for all but one of the columns (see Table 5-2).

Table 5-2. *Non-Normalized Table with a Professor Who Teaches Two Classes*

Name	Email	Hire_date	Class
Jane Doe	jane.doe@example.org	2004-08-09	ECON-101
Jane Doe	jane.doe@example.org	2004-08-09	ECON-201
Tom Jones	tom.jones@example.org	2007-01-15	MATH-315

There's also the issue of deleting info: If Tom Jones stops teaching MATH-315, and that row is removed from the database, his other info is lost as well, which probably wasn't the desired outcome.

---

[3]http://en.wikipedia.org/wiki/Database_normalization

Normalizing the Database

To make this database more manageable, it should be normalized, which would break the data into two tables: one for professor data (see Table 5-3) and one to map professors to the classes they teach (see Table 5-4).

Table 5-3. *Professors Table Without the Class Information*

Name	Email	Hire_date
Jane Doe	jane.doe@example.org	2004-08-09
Tom Jones	tom.jones@example.org	2007-01-15

Table 5-4. *New Table Maps Professors to the Classes They Teach*

Professor	Class
Jane Doe	ECON-101
Jane Doe	ECON-201
Tom Jones	MATH-315

By splitting the data into two tables, it's now possible to remove Tom Jones as the teacher of Math 315 without losing his personal data, and it's also possible to have Jane Doe teach two classes without duplicating all her other data.

This table still isn't ideal, however, because it presents difficulties in updating the professor's name. For instance, if another teacher called Jane Doe is hired, how do you uniquely identify which one was being referred to in the table that maps professors to classes being taught? It could be further normalized to use a numeric ID for the professors rather than their names, which solves that issue (see Tables 5-5 and 5-6).

Table 5-5. *The Professors Table with an ID Field Added*

ID	Name	Email	Hire_date
1	Jane Doe	jane.doe@example.org	2004-08-09
2	Tom Jones	tom.jones@example.org	2007-01-15

Table 5-6. *Class Info Table Now Uses the Professors' IDs Rather Than Their Names*

Professor_ID	Class
1	ECON-101
1	ECON-201
2	MATH-315

At this point, this database is adequately normalized and shouldn't present any issues when adding, modifying, or deleting data in the future.

Determining the Tables and Structure

With normalization in mind, let's define the tables for your app. To recap, the data that you need to store is the following:

- The room's name
- A unique identifier for the room
- Whether or not the room is active
- The presenter's name
- A unique identifier for the presenter
- The presenter's email
- The question
- A unique identifier for the question
- Whether or not the question is answered
- The number of votes for the question

If you group this data normally, you should end up with four tables:

- Presenters
- Rooms
- Questions
- Votes

Presenters Table

The first table, presenters, stores the presenter's name, email, and a unique ID (see Table 5-7).

Table 5-7. presenters Table

id	name	email

Rooms Table

The rooms table will store a room's unique ID, its name, and whether or not it's active (see Table 5-8).

Table 5-8. rooms Table

id	name	is_active

Questions Table

The questions table will store a question's unique ID, the room to which it belongs, the question text, and whether or not it's been answered (see Table 5-9).

Table 5-9. *questions Table*

id	room_id	question	is_answered

Question Votes Table

The question_votes table will store the question's ID and the current vote count (see Table 5-10).

Table 5-10. *question_votes Table*

question_id	vote_counts

Room Owners Table

The Room_owners table will store the IDs of the room and the presenter (see Table 5-11).

Table 5-11. *room_owners Table*

room_id	presenter_id

Putting Everything Together in a Wireframe

At this point, we have most of our planning completed; all that's left is to wireframe the app quickly to get a general idea of the layout.

Organizing the Home Page

The home page needs to serve two purposes in order to meet the needs of our two user roles.

First, it needs to provide a way for a presenter to create a new room. This will require a form that asks for the necessary information.

Second, attendees need to be able to join a room if they don't have a direct link to the session. This also requires a form that will accept the room's ID.

In addition to the two forms, there should also be a header to identify the app and a footer to provide additional information, such as copyright.

Wireframing for Wider Screens

On wider screens, it makes sense to set these two forms side by side because neither is more or less important than the other. When we put this all into a basic wireframe, it looks like Figure 5-4.

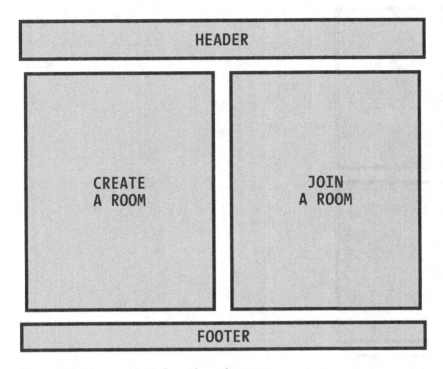

Figure 5-4. Home page wireframe for wider screens

Wireframing for Narrower Screens

On narrower screens, a two-column layout isn't feasible, so we have to reflow the content into a single column. The form for attendees to join a room should be on top for two reasons: It will be much shorter than the presenter form, and it's reasonable to assume that more people will be using the app to attend sessions than to present.

After reflowing the content, it will look like Figure 5-5.

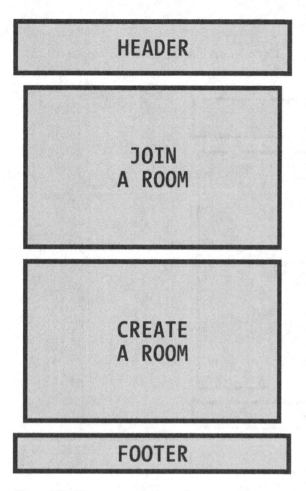

Figure 5-5. Home page wireframe for narrower screens

Organizing the Q&A Page for Attendees

After an attendee has joined a room, the app needs to display the room's name and who the presenter is, as well as showing her the form to ask a question and the list of existing questions.

The header and footer will stay consistent across the app, so only the main content area needs to change.

Wireframing for Wider Screens

Again, on a wider screen, the content can flow to two columns, but in this case one of the columns should be wider than the other because not much will be displayed in the sidebar.

The form to ask a new question should be prominently featured at the top of the main column with questions underneath.

On the right side, the name of the room and the presenter's information should be displayed.

With this information plugged in, the wireframe looks like Figure 5-6.

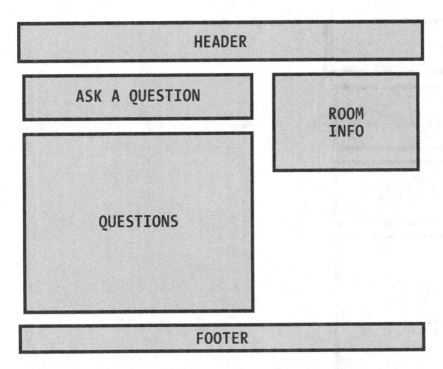

Figure 5-6. *The Q&A page for attendees wireframed for wider screens*

Wireframing for Narrower Screens

For the single-column layout, we're actually going to put the sidebar containing room information at the top. The reason for doing this is the content is important—without it, attendees wouldn't know which session they had joined—and very short, so it won't push the rest of the content too far down.

After reflowing the content, you'll see something similar to Figure 5-7.

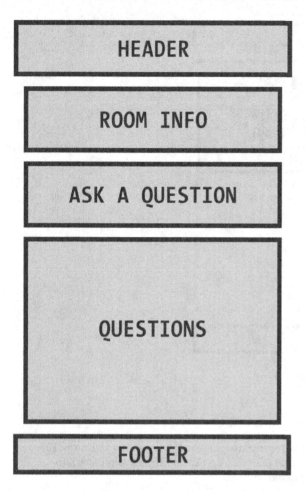

Figure 5-7. *The Q&A page for attendees wireframed for narrower screens*

Organizing the Q&A Page for Presenters

There are only a few small differences between the Q&A page for attendees and the one for presenters. Namely, the "ask a question" form is removed, and some controls for the presenter are added.

Wireframing for Wider Screens

After swapping out the "ask a question" form for presenter controls, the layout doesn't change too much in the two-column view. However, instead of placing the controls at the top of the list of questions, they'll be below the room info to place the focus more heavily on answering questions (see Figure 5-8).

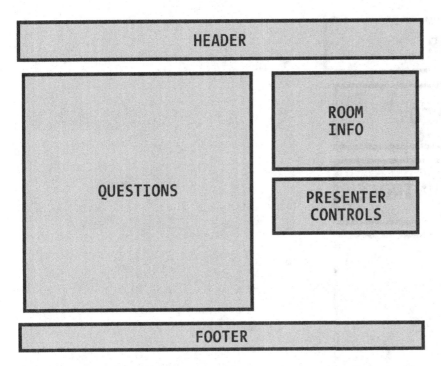

Figure 5-8. *The Q&A page for presenters wireframed for wider screens*

Wireframing for Narrower Screens

Similarly to the layout for attendees, the room info and controls will move to the top of the list of questions in single-column view (see Figure 5-9).

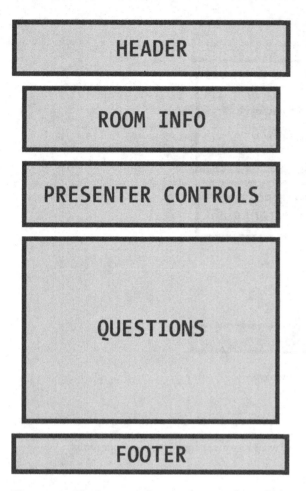

Figure 5-9. The Q&A page for presenters wireframed for narrower screens

Summary

At this point, you're familiar with all the required technologies, you've got a plan of attack for both the front- and back-end development of the site, and you have a wireframe to inform your design.

In the next chapter, you'll design and build the app from the ground up according to the plan laid out in this chapter.

■ ■ ■

PART III

Building the Basics

You are now armed with the required tools, a wireframe, and a solid plan of attack. In this section, you will build the basics of your application.

At the end of this section, you will have a functioning app with a front end for displaying information on multiple screen sizes and a back end for storing and retrieving room data and question information dynamically.

CHAPTER 6

■ ■ ■

Designing the App

Because this is a book about development and not about design, this chapter will be short. It discusses a few design considerations that are unique to web apps. In addition, we'll talk a bit about how to make sure that a design made in Photoshop will translate well to the web.

■ **Note** This chapter assumes that you have access to Adobe Photoshop, are reasonably familiar with its interface, and—perhaps most importantly—that you care about design. You will be able to create the same artwork in an alternative program (such as GIMP), but the following steps won't match up properly.

■ **Caution** If you're a hard-core developer and are thinking about skipping this chapter, consider that besides walking you through the app's design, it also offers some tips on tweaking Photoshop settings to make sure that the coded design looks like what was laid out in Photoshop. If you work in a team and do any front-end work, it might save you some headaches when your creative team wants to know why a font looks slightly different or other minor layout inconsistencies.

Setting Goals for the Design

It's important for any design project to start with clearly defined goals. This helps to prevent the design from wandering off-course or conflicting with the intentions of the app.

Because this design is for an app that needs to work both on standard web browsers and on handheld devices, the goals for this design are the following:

- To require as few images as absolutely necessary

- To keep the design minimal and focused only on the required content

- To use large user interface (UI) elements that make the app easy to use on touch screens

If the design adheres to just these three goals, it will be easy to transition from the desktop to mobile, simple to use, and very easy to navigate.

Defining the Color Palette

Next, you need to choose a color palette for the app. This is an entirely subjective decision, but the colors chosen should fall within certain guidelines:

- The background color and the text color should have a high contrast difference to make sure it's easy to read

- Lighter backgrounds tend to be a bit easier on the eyes, legibility-wise

- It's typically a good idea to include an accent color to draw attention to important elements, such as links and buttons

For this app, let's use simple earth tones with a bright orange accent color (see Figure 6-1). Keeping it neutral makes it easy on the eyes and prevents the colors from clashing, which could make text on the site harder to read. The accent color won't show up properly in this book because it's greyscale. To see the accent color properly, set the color picker in Photoshop to the hex value shown in the figure.

Figure 6-1. *The chosen color palette for the app Light will be used for the background and Dark for the text*

Choosing Fonts

The relatively recent widespread support of @font-face has opened up a whole new world of possibilities for designers. No longer are web-based apps limited to a tiny subset of web-safe fonts; instead, interactive designers are now limited only by their imaginations (and the OFL license[1]).

Taking advantage of your newfound freedom, you now need to choose fonts for the app. Like the color palette, this is an entirely subjective decision, but there are some general guidelines that help inform solid font choices:

- Headlines can use a more interesting font than other copy on the site.

- Body text should use a simple, legible font to make sure it's not difficult to read.

- Design consistency is important. Don't go overboard on different fonts; stick to one or two that work well together.

- If one of the fonts chosen is very distinctive, other fonts used in the document should be more demure to prevent clashing.

- Bonus tip: When in doubt, use Helvetica.[2]

To create visual interest, headlines in our app will be in Cooper Black,[3] which is a very distinctive font that was heavily used in the *Mad Men* era of advertising. It's classic and bold without looking silly, which makes it ideal for large type.

---

[1]http://scripts.sil.org/cms/scripts/page.php?site_id=nrsi&id=OFL_web
[2]http://www.webdesignerdepot.com/2009/03/40-excellent-logos-created-with-helvetica/
[3]http://www.fonts101.com/fonts/view/Standard/2436/CooperBTBlack

Tight kerning—the spacing between characters—adds to the visual interest due to Cooper Black's round serifs. By smushing letters together, we get a neat visual appeal.

In contrast, the rest of the site's text will be set in News Gothic[4], which is significantly less outspoken as far as fonts go. It has clean, strong lines and is extremely legible—even at small sizes—but doesn't jump out at the reader like Cooper Black.

To assist with legibility, the kerning should be adjusted outward a bit to let the characters "breathe." It also forms a nice contrast with the headline font.

These two fonts complement each other well, and will make for a cohesive presentation that doesn't blend in with the rest of the sites on the Internet using traditionally web-safe fonts, such as Arial and Georgia.

The final font choices look very nice when we put them together in a sample (see Figure 6-2).

Cooper Black for titles.

News Gothic for body text.

Figure 6-2. A sample of the chosen fonts together

FONT RENDERING: PHOTOSHOP VS. @FONT-FACE

A common complaint from designers who don't have experience with web-based fonts is that they don't look the same as they did in Photoshop. This happens because Photoshop uses different antialiasing than most web browsers, which means the fonts will be rendered a bit differently. Most people won't notice the difference, but the difference is enough to cause some heartache for a creative type who has just spent a week getting his design just right (see Figure 6-3).

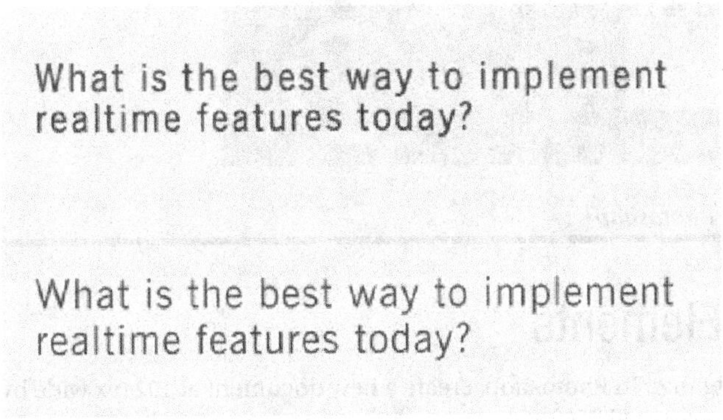

What is the best way to implement
realtime features today?

What is the best way to implement
realtime features today?

Figure 6-3. News Gothic rendered in the browser (top) and in Photoshop (bottom)

Fortunately, Photoshop provides options to change the antialiasing for fonts in layouts. One of these options—strong—is similar enough to the antialiasing used by most browsers that it eliminates the noticeable difference between a Photoshop layout and its appearance on the Web (see Figure 6-4).

---

[4] http://www.fontpalace.com/font-details/News+Gothic+BT/

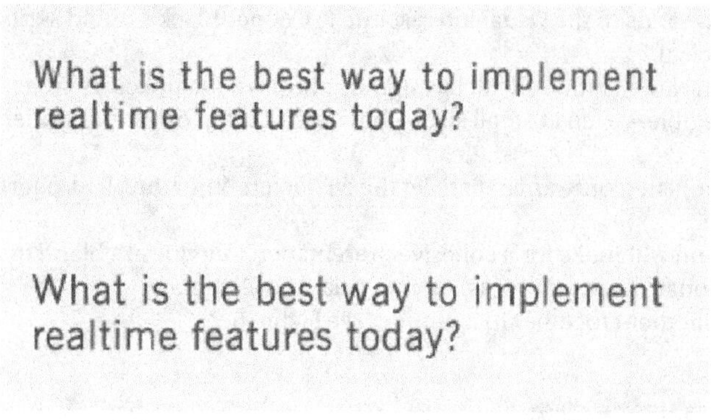

What is the best way to implement
realtime features today?
What is the best way to implement
realtime features today?

Figure 6-4. *With the strong antialiasing type, the fonts matches more closely*

To change the antialiasing mode in Photoshop, select the text layer (or layers; this can be changed in bulk without affecting other settings) and open the Character panel. At the bottom right, there is a drop-down menu that probably has Smooth selected by default. Change it to Strong and you're all set (see Figure 6-5).

What is the best way to implement
realtime features today?
What is the best way to implement
realtime features today?
Character
Paragraph
News Cothic BT
Roman
24 pt
27 pt
Metrics
40
100%
0 pt
Color:
English: USA
Strong

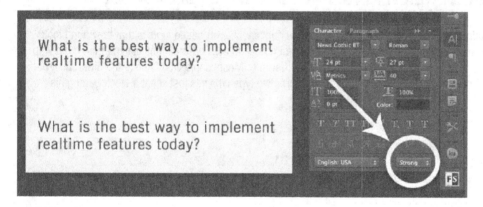

Figure 6-5. *Changing the antialiasing of type in Photoshop*

Designing the Common Site Elements

Armed with your colors and fonts, you can start designing. In Photoshop, create a new document at 1024px wide by 840px tall. Start by setting the background to the light color, #FBF7E7.

Creating the Header

The first element to design is the header, which will be set apart from the body of the design with the dark color, #1F1B0C, as its background color.

1. For the header, select the Rectangle Tool and draw a rectangle that is 1024px wide and 240px tall. Align it with the top and left of the document.

2. Next, select the Horizontal Type Tool and draw a text area on the page that will contain the main headline. Open the Character panel and put in the following settings:

   - Font: Cooper Black
   - Size: 110 pt
   - Tracking: -80
   - Color: #FBF7E7
   - Antialiasing: Strong

3. Add the title of the app, **Realtime Q&A**, and center it in the header.

4. To add the subhead line, use the Horizontal Type Tool to draw another text area below the headline. In the Character panel, change the settings to the following:

   - Font: News Gothic Light
   - Size: 18 pt
   - Tracking: 100
   - Color: #FBF7E7
   - Antialiasing: Strong

5. Add the subtitle, **A live feedback system for classes, presentations, and conferences**.

Save your work so far; you've now got the app's header (see Figure 6-6).

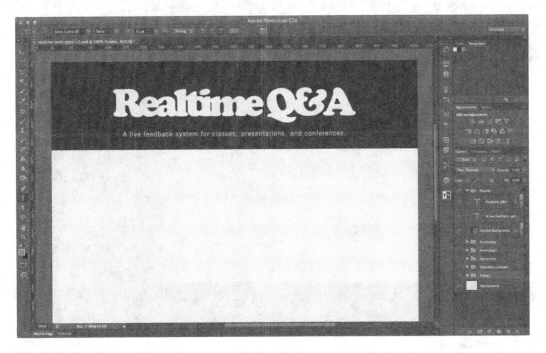

Figure 6-6. *The work in progress with the header designed*

Creating the Footer

Next up, let's add the site footer. Draw another rectangle (like the one you made for the header) at 1024px wide by 50px tall and align it with the bottom and left sides; this will be the background of the footer.

1. Using the Horizontal Type Tool, draw a text area centered on the footer background; then change the settings in the Character panel to the following:

   - Font: News Gothic Light

   - Size: 13 pt

   - Tracking: 25

   - Color: #FBF7E7

   - Antialiasing: Strong

2. Add the copyright info, **© 2013 Jason Lengstorf & Phil Leggetter**; then press Tab and choose the right align option. The tab allows the copyright info to align left while the text after the tab aligns right. Now add the rest of the footer text: **Part of** *Realtime Web Apps:* *With HTML5 WebSocket, PHP, and jQuery.* **Get the Book | Source Code (on GitHub)**.

3. For the links Get the Book and Source Code (on GitHub), select each one in turn and set the font to News Gothic Medium, turn on underlining, and set the color to your accent color, #E06F00.

Save again; the footer is good to go (see Figure 6-7).

Figure 6-7. *The footer for the app*

Form Elements

Now that you have a basic wrapper for the app, you can start putting together the look and feel of the user interface. Because this app is all about interaction, it relies heavily on forms to send information between the attendees and the presenter.

Because this app will be leaning on its form elements for most of its aesthetic, let's start by designing the inputs and buttons styles that we can use on all views in the application.

Text and E-mail Inputs

Text inputs will be used for nearly all the interaction on this app, so they're a logical starting point. I tend to keep all the elements on different layers in Photoshop and then group them into folders. Feel free to use whatever organizational method works for you.

1. Playing off the roundness of our headline font, grab the rounded rectangle tool and set the border radius to 6px. Draw a rectangle 430px wide by 40px tall and make it white (#FFFFFF). This will serve as the base for the input (see Figure 6-8).

Figure 6-8. *A white rectangle with 6px rounded corners*

2. Next, we need to make it look a little more like an input. To start, let's give it a border. Bring up the Layer Style panel by clicking the Layer Style (fx) button at the bottom of your layers panel while the rectangle layer is active (see Figure 6-9).

Figure 6-9. *The Layer Style button in Photoshop*

3. After the Layer Style button is clicked, several options will be listed. Click Stroke and the Effects dialog will open.

■ **Tip**   Hide the Target Path—the outline of the rectangle that Photoshop shows when you select the layer
(see Figure 6-9 for an example)—to get a better idea of what your effects look like as you edit them. To hide, press
Command + Shift + H or click View ➤ Show and uncheck Target Path.

---

4.   In the Effects dialog, give the input a 2px stroke and place it outside the shape. Use the
     dark color for this. The rest of the settings should remain at their default values
     (see Figure 6-10).

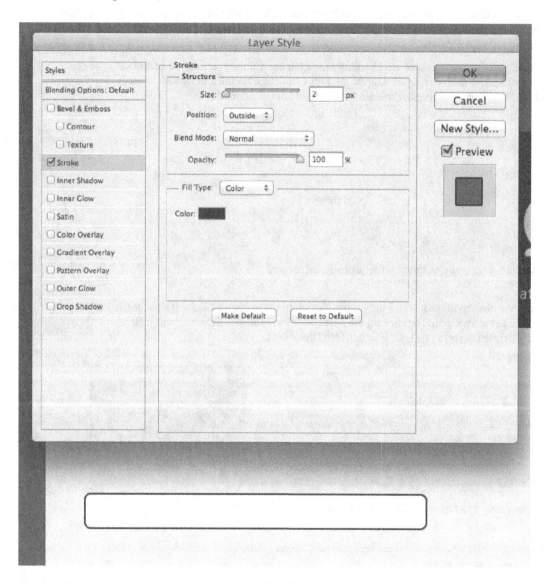

Figure 6-10.   *The input with a stroke added, plus all the settings*

5.   Next, add an inner shadow to the input, which will give it some dimension. Click the Inner Shadow check box below Stroke in the Layer Style panel, which brings up new settings (if it doesn't, click the actual label next to the check box). Set the shadow color to dark (#1F1B0C), the angle to 135°, distance to 2px, and the size to 14px. Change the blending mode to Normal as well, and drop the opacity to 30%, which gives you an input-looking rectangle (see Figure 6-11).

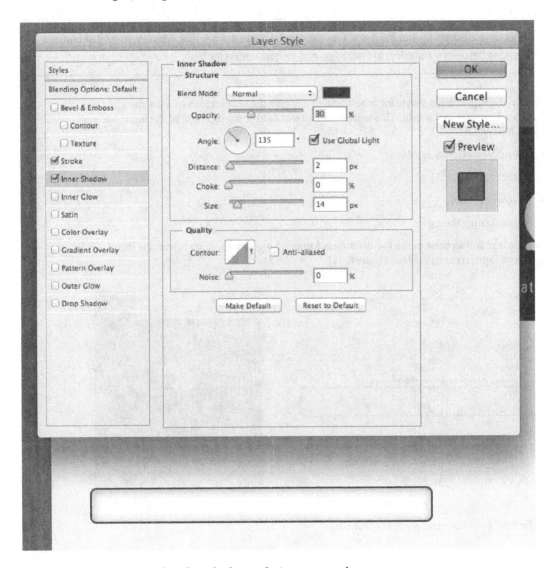

Figure 6-11. *Settings to apply a drop shadow to the input rectangle*

■ **Tip**   Setting the blending mode to Normal ensures that the drop shadow translates well to HTML/CSS. Although blending modes are in the works[5] (hopefully soon), they're not currently supported by CSS3, and therefore should be avoided in web layouts for the time being.

■ **Tip**   Use 135° for drop shadows so that the X and Y offsets are the same in CSS. This, typically, looks just fine and prevents inconsistencies between the shadow in Photoshop and the shadow on the Web.

---

6. Finally, the input needs a style for labels, which will give the user an idea of what she's supposed to enter in the field. This will be a small text field at the top right of the input, set to the following:

    •   Font: News Gothic Bold

    •   Tracking: 25

    •   Color: #1F1B0C

    •   Antialiasing: Strong

7. Use the text **Tell us your name (so attendees know who you are)**. Align it with the input, and your input is complete (see Figure 6-12).

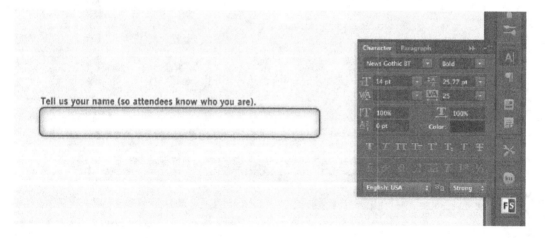

Figure 6-12.   *The label for the input completes the styling*

---

[5]http://www.w3.org/TR/compositing/

Submit Buttons

Forms won't do us much good if they can't be submitted, so we'll need a submit button designed to go along with the inputs.

1. Just like the text input, use the rounded rectangle tool with the border radius set to 6px. Create a box 310px wide by 54px tall and set it to the dark color (#1F1B0C). This will be the base of your button.

2. Next, use the Text tool with the following settings:
   - Font: Cooper Black
   - Size: 30 pt
   - Tracking: -50
   - Color: #FBF7E7
   - Antialiasing: Strong

3. Use the text **Create Your Room** and center the text on the submit button.

4. To give it a little dimension, open the Layer Style panel and add a drop shadow using the dark color (#1F1B0C) at 30% opacity, angled at 135°, and set at a size of 10px (see Figure 6-13).

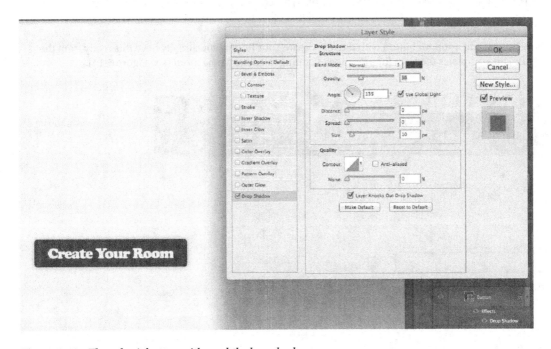

Figure 6-13. *The submit button with a subtle drop shadow*

Designing the Home View

Now that the basic elements of the site are designed, you can start assembling them into the home page design.

This page provides users with two options: They can create a room as a presenter or join an existing room. To keep things simple, these two options should be the only things on the page aside from the header and footer.

Create-a-Room Form

Start by placing the inputs needed to create the *create-a-room form*, which allows a soon-to-be presenter to create a room for Q&A:

- Name

- E-mail

- Session name

Because there are two forms on this page, use only the left half of your available space. Be a little more descriptive with your labels to explain to the user why she needs to provide this information. Instead of just listing what data they accept, use the following, more human-sounding labels:

- Tell us your name (so attendees know who you are).

- Tell us your e-mail address (so attendees can get in touch with you).

- What is your session called?

Below these inputs, add a submit button with the text Create Your Room (you already have this ready from the previous section). This completes the form for presenters wanting to create a new room (see Figure 6-14).

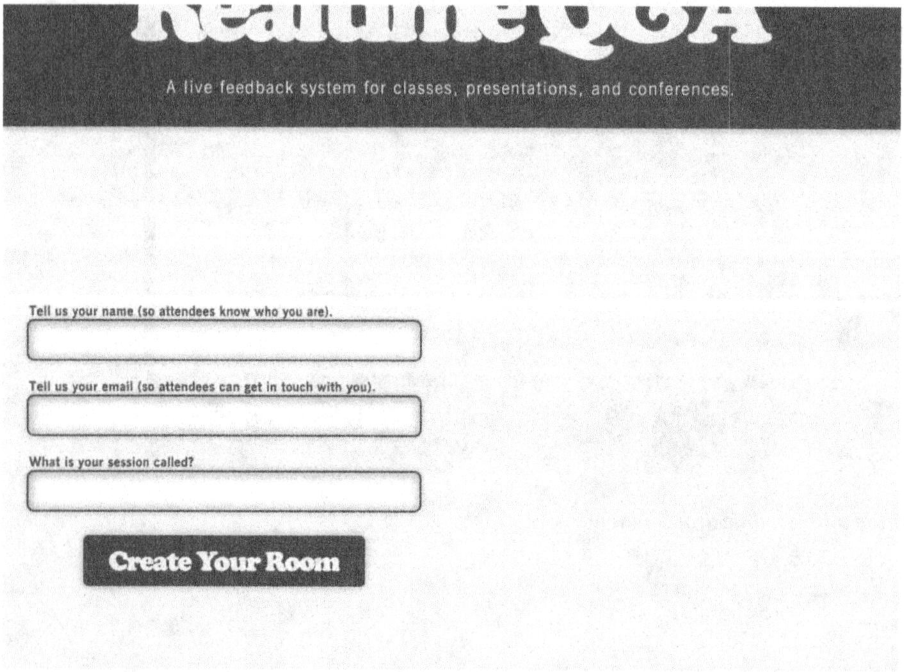

Figure 6-14. The form for presenters on the home view

However, this form is still missing something. Let's add a headline and a snippet of descriptive copy to make it very clear what this form is for. Start by adding a headline above the form with the following settings:

- Font: Cooper Black
- Size: 48 pt
- Tracking: -50
- Color: #1F1B0C
- Antialiasing: Strong

Simply use the text Presenting? for the headline, which poses a clear question to the user that should quickly direct him to the proper form. Give this a little dimension by adding the same drop shadow as you used on the submit buttons: color #1F1B0C at 30% opacity, 135°, and a size of 10px.

Tip You can quickly and easily copy layer styles to other elements by right-clicking (or Control + clicking) on the layer in the Layers panel that has the styles to be copied; then selecting Copy Layer Style from the context menu. After it's copied, right-click on the layer to which you want to apply the styles; then select Paste Layer Style from the context menu, and the styles will be applied. This will save you hours when a finicky client wants to see multiple variations of every element of the design.

Next, add a bit of copy below the headline that says, Create a room to start your Q&A session. Use the following settings:

- Font: News Gothic Roman
- Size: 24 pt
- Tracking: 25
- Color: #1F1B0C

Center the headline and copy above the form, and you should now have a finished form for creating a new room (see Figure 6-15).

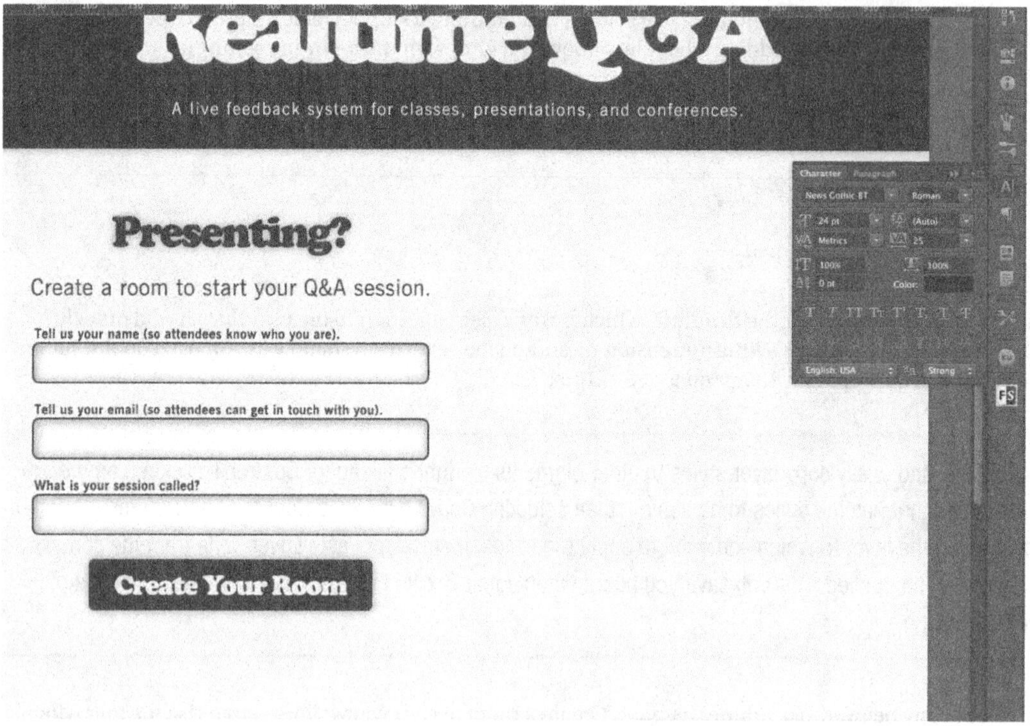

Figure 6-15. *The completed create-a-room form for the home view*

Join-a-Room Form

To keep the design consistent, the join-a-room form will be stylistically identical to the create-a-room form; only the inputs and copy will change.

In the interest of minimizing the barrier to entry for attendees, the only information required to join a room is the room's number.

1. Jump start this form by copying the create-a-room form into the right half of the page and then eliminating two of the three inputs.

2. Change the headline to read Attending? and the copy at the top to read, Join a room using its ID.

3. The label for the input should change to, What is the room's ID?

4. Finally, the submit button's text should read, Join This Room.

5. With those changes in place, the home page view should be complete with both forms (see Figure 6-16).

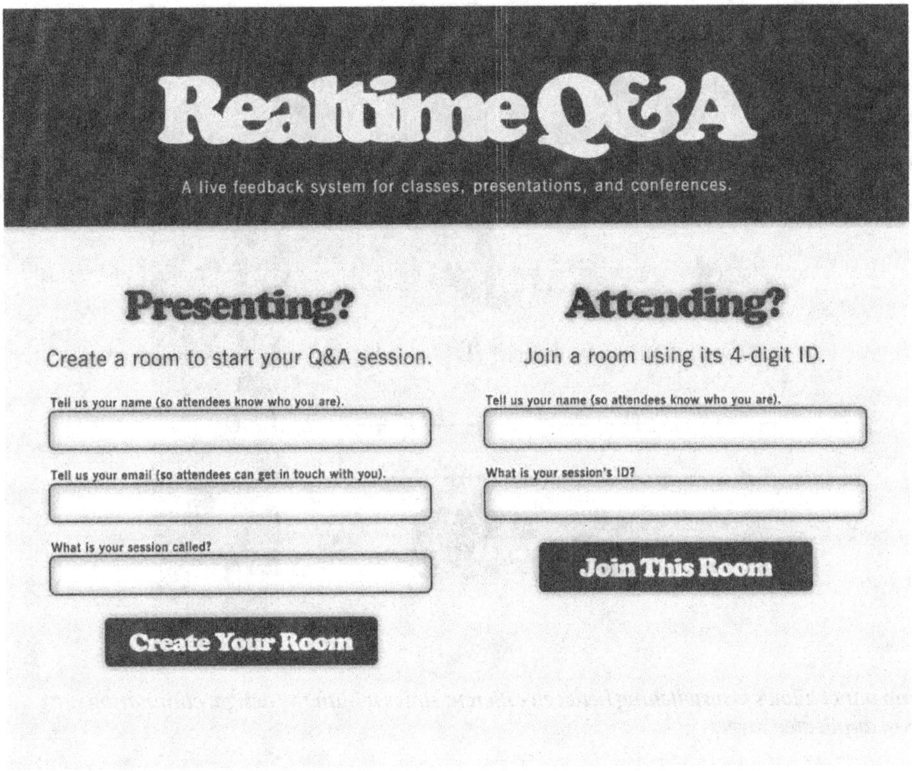

Figure 6-16. *The completed home view*

■ **Tip** Now that you have the home view completed, save it as a Layer Comp to create a snapshot of the document in this state (see Figure 6-17). This allows you to hide all your home view layers and start working on the questions view without losing any of your layout. If you've ever had to save multiple versions of a PSD or lost a half-day's work due to overwriting part of your layout, layer comps will be your new best friend.

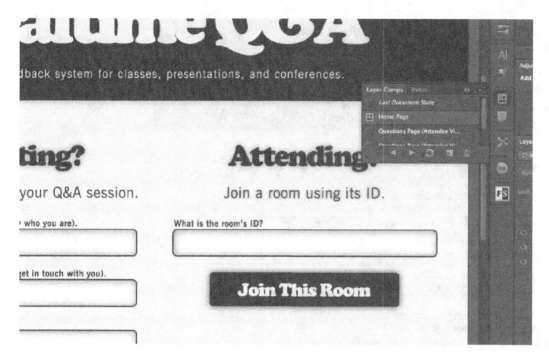

Figure 6-17. *The Layer Comp panel allows fast switching between different states within the design, eliminating the need for multiple files or lots of duplicated layers*

Designing the Room View(s)

The room view borrows several elements from the home view, which will simplify the process a bit, but it also has multiple states: There's a version for attendees, one for the presenter, and a "closed" room look for after the presenter has ended his session.

Designing the Attendee View

The attendee view has three distinct pieces:

- The ask-a-question form

- The room information (where they are and who's in charge)

- The questions

To organize this information, you'll be using a two-column layout in which the left column will be larger and will feature the important information (where *important* means most immediately useful; in this case, the ask-a-question form and the questions themselves), and the right column will contain less important information—the name of the session and speaker, which attendees presumably know before they join—and be smaller.

The ask-a-question form will be at the top of the main column and won't stray from the standard form element designs.

The room info will follow the standard of a Cooper Black headline and News Gothic body copy; the only difference is that it will be smaller, using 30 pt text for the headline and 18 pt for the body.

The questions are different from anything you've designed so far, so they'll require a bit more thought. The information that needs to be displayed is as follows:

- The question itself
- The number of votes the question has received
- A button that allows the attendee to vote for that question

The question will be displayed using News Gothic at 24 pt, which should be a good size for reading on any screen size, even if the device is a little farther away like, for instance, a phone laid on a desk. The text will sit at the right side of the question layout.

The vote count will be in Cooper Black at 24 pt and will sit at the far left of the question.

Between the count and the question sits a large button for voting the question up. Use the Ellipse tool to draw a circle with a 60px diameter in our dark color, #1F1B0C; then use the Custom Shape tool to draw an arrow in the light color, #FBF7E7, in the center of it. Add the same drop shadow as the submit button to the dark circle, and you now have a vote button.

Add a second question below the first to make sure the design works with multiple questions. A subtle divider between the questions—a 2px by 500px dark-colored rectangle at 10% fill opacity with the drop shadow from the submit button—completes the attendee page view (see Figure 6-18).

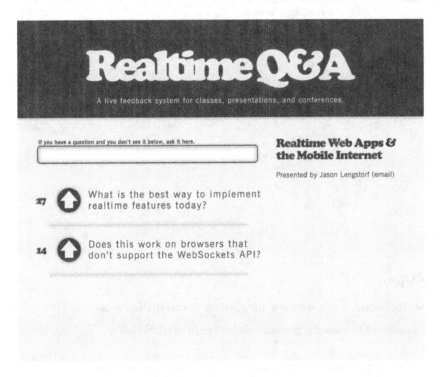

Figure 6-18. *The room view for attendees*

Designing the Closed Room View

The closed room view is very similar to the standard attendee view, with two notable exceptions:

- The ask-a-question form has been replaced with a notice about the room being closed.

- The questions have been faded to 60% opacity (and the vote button to 15% opacity) to make it visually apparent that this room is closed.

Aside from those two changes, the closed room view barely changes at all (see Figure 6-19).

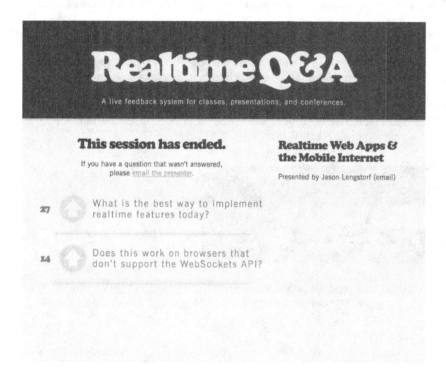

Figure 6-19. *The closed room view*

Designing the Presenter View

Finally, the app needs a presenter view. This, again, is very similar to the attendee view with a few exceptions:

- The ask-a-question form is removed because the presenter doesn't need to ask herself a question.

- A link to the room is present so the presenter can easily share the room with whomever she chooses.

- There is a button to close the room.

- The vote button is removed, and in its place—albeit on the right of the question instead of the left—is a button to mark the question answered.

The room link and the close button both use the standard form elements we've already designed, but the answer button needs a bit of new design:

1. Using the rounded rectangle tool, draw a shape 72px square using the dark color, #1F1B0C. Next, command + click on the shape in the Layers panel, which will draw a marquee selection around the shape.

2. Choose the Rectangular Marquee tool and hold Alt; then click and drag on the left side of the marquee, overlapping it from top to bottom by 12px. When you release the click, the marquee should now be 60px wide by 72px tall, leaving the left side of the rectangle unselected.

3. With the marquee still on the shape, make sure the shape layer is selected in the Layers panel; then click the Add layer mask button at the bottom of the Layers panel (it is next to the Layer Styles button) to create a mask. This gives the shape the appearance of having the upper- and lower-right corners rounded, but the left side squared (see Figure 6-20).

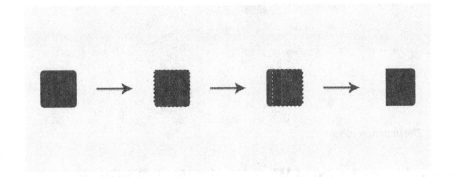

Figure 6-20. *From left-to-right, the rounded rectangle, a marquee selection around the rectangle, 12px deselected from the left-hand side, and the final masked shape*

4. Apply the same drop shadow to this shape as to the submit buttons; then use the Custom Shape tool with the check box selected to draw a check box in the light color, #FBF7E7, centered on the dark shape. This gives you an answer button.

5. Position the room link and end this session buttons in the right-hand column, and the presenter view is good to go (see Figure 6-21).

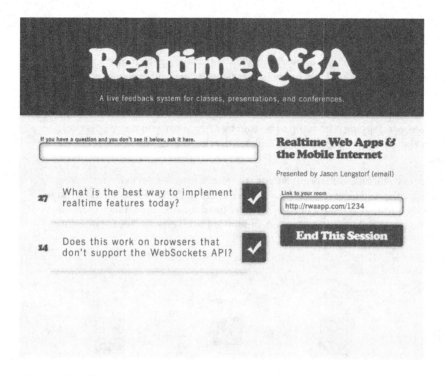

Figure 6-21. *The presenter view*

Smaller Screen Layouts (and Why You're Not Designing Them Here)

We spent a lot of time in the last chapter discussing the benefits of a mobile-friendly web app versus a suite of native apps. So why aren't you designing the mobile version now?

The main reason is that mobile design is, by its very nature, too fluid to really lend itself to traditional design. It requires a little more of a hands-on, try-it-and-see approach that would take way too long in Photoshop.[6]

Due to the simplicity of this particular layout, another reason not to do mobile-specific layouts is for the purposes of time. If it's easy to make the changes in CSS, that time is better spent coding. No need to double the effort required.

Summary

In this chapter, you applied all the planning from the previous chapters and created a design for the app. Because you're organized and you thought ahead, your PSD contains styles and fonts that can be replicated very closely using CSS.

In the next chapter—at long last—you will finally start coding this app. More specifically, you'll be building the front end, including the advanced CSS that will make this design adapt to any screen size.

---

[6]It would appear that Adobe knows this as well because they're working on a new tool to address the issue: http://html.adobe.com/edge/reflow/.

■ ■ ■

CHAPTER 7

Creating HTML and CSS Markup

Now that the design is ready, you can start coding. In this chapter, you will convert the PSD you've created into a web-ready HTML and CSS layout. You'll also implement CSS3 media queries to make sure the layout looks good on tablet- and handheld-size screens.

Starting with the Basics: Setting Up an HTML5 Document

Before we write a line of code, let's remind ourselves about the design we're creating (see Figure 7-1).

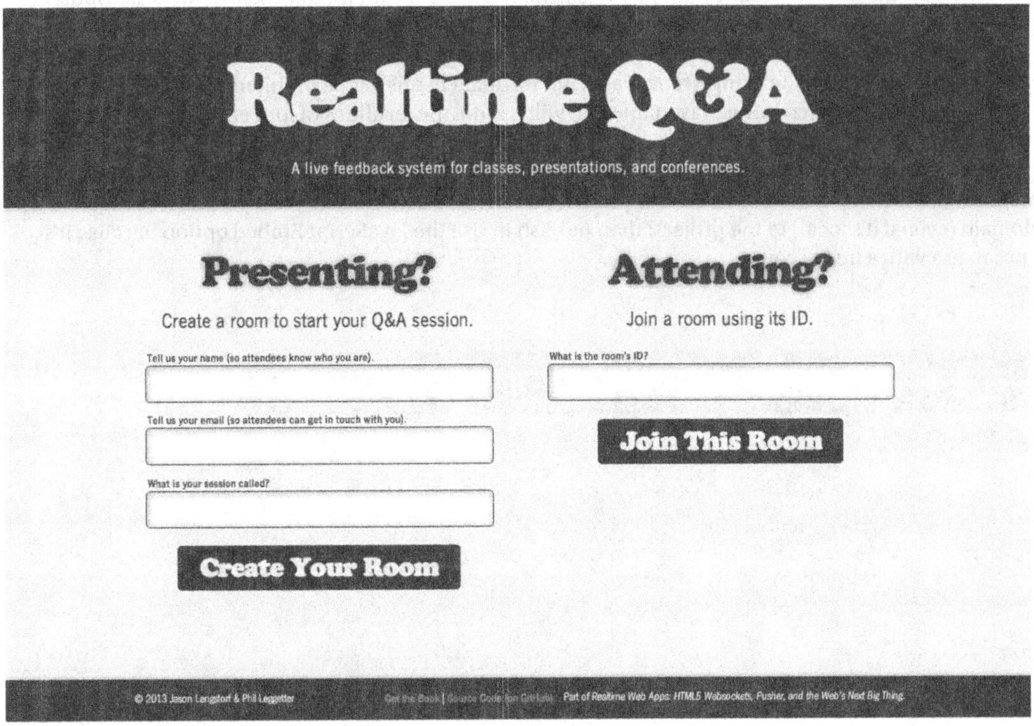

Figure 7-1. A reminder of how the application should look

Now you can start out by creating a new HTML document in the root folder of your project. Name it **index.html** and insert the doctype and other required elements:

```
<!doctype html>
<html lang="en">

<head>

<meta charset="utf-8" />

<title>Realtime Q&amp;A</title>

</head>

<body>

</body>

</html>
```

Getting Fonts Ready to Go

Next, you need the fonts for the design. Because Cooper Black and News Gothic aren't traditionally web-safe fonts such as Tahoma and Georgia, you'll need to use the @font-face capability of CSS to load them.

However, Cooper Black and News Gothic aren't released under the Open Font License,[1] which means it's not legal to simply toss the font up on the site using @font-face. But fortunately this isn't a problem due to the emergence of companies such as Fonts.com, which (for a reasonable fee) will handle the legalities of font embedding and just let us get on with the design.

For this app, create a free account at Fonts.com, create a new project in the "Manage Web Fonts" section, and add Cooper Black Regular and the News Gothic No. 2 Family fonts (search for "News Gothic") to a project (see Figure 7-2). Add your dev domain (even if it's local) to the project; then publish it. Use the JavaScript Embed option because it's the only one you can use with a free account.

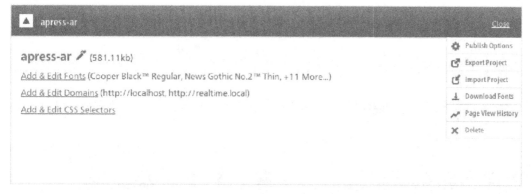

Figure 7-2. *Fonts.com project details*

---

[1]http://scripts.sil.org/OFL

Add the new `<script>` tag to index.html in the `<head>` section:

```
<head>

<meta charset="utf-8" />

<title>Realtime Q&amp;A</title>

<!-- Fonts via fonts.com -->
<script type="text/javascript" src="http://fast.fonts.com/jsapi/a09d5d16-57fd-447d-a0f6-73443033d2de.js">
</script>

</head>
```

Next, create a subdirectory in your app's root called `assets`, and another inside that called `styles`. Inside, create a new stylesheet called `main.css`.

Inside `main.css`, add a comment block with the `font-family` rules from Fonts.com for later reference:

```
/**
 * Styles for the Realtime Q&A app
 */

/*
fonts.com font-family rules.

Cooper Black
font-family:'Cooper Black W01';

News Gothic:
light: font-family:'NewsGothicNo.2W01-Light 710401';
light-italic: font-family:'NewsGothicNo.2W01-Light 710404';
roman: font-family:'NewsGothicNo.2W01-Roman';
italic: font-family:'News Gothic No.2 W01 It';
demi: font-family:'NewsGothicNo.2W01-Mediu 710407';
demi-italic: font-family:'NewsGothicNo.2W01-Mediu 710410';
bold: font-family:'NewsGothicNo.2W01-Bold';
bold-italic: font-family:'NewsGothicNo.2W01-BoldI';
*/
```

Include the new stylesheet below the Fonts.com script tag in the `<head>` section of index.html:

```
<head>

<meta charset="utf-8" />

<title>Realtime Q&amp;A</title>

<!-- Fonts via fonts.com -->
<script type="text/javascript" src="http://fast.fonts.com/jsapi/a09d5d16-57fd-447d-a0f6-73443033d2de.js">
</script>
```

```
<!-- Main site styles -->
<link rel="stylesheet" href="./assets/styles/main.css" />

</head>
```

@FONT-FACE AND SAAS

Though it seems as if it's been around for only a year or two, @font-face was actually introduced back in 1998 with the CSS2 specification.[2] However, it wasn't really used until recently due to lack of support, browser incompatibility issues, and—most of all—legal concerns.

The use of @font-face creates a pointer to the font, which allows the browser to download it and use it for rendering the font on the user's machine. This is great for design, but it opens the door for anyone to simply download the font illegally. Type foundries, predictably, were not okay with this.

In recent years, however, big steps were made toward increasing the security of fonts on the Web. In addition to new formats for web fonts, such as Embedded Open Type (EOT) and Web Open Font Format (WOFF), companies sprang up that provided web font embedding software as a service (SaaS).

There are many benefits to using SaaS, and only one downside (that isn't really a downside at all). The primary benefits are these:

- The font is available to you without having to purchase it.

- You no longer have to navigate murky legal waters to protect yourself and your clients.

- The finickiness of cross-browser font embedding is handled for you.

The only "downside" to using SaaS for font embedding is that it's not free. But if you look at the numbers, using SaaS is actually a huge bargain. For example, the popular Futura font is available for purchase as a web font from MyFonts[3] for $24.95 *per style* or $445.50 to buy the whole family (limited to 10,000 pageviews per month).

Fonts.com[4] charges $10 per month to embed the entire Futura family (as well as any of the other fonts in its library) for up to 250,000 pageviews per month.

When we do the math, that means that if the *only* font being embedded was the Futura family, it would take more than 3-1/2 years of using SaaS to equate purchasing a web font license.

Considering that you also get 25 times the number ofpageviews and that you'll probably be using more than one font from the service, it's pretty obvious that SaaS is a great deal.

---

[2]http://www.w3.org/TR/2008/REC-CSS2-20080411/fonts.html#font-descriptions
[3]http://www.myfonts.com/fonts/bitstream/futura/
[4]http://www.fonts.com/font/linotype/futura

Web Font SaaS Options

For this app, we're using Fonts.com to load Cooper Black and News Gothic into our design. There are many options available, but a few of the most popular options are these:

- `http://fontdeck.com/`

- `http://fonts.com/`

- `https://typekit.com/`

If you choose to use something other than `Fonts.com`, you'll still be able to complete the app in this book without issue, but note that the `font-family` names will probably vary.

■ **Note**   The Fonts.com free account requires a banner to be placed in your app, which the JavaScript include automatically does. A free account at Fontdeck will allow you to develop the app in this book without any added cost. They charge only when a site is taken "live," which they consider to be when more than 20 unique IP addresses need to access the site.

Common Elements

This app, like most others, has common elements that don't change from page to page. Let's start by developing those.

The Header Markup

Every view this app will offer features the header at the top. This is structurally simple: it's a box with the app title and a tagline inside.

Using the HTML5 `<header>` element, add the header markup to the `<body>` section of `index.html`:

```
<body>

<header>
    <h1>Realtime Q&amp;A</h1>
    <p class="tagline">
        A live feedback system for classes, presentations, and conferences.
    </p><!--/.tagline-->
</header>

</body>
```

■ **Tip**   Using a comment at the closing of elements with classes or IDs can help with scannability, especially when dealing with nested elements or layouts that nest the same tags, such as `<div>` elements. These comments are entirely optional.

If you view this in your browser, it makes sense semantically (see Figure 7-3). This should be a secondary goal for the app: if all the styles are ripped away, is it still legible?

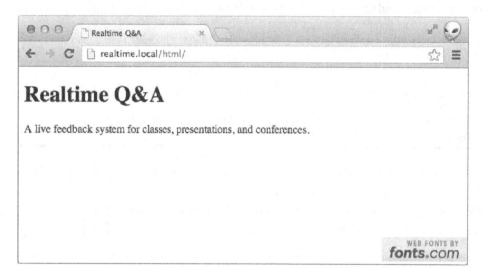

Figure 7-3. *The unstyled header markup*

The Footer Markup

Similar to the header, the footer is semantically simple. It breaks down to a box with legal copy and a couple of links. Because copy like that makes sense in a list, let's use an unordered list to display it inside the `<footer>` element. Add the code in bold to the body of `index.html`:

```
<body>

<header>
    <h1>Realtime Q&amp;A</h1>
    <p class="tagline">
        A live feedback system for classes, presentations, and conferences.
    </p><!--/.tagline-->
</header>

<footer>
    <ul>
        <li class="copyright">
            &copy; 2013 Jason Lengstorf &amp; Phil Leggetter
        </li><!--/.copyright-->
        <li>
            Part of <em>Realtime Web Apps: HTML5 Websockets, Pusher, and the
            Web&rsquo;s Next Big Thing</em>.
        </li>
        <li>
            <a href="http://amzn.to/XKcBbG">Get the Book</a> |
            <a href="http://cptr.me/UkMSmn">Source Code (on GitHub)</a>
        </li>
```

```
    </ul>
</footer>
```

```
</body>
```

Reload index.html in your browser. The footer info is displayed logically (see Figure 7-4).

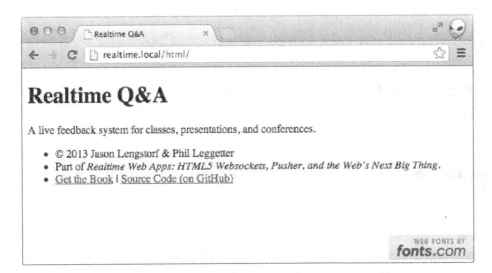

Figure 7-4. *The unstyled footer markup added*

The Styles

With the markup in place, you can start styling up the elements. Starting with the basics, add the font rules. Each element will have its font size set in ems to make it more flexible when media queries come into play later. The trick is to set the body font-size to a px value, use relative sizes for all other elements. If you need to bump the font size up or down later, all you'll need to do is adjust the body setting and the whole design will adjust proportionally.

Using the design as a guide, set colors, sizes, and letter spacing for each of the elements in the header and footer. Don't forget to reset the fonts to normal styles and weights when using a bold or italicized font; if you forget, the browser will apply its own bold or italics to the already bold or italicized text, which looks bad in most cases. When you've done this, the CSS will look like the following:

```
/**
 * Styles for the Realtime Q&A app
 */

/*
fonts.com font-family rules.

Cooper Black
font-family:'Cooper Black W01';

News Gothic:
light: font-family:'NewsGothicNo.2W01-Light 710401';
light-italic: font-family:'NewsGothicNo.2W01-Light 710404';
```

```
roman: font-family:'NewsGothicNo.2W01-Roman';
italic: font-family:'News Gothic No.2 W01 It';
demi: font-family:'NewsGothicNo.2W01-Mediu 710407';
demi-italic: font-family:'NewsGothicNo.2W01-Mediu 710410';
bold: font-family:'NewsGothicNo.2W01-Bold';
bold-italic: font-family:'NewsGothicNo.2W01-BoldI';
*/

/* Basic Font Styles
 -----------------------------------------------------------------------*/

body {
    font: 18px/24px 'NewsGothicNo.2W01-Roman';
    color: #1f1b0c;
    letter-spacing: .06em;
}

h1 {
    font-family: 'Cooper Black W01';
    font-weight: normal;
}

h1 {
    margin: 0;
    color: #fbf7e7;
    font-size: 6em;
    line-height: 1em;
    letter-spacing: -.1em;
}

.tagline {
    font-family: 'NewsGothicNo.2W01-Light 710401';
    font-size: 1.1em;
    line-height: 1em;
    color: #fbf7e7;
    letter-spacing: .12em;
}

a {
    font-family: 'NewsGothicNo.2W01-Mediu 710407';
    color: #e06f00;
    text-decoration: none;
}

a:active,a:hover,a:focus {
    text-decoration: underline;
    outline: none;
}
```

```css
footer li {
    font-family: 'NewsGothicNo.2W01-Light 710401';
    font-size: .75em;
    line-height: 1em;
    letter-spacing: .04em;
    color: #fbf7e7;
}

footer li em {
    font-family: 'NewsGothicNo.2W01-Light 710404';
    font-style: normal;
}
```

■ **Note**   There are two rules set up for h1 right now. This is intentional because later in the design there will be other elements added to the first rule that should not receive the styles from the second set.

If you load index.html in your browser at this point, it won't look right until you add a dark background (see Figure 7-5).

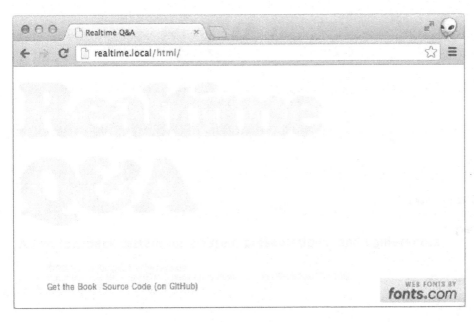

Figure 7-5. *The markup with only the font styling rules applied*

To correct this, now you need to add the layout rules to give background colors, alignment, and other box model rules. Add the new layout code to finish the header and footer styles:

```css
/* Layout
  ------------------------------------------------------------------------*/

html { background-color: #fbf7e7; }

body { margin: 0; }

header,footer {
    -webkit-box-shadow: 0 0 10px rgba(31, 27, 12, .3);
            box-shadow: 0 0 10px rgba(31, 27, 12, .3);
}

header,footer {
    overflow: hidden;
    background: #1f1b0c;
    margin: 0;
    padding: 1em;
    text-align: center;
}

header {
    margin-bottom: 3em;
    padding: 3em 0 2em;
}

header h1,header p {
    width: 960px;
    margin: 0 auto;
    padding: 0;
}

header h1 { margin-bottom: .25em; }

footer { margin-top: 6em; }

footer ul {
    overflow: hidden;
    width: 960px;
    margin: 0 auto;
    padding: 0;
}

footer li {
    float: right;
    margin-left: 1em;
    list-style: none;
}

footer li.copyright { float: left; margin-left: 0; }
```

Most of this code is fairly self-explanatory, but there are a couple of rules worth noting. The box shadow only uses the -webkit- prefix. This is because all the other browsers now support the standard box-shadow rule (even IE9), so it's no longer required to include prefixed versions of the rule to make it work. In fact, the -webkit- prefix is only required to add support for older versions of Safari, iOS, and Android. Because it's not uncommon to see older versions of iOS and Android, though, it's a good idea to keep this rule.

The box-shadow rule also uses rgba, which is new as of CSS3. This allows you to set the alpha—or opacity—of a color. The RGB values used match the site's dark color.

Finally, a trick that solves the need for "clearfixes": set the containing element to overflow: hidden and it will grow to contain floated elements. This works on all browsers, so it's a very simple trick to eliminate a lot of non-semantic elements. This trick is used on the footer elements to force the <footer> element to properly apply padding around the floated <li> elements.

Reload your browser to see the completed header and footer (see Figure 7-6).

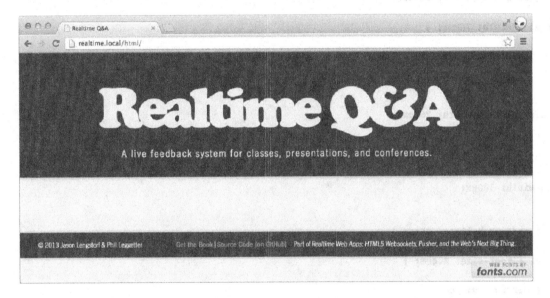

Figure 7-6. *The styled header and footer*

Making the Header and Footer Responsive

The final step of completing the header and footer is to add media queries that will adjust their display on tablets and handheld devices.

Rather than doing anything fancy, such as checking for device orientation or pixel density, you're simply going to be adjusting the layout based on the viewport width. The reason for this approach is that nothing fancy needs to happen on smaller screens; the layout simply needs to readjust a bit to fit within the provided screen real estate.

In the interest of simplicity, there will only be two adjustments made to the layout: devices under 960px wide (tablets) and devices under 768px wide (handheld devices).

For the header, all that needs to change is the font size and maximum width of the elements. Changing the padding helps keep the layout from looking too spacious.

The footer needs the same adjustments. In addition, it also needs the float turned off for the list elements so they can be centered.

Add the media to the bottom of main.css to adjust the header and footer for smaller screens:

```css
/* Media queries
   --------------------------------------------------------------------------*/

@media screen and (max-width: 960px)
{

    header h1,header p { width: 760px; }

    header { padding: .75em 0 1.2em; }

    footer { margin-top: 4em; padding: 0;}

    footer ul { width: 740px; }

    footer li,footer li.copyright { float: none; margin: .75em 0;}

}

@media screen and (max-width: 768px)
{

    header h1,header p {
        width: 90%;
        min-width: 300px;
    }

    header { padding-bottom: .75em; }

    header h1 { font-size: 2.4em; }

    footer { margin-top: 3em; }

    footer ul { width: 300px; }

}
```

Reload the file in your browser. At a glance, it will appear that nothing has changed, but if you resize your browser window, you'll see that the elements adjust for the different screen sizes (see Figure 7-7).

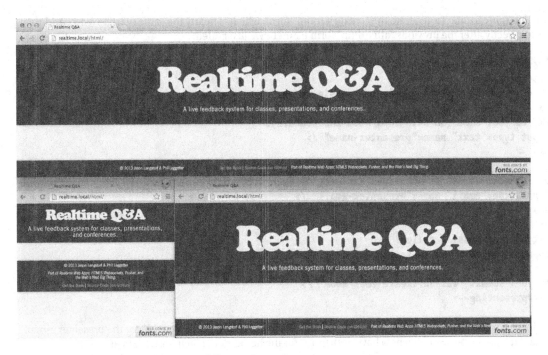

Figure 7-7. *The header and footer at different screen sizes*

Developing the Home Page View

With the app's frame ready, you can now start plugging in the guts of individual views, starting with the home page.

Writing the Markup

The home page consists of two forms, so let's start with the simpler of the two to get the basics in place.

The "join a room" form has a headline, a short blurb of copy, an input with a label, and a submit button. Add the following markup to index.html, in between the <header> and <footer> tags, to create this form:

```
<section>

    <form id="attending">
        <h2>Attending?</h2>
        <p>Join a room using its ID.</p>
        <label>
            What is the room's ID?
            <input type="text" name="room_id" />
        </label>
        <input type="submit" value="Join This Room" />
    </form><!--/#attending-->

</section>
```

Next, use that same format to generate the "create a room" form, which is nearly the same markup-wise. Add this `<form>` element directly after the previous "attending" form element we just added:

```
<form id="presenting">
    <h2>Presenting?</h2>
    <p>Create a room to start your Q&amp;A session.</p>
    <label>
        Tell us your name (so attendees know who you are).
        <input type="text" name="presenter-name" />
    </label>
    <label>
        Tell us your email (so attendees can get in touch with you).
        <input type="email" name="presenter-email" />
    </label>
    <label>
        What is your session called?
        <input type="text" name="session-name" />
    </label>
    <input type="submit" value="Create Your Room" />
</form><!--/#presenting-->
```

There is nothing remarkable about this code, with the exception of the use of `type="email"` for the presenter e-mail input. Save it and reload the browser; you now have both forms for the home view, albeit unstyled (see Figure 7-8).

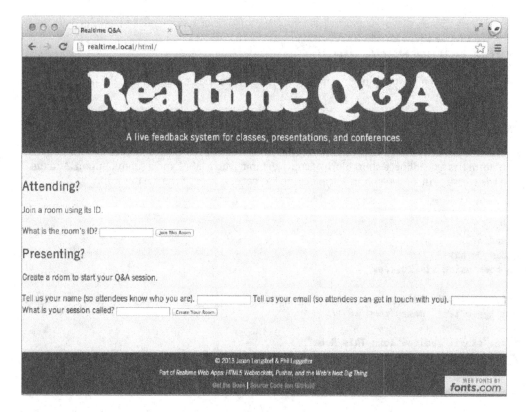

Figure 7-8. *All the markup for the home view is in place, but it needs styling*

Implementing the CSS

Update the existing h1 rule containing font-family and font-weight so the font-family and weight is also applied to h2 tags. Also add additional rules for the second-level headings; general paragraphs; and form, inputs, and labels:

```css
/* Basic Font Styles
  --------------------------------------------------------------------------*/

/* Update */
h1, h2 {
    font-family: 'Cooper Black W01';
    font-weight: normal;
}

/* Unchanged */
h1 {
    margin: 0;
    color: #fbf7e7;
    font-size: 6em;
    line-height: 1em;
    letter-spacing: -.1em;
}

/* New rules */
h2 { text-shadow: 0 0 10px rgba(31, 27, 12, .3); }

h2 {
    margin: 0 0 .5em;
    font-size: 2.75em;
    line-height: 1em;
    letter-spacing: -.08em;
}

p {
    text-align: center;
}

form p {
    margin: 0 0 1em;
    padding: 0;
    font-size: 1.375em;
}

label {
    font-family: 'NewsGothicNo.2W01-Bold';
    font-size: .75em;
    line-height: 1.25em;
    letter-spacing: .04em;
}

input {
    font-family: 'Cooper Black W01';
    color: #fbf7e7;
```

```
    background-color: #1f1b0c;
    border-radius: 6px;
    border: none;
    font-size: 1.75em;
    line-height: 1em;
    letter-spacing: -.08em;
    text-shadow: 0 0 10px rgba(31, 27, 12, .3);
}

label input {
    font-family: 'NewsGothicNo.2W01-Light 710401';
    font-size: 1.75em;
    letter-spacing: .08em;
    color: #1f1b0c;
    background-color: #fff;
}

/* Existing rules e.g. .tagline */
```

After saving, the home view should have the proper fonts in place (see Figure 7-9).

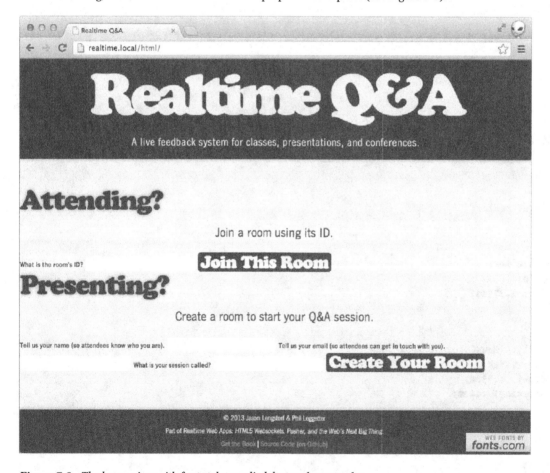

Figure 7-9. The home view with font styles applied, but no layout rules

The layout rules are fairly straightforward: the "join a room" form will float right, the "create a room" form will float left, and the labels and inputs need to stack vertically. Implement these rules by inserting the code shown below before the first footer rule in the "Layout" section of main.css:

```
section {
    width: 960px;
    margin: 0 auto;
    overflow: hidden;
}

form {
    float: left;
    width: 460px;
    text-align: center;
}

form#attending { float: right; }

label {
    display: block;
    width: 430px;
    margin: 0 auto 1em;
    text-indent: 2px;
    text-align: left;
}

input {
    margin: .25em 0 0;
    padding: .375em .875em;
}

label input {
    display: block;
    width: 400px;
    margin: 0;
    padding: .375em 15px;
    border: 2px solid #1f1b0c;
    -webkit-border-radius: 6px;
            border-radius: 6px;
    -webkit-box-shadow: inset 2px 2px 14px rgba(31, 27, 12, .3);
            box-shadow: inset 2px 2px 14px rgba(31, 27, 12, .3);
}
```

Save these changes and reload the page in your browser. At this point, the home view is nearly complete (see Figure 7-10).

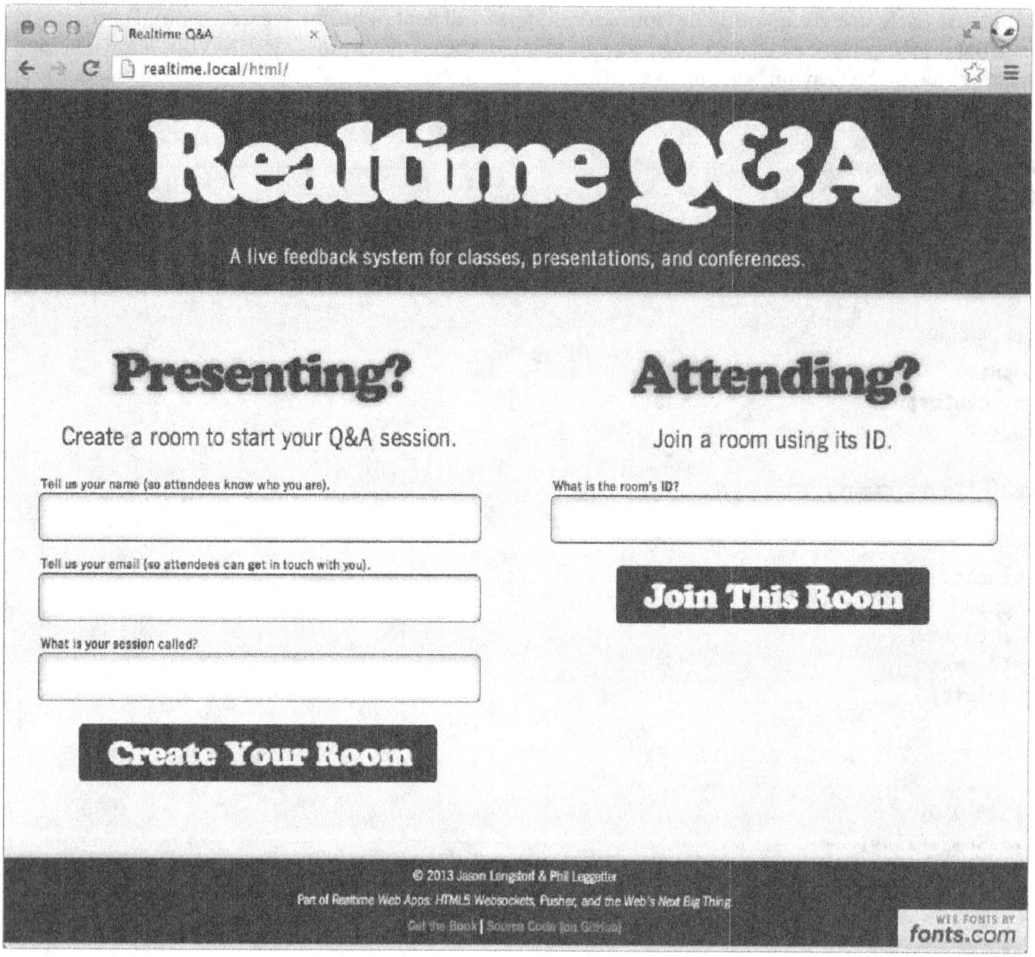

Figure 7-10. *The home view now looks like the mockup*

Creating Styles for Active and Hovered Form Elements

Because forms are interactive, it's a good idea to provide visual feedback for the users as they hover, click, and tab through the form elements. To do this, you need to add styles for the :active, :hover, and :focus states of inputs.

Using the highlight color #E06F00, change the border color of active inputs to indicate where the user is currently focused, and make the submit buttons turn orange when active or hovered. Include the following code to accomplish this:

```
/* Highlights
    -------------------------------------------------------------------------*/
input:active,input:hover,input:focus {
    background-color: #e06f00;
    outline: none;
}

input::-moz-focus-inner { border: 0; }
```

```
label input:active,label input:focus {
    border-color: #e06f00;
    background-color: #fff;
    outline: none;
}
```

```
label input:hover { background-color: #fff; }
```

This code overrides browser default behavior and replaces it with a custom highlight. Worth noting is the `input::-moz-focus-inner` rule; this addresses a behavior in Firefox that causes the input to get a small dotted line on the inside of the input when it is active.

■ **Caution** If you override default browser styles, make sure you replace them with styles of your own. Users who navigate the Web with their keyboards rely on the `:focus` and `:active` states to see where the cursor currently rests, so removing those states altogether will have a negative effect on the user experience.

After the styles are overridden, reload the page in your browser and use the Tab key to navigate through the form. The inputs now get highlighted with orange when they're active (see Figure 7-11), and the submit buttons turn orange when they have focus or when hovered over (see Figure 7-12).

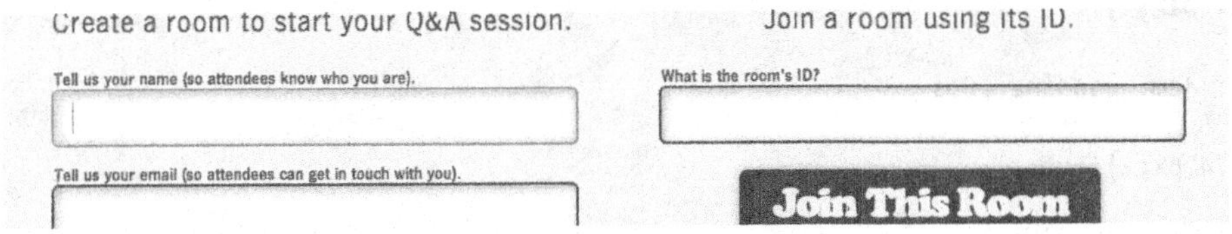

Figure 7-11. *A text input that has focus is now highlighted with orange*

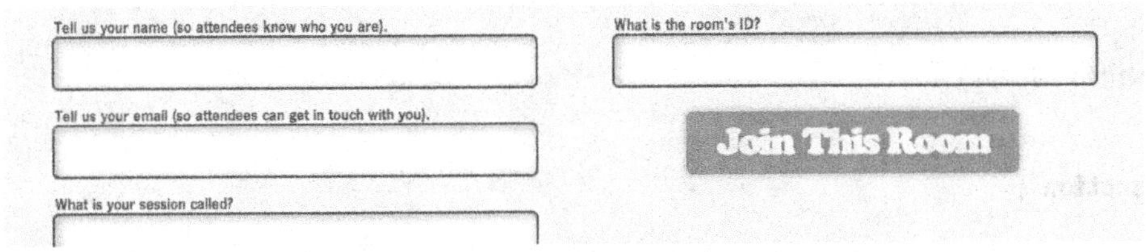

Figure 7-12. *The submit button turns orange when hovered or focused*

Adding Media Queries

The media queries for the home page stay fairly bare-bones. On tablets, you can still fit the forms side by side if they shrink a bit, and on handheld devices they should stack one on top of the other.

The "join a room" form should be on top because it's shorter and because it's more likely to be used (more people are likely to be attending than presenting).

The following code adds extra rules for smaller viewports:

```
@media screen and (max-width: 960px)
{

    header h1,header p { width: 760px; }

    header { padding: .75em 0 1.2em; }

    section { width: 740px; }

    p { margin: 0 0 2em; padding: 0; }

    header>p,section>p { font-size: .875em; }

    form { width: 340px; padding: 0 8px; }

    form p { font-size: 1em; }

    label { width: 100%; }

    input { font-size: 1.5em; }

    label input { width: 91%; }

    footer { margin-top: 4em; padding: 0;}

    footer ul { width: 740px; }

    footer li,footer li.copyright { float: none; margin: .75em 0;}

}


@media screen and (max-width: 768px)
{

    header h1,header p,section {
        width: 90%;
        min-width: 300px;
    }

    header { padding-bottom: .75em; }

    header h1 { font-size: 2.4em; }

    form,form#attending {
        float: none;
        width: 90%;
        margin: 0 auto 3em;
    }
```

```
form p { font-size: .75em; }

label input { width: 88%; font-size: 1.6em; }

footer { margin-top: 3em; }

footer ul { width: 300px; }
}
```

Save and reload the page; then change the browser size to see the layout adapt (see Figure 7-13).

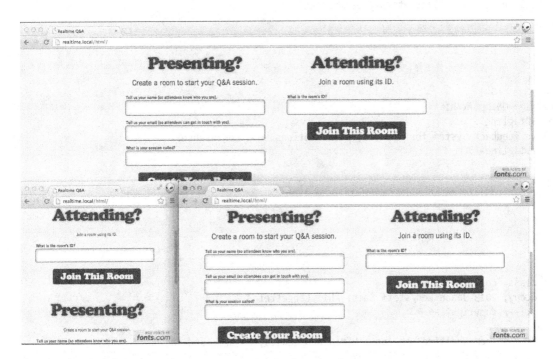

Figure 7-13. The home view, complete with responsive layout rules

Developing the Active Room View for Attendees

The next step is to create the markup for the active room view as it will be seen by attendees. This is where they will ask and vote for questions.

Writing the Markup

To start, grab the same header and footer markup used in `index.html` and save it to a new file called `attendee-active.html`:

```
<!doctype html>
<html lang="en">
```

```html
<head>

<meta charset="utf-8" />

<title>Realtime Q&amp;A</title>

<!-- Fonts via fonts.com -->
<script type="text/javascript" src="http://fast.fonts.com/jsapi/a09d5d16-57fd-447d-a0f6-73443033d2de.js">
</script>

<!-- Main site styles -->
<link rel="stylesheet" href="./assets/styles/main.css" />

</head>

<body>

<header>
    <h1>Realtime Q&amp;A</h1>
    <p class="tagline">
        A live feedback system for classes, presentations, and conferences.
    </p><!--/.tagline-->
</header>

<section>

</section>

<footer>
    <ul>
        <li class="copyright">
            &copy; 2013 Jason Lengstorf &amp; Phil Leggetter
        </li><!--/.copyright-->
        <li>
            Part of <em>Realtime Web Apps: HTML5 Websockets, Pusher, and the
            Web&rsquo;s Next Big Thing</em>.
        </li>
        <li>
            <a href="http://amzn.to/XKcBbG">Get the Book</a> |
            <a href="http://cptr.me/UkMSmn">Source Code (on GitHub)</a>
        </li>
    </ul>
</footer>

</body>

</html>
```

The content of this view is separated into three sections:

- The header, with the room name and presenter information
- The "ask a question" form
- The list of questions

The first two markup elements aren't anything wild, so let's get those out of the way first. Add the two additional elements in the `<section>`:

```
<section>

    <header>
        <h2>Realtime Web Apps &amp; the Mobile Internet</h2>
        <p>
            Presented by Jason Lengstorf
            (<a href="mailto:jason@lengstorf.com">email</a>)
        </p>
    </header>

    <form id="ask-a-question">
        <label>
            If you have a question and you don't see it below, ask it here.
            <input type="text" name="new-question" tabindex="1" />
        </label>
        <input type="submit" value="Ask" tabindex="2" />
    </form><!--/#ask-a-question-->

</section>
```

Using HTML5's data Attribute

The questions are going to be presented in an unordered list, but there's a twist: instead of creating an extra element for the vote count, you're going to use the HTML5 data- attribute.

This serves two purposes:

- jQuery has built-in support for accessing this attribute
- CSS can use this attribute to generate content that is unimportant to the document

---

■ **Note** "Unimportant" in the context of the previous statement means that the vote count is not vital to the information being displayed. For that reason, it's being left out of the markup and displayed by CSS instead, thereby keeping the markup clean and semantic.

Add the questions unordered list markup to the bottom of the existing `<section>`:

```html
<ul id="questions">

    <li id="question-1"
        data-count="27">

        <p>
            What is the best way to implement realtime features today?
        </p>

        <form class="vote">
            <input value="I also have this question."
                   type="submit"  />
        </form>

    </li><!--/#question-1-->

    <li id="question-2"
        data-count="14">

        <p>
            Does this work on browsers that don't support the
            WebSockets API?
        </p>

        <form class="vote">
            <input value="I also have this question."
                   type="submit"  />
        </form>

    </li><!--/#question-2-->

</ul><!--/#questions-->
```

With the markup in place, load `attendee-active.html` in your browser. It doesn't look good, but all the pieces are in place (see Figure 7-14).

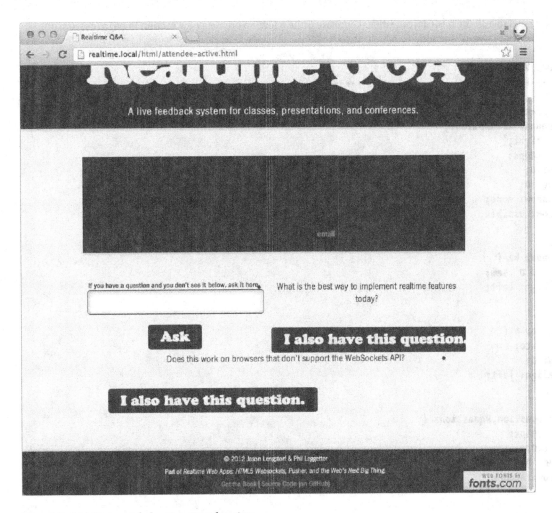

Figure 7-14. *The unstyled active attendee view*

Implementing the CSS

First, add the font styles for questions and the heading by inserting the following code before the first footer rule in the "Basic Font Styles" section of `main.css`:.

```css
section header h2 {
    font-size: 1.5em;
    line-height: 1.125em;
    letter-spacing: -.06em;
}

#questions li {
    font-size: 1.33em;
    letter-spacing: .1em;
}
```

Next, you need to add the basic layout rules. There are quite a few, so create a new section in `main.css` starting just after the existing "Layout" section:

```css
/* Questions View
   -------------------------------------------------------------------------*/

section header {
    background: transparent;
    float: right;
    width: 340px;
    margin: 0;
    padding: 0;
    box-shadow: none;
    overflow: visible;
}

section header h2 {
    margin: 0 0 .5em;
    text-align: left;
}

section header p {
    width: auto;
    margin: 0;
    text-align: left;
}

form#ask-a-question,#questions {
    width: 596px;
    margin: 0;
    padding: 0;
    overflow: hidden;
}

#questions { padding-bottom: 1em; }

#ask-a-question label,#ask-a-question>input { float: left; }

#ask-a-question label { width: 460px; }

#ask-a-question label input {
    width: 430px;
    height: 1.7em;
    margin: 0;
    padding-left: 15px;
    padding-right: 15px;
}
```

```css
#ask-a-question input {
    height: 1.55em;
    margin: 0.5em 0 0 0.5em;
    padding: 0.1em 0.75em;
}

#questions li {
    position: relative;
    list-style: none;
    margin: 0;
    padding: 1em 0 1em;
    overflow: hidden;
    -webkit-box-shadow: 0  12px 16px -16px rgba(31, 27, 12, .3),
                        0 -12px 16px -16px rgba(31, 27, 12, .3);
            box-shadow: 0  12px 16px -16px rgba(31, 27, 12, .3),
                        0 -12px 16px -16px rgba(31, 27, 12, .3);
}

#questions p {
    float: right;
    width: 77%;
    margin: .75em 0;
    padding: 0;
    text-align: left;
}

#questions .vote {
    position: relative;
    display: block;
    width: 76px;
    height: 76px;
    margin: 0 0 0 2em;
    padding: 0;
    overflow: hidden;
}
```

These rules are all fairly basic; they fix the issue with the <header> element being the same color as the text, float the sections to their proper places, and add margin and spacing where appropriate to get the elements to lay out properly (see Figure 7-15).

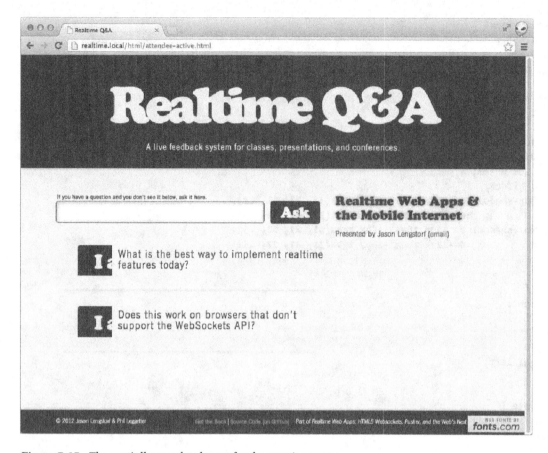

Figure 7-15. *The partially complete layout for the questions page*

Slicing PSDs and Creating Sprites

With the layout mostly complete, we need to get the images for the buttons into the site. This will require slicing the PSD and creating a sprite, which is a large image made up of smaller images. Sprites are used to reduce the number of requests and the overall download size of a site.

Open the PSD in Photoshop in the attendee question view and grab the Slice tool. Draw a slice that's 76 px by 76 px around the vote up button. Make sure it is centered horizontally and vertically.

On the second vote up button, go into the layers styles on the dark circle shape and add a color overlay using our highlight color, #E06F00. This will be the hover and active state for the button.

Draw another slice on top of that button at 76 px by 76 px (see Figure 7-16).

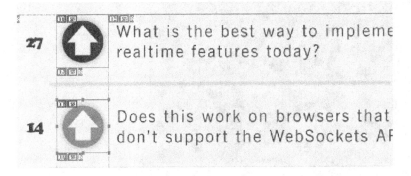

Figure 7-16. *The buttons in the PSD with slices*

Save for the Web (command + option + shift + S or "Save for Web…" in the File menu). Save the two button slices as PNG files. Name them whatever you want because you'll be combining them into a different image in the next step.

To be ready for the presenter view, do the same thing for the answer button and its hover state by drawing slices that are 78 px wide by 88 px high (see Figure 7-17).

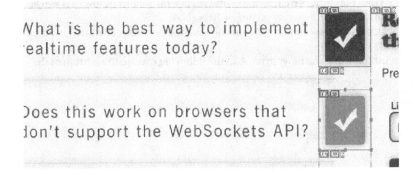

Figure 7-17. *The answer buttons in the PSD with slices*

Next, create a new PSD at 154 px wide by 176 px tall. Set the background to the light color #FBF7E7.

Place the four PNGs you just created into the document, placing the "off" vote button at the top left, the "on" vote button at the bottom left, the "off" answer button at the top right, and the "on" answer button at the bottom right (see Figure 7-18).

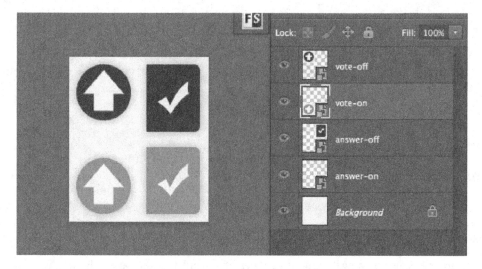

Figure 7-18. *The sprite in Photoshop*

The last step is to save this image for the Web. This time, save it as a JPG and reduce the quality as low as it will go without noticeably losing quality. In the case of this image, a quality setting of 70 is good.

To save this image for use with the project, create a new subdirectory inside the `assets` folder called `images`; then save this image as `sprite.jpg`.

Back in `main.css`, let's style up the vote button using the new sprite. Add the following code to the bottom of the "Questions View" section:

```
#questions .vote input[type=submit] {
    margin: 0;
    width: 100%;
    height: 100%;
    cursor: pointer;
    text-indent: -9999px;
    background: url(../images/sprite.jpg) left top no-repeat;
    -webkit-box-shadow: none;
            box-shadow: none;
}

#questions .vote input:active,
#questions .vote input:hover,
#questions .vote input:focus {
    background-position: left bottom;
}
```

This code sets up the input to work like a small viewing window that shows only a portion of the sprite. On hover—or when the user tabs to the input—the sprite moves, showing a different portion of itself in the viewing window of the input. This saves an additional HTTP request to load the "over" image, improving the load time and overall user experience.

Save and reload the document in your browser. The input now looks like the button you designed, and hovering or tabbing to the button causes it to highlight with orange (see Figure 7-19).

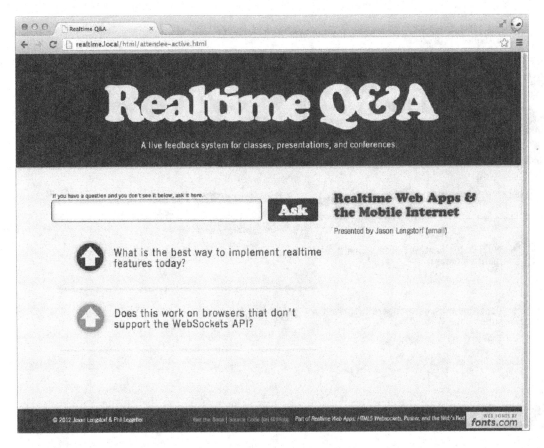

Figure 7-19. The styled button, including its highlighted state

Using :before

The final step in this view is to retrieve the vote count from the data-count attribute. This is accomplished using the :before pseudo-element and the content rule, which lets you pass in an attribute name to be displayed in the pseudo-element. Use the data-count attribute, move it to the left, and position it vertically at the center using the following code (to be added to the bottom of the "Questions View" section in main.css):

```css
#questions li:before {
    content: attr(data-count);
    position: absolute;
    left: 0;
    top: 50%;
    margin-top: -.5em;
}
```

Save and reload; now the vote count is displayed on the left of each question (see Figure 7-20).

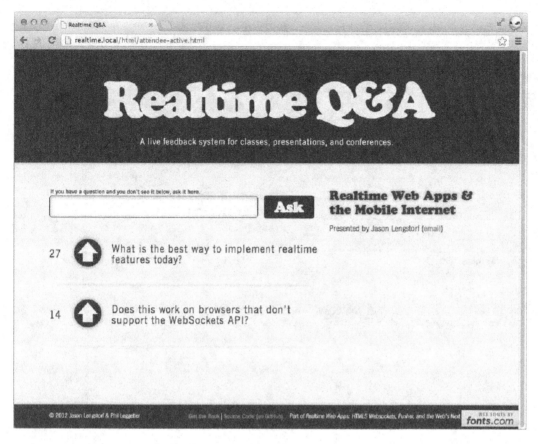

Figure 7-20. *The vote count displayed on the left of the questions*

Finally, you need to make the font match the design, so add a selector for the pseudo-element to the font rule already applied to h1 and h2 in the "Basic Font Styles" section of main.css:

```
h1,h2,#questions li:before {
    font-family: 'Cooper Black WO1';
    font-weight: normal;
}
```

Now the font looks correct if you reload (see Figure 7-21).

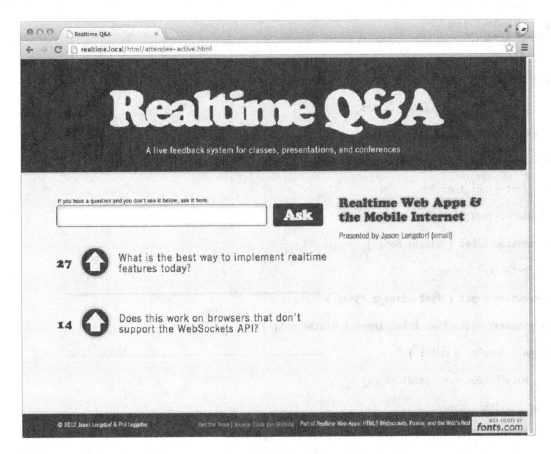

Figure 7-21. *The styled vote count*

Adding Media Queries

The layouts for smaller screens are fairly simple. On tablets, the room description moves to the top of the layout, and the form and questions sit below, creating a one-column layout.

On handheld devices, the one-column layout persists, and the vote count moves above the vote button to save even more horizontal space.

Update the "Media queries" section in main.css to match the code shown in bold in order to implement the changes:

```
@media screen and (max-width: 960px)
{

    header h1,header p { width: 760px; }

    header { padding: .75em 0 1.2em; }

    section header {
      float: none;
      width: 680px;
```

```
        margin: 0 auto 1.5em;
        overflow: hidden;
    }

    p { margin: 0 0 2em; padding: 0; }

    header>p,section>p { font-size: .875em; }

    form { width: 340px; padding: 0 8px; }

    form#ask-a-question { float: none; width: 680px; margin: 0 auto 1em; }

    form p { font-size: 1em; }

    label { width: 100%; }

    #ask-a-question label { width: 80%; }

    input { font-size: 1.5em; }

    #ask-a-question input { font-size: 1.75em; }

    label input,#ask-a-question label input { width: 91%; }

    #questions { margin: 0 auto; }

    footer { margin-top: 4em; padding: 0;}

    footer ul { width: 740px; }

    footer li,footer li.copyright { float: none; margin: .75em 0;}
}

@media screen and (max-width: 768px)
{

    header h1,header p {
        width: 90%;
        min-width: 300px;
    }

    section,section header,form#ask-a-question,#questions { width: 300px; }

    header { padding-bottom: .75em; }

    header h1 { font-size: 2.4em; }

    form,form#attending,form#ask-a-question {
        float: none;
        width: 90%;
        margin: 0 auto 3em;
    }

    form#ask-a-question { overflow: visible; }
```

```
form p { font-size: .75em; }

label input { width: 88%; font-size: 1.6em; }

#ask-a-question label { width: 270px; }

#ask-a-question label input { width: 87%; }

#ask-a-question input {
    float: none;
    margin: 0 auto;
}

#questions li { font-size: 1.125em; line-height: 1.125em; }

#questions li:before { top: 20px; left: 24px; margin-top: 0; }

#questions .vote { margin: 20px 0 0;}

#questions p { width: 210px; margin: 0; }

footer { margin-top: 3em; }

footer ul { width: 300px; }
```
}

Save, reload, and resize your browser window. The layout is now responsive (see Figure 7-22).

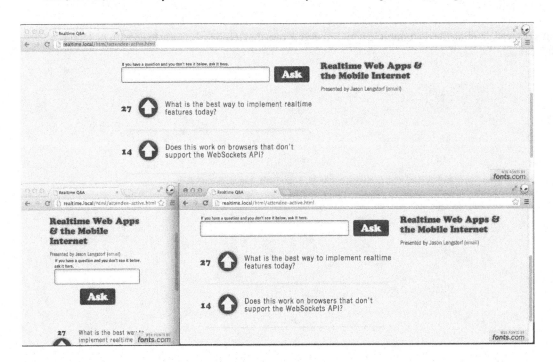

Figure 7-22. *The questions view at multiple viewport sizes*

Developing the Closed Room View for Attendees

The next step is to create the view for a room that was closed by its presenter. Attendees will no longer be able to vote, and there will be a notice to let them know both that the room is closed and that they can contact the presenter by e-mail.

Create a new file called `attendee-closed.html` in the root of the app; this is where you'll save the markup for this step.

Striving for as Little New Markup as Necessary

Because it's always better to write less code, the only change made to the markup is to replace the "ask a question" form with the closed room notice and to add a class of "closed" to the list of questions. Copy the contents of `attendee-active.html` into the new `attendee-closed.html` file, replace the "ask a question" form with the closed notice markup and add the `class="closed"` attribute, as shown here:

```
<h3>This session has ended.</h3>
<p>
    If you have a question that wasn't answered, please
    <a href="mailto:jason@copterlabs.com">email the presenter</a>.
</p>

<ul id="questions" class="closed">

    <!-leave existing elements here -->

</ul><!--/#questions-->
```

After this is saved, loading the document in your browser shows that it is nearly ready to go with no changes (see Figure 7-23).

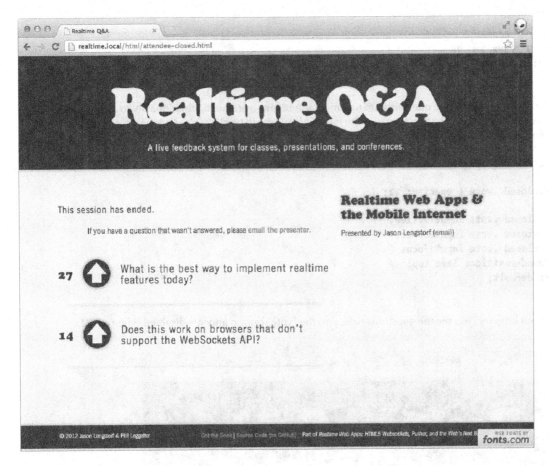

Figure 7-23. The closed view with no new styles applied

Adding Styles

Tweak the headline and copy styles by updating the two existing rules to include h3, add a new h3 rule, and amend p, as shown in the following "Basic Font Styles" section of main.css:

```
h1,h2,h3,#questions li:before {
    font-family: 'Cooper Black W01';
    font-weight: normal;
}

h2,h3 { text-shadow: 0 0 10px rgba(31, 27, 12, .3); }

h3 {
    margin: 0 365px .75em 0;
    font-size: 1.875em;
    line-height: 1em;
    letter-spacing: -.08em;
    text-align: center;
}
```

```
p {
    text-align: center;
    margin: 0 365px 2em 0;
    padding: 0 6em;
}
```

Next, make it obvious that the questions are no longer interactive by reducing their opacity to .2. Remove the active and hover states from the button to make sure it doesn't appear to be clickable. Add the #questions.closed rules to the end of the "Questions View" section in main.css:

```
#questions.closed { opacity: .4; }

#questions.closed .vote { opacity: .2; }

#questions.closed .vote input:active,
#questions.closed .vote input:hover,
#questions.closed .vote input:focus {
    background-position: left top;
    cursor: default;
}
```

Reload your browser; you see the questions fade, and the "vote" button appears disabled (Figure 7-24).

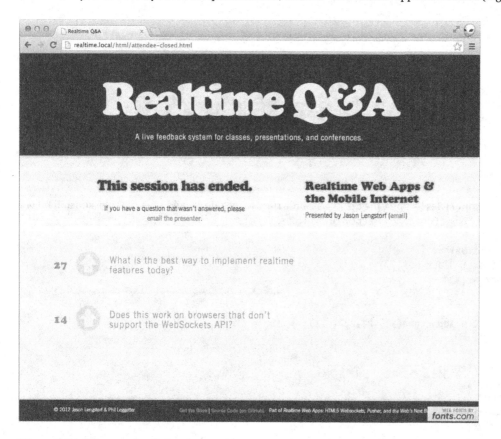

Figure 7-24. *The completed closed room view*

146

What About the Media Queries?

Because you kept the changes so simple, no updates to the media queries are required; it will work as expected right out of the box.

Developing the Room View for Presenters

The final step before moving on to the back-end functionality is to create the markup for the presenter view. This view is the same as the attendee view in every way except for three things:

- There is no "ask a question" form

- There is an "answer" form and button instead of a "vote" button

- There is a form beneath the room information with a link to the room and a button to close the form

Reworking the Existing Markup

Create a new file called `presenter.html` and copy the contents of `attendee-active.html` into it.

Next, remove the "ask a question" form markup from above the questions and remove the "vote" form from each question, replacing it with an "answer" form and button. Add a new form inside the `<header>` tag with the room information that has a disabled text input with the room's uniform resource indicator (URI) as its value and add a submit button with the copy "Close This Room" that will allow the presenter to end the session.

All in all, there are very few changes. The only differences are those within the `<section>` element:

```
<section>

    <header>
        <h2>Realtime Web Apps &amp; the Mobile Internet</h2>
        <p>
            Presented by Jason Lengstorf
            (<a href="mailto:jason@lengstorf.com" tabindex="100">email</a>)
        </p>

        <form id="close-this-room">
            <label>
                Link to your room.
                <input type="text" name="room-url"
                        value="http://realtime.local/room/1234"
                        disabled />
            </label>
            <input type="submit" value="Close This Room" />
        </form><!--/#close-this-room-->

    </header>

    <ul id="questions" class="presenter">

        <li id="question-1"
            data-count="27">
```

```
        <form class="answer">
            <input type="submit" value="Answer this question." />
        </form>

        <p>
            What is the best way to implement realtime features today?
        </p>

    </li>

    <li id="question-2"
        data-count="14">

        <form class="answer">
            <input type="submit" value="Answer this question." />
        </form>

        <p>
            Does this work on browsers that don't support the
            WebSockets API?
        </p>

    </li>

</ul><!--/#questions-->

</section>
```

View this file in your browser; it needs a little tweaking, but it is close (see Figure 7-25).

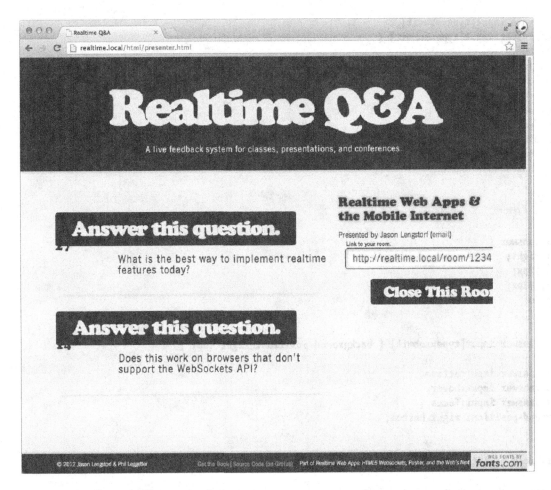

Figure 7-25. *The unstyled presenter view*

Updating the CSS

As you can see in Figure 7-25, the only things that need tweaking are the "answer" button and the form in the sidebar. The "answer" button uses the sprite, similar to the "vote" button, and floats to the right of the question. The form in the sidebar simply needs to be a little narrower to fit in the available space.

Update the existing #questions .vote and #questions .vote input[type=submit] rules to also apply to the presenter view and add some specific answer and close rules to the bottom of the "Questions View" section in main.css:

```css
/* Updated rules */
#questions .vote,#questions .answer {
    position: relative;
    display: block;
    width: 76px;
    height: 76px;
    margin: 0 0 0 2em;
    padding: 0;
    overflow: hidden;
}
```

149

```
#questions .vote input[type=submit],
#questions .answer input[type=submit] {
    width: 100%;
    height: 100%;
    margin: 0;
    padding: 0;
    cursor: pointer;
    text-indent: -9999px;
    background: url(../images/sprite.jpg) left top no-repeat;
    -webkit-box-shadow: none;
            box-shadow: none;
}

/* new rules */

#questions .answer {
    float: right;
    width: 78px;
    height: 88px;
    margin: 0;
}

#questions .answer input[type=submit] { background-position: right top; }

#questions .answer input:active,
#questions .answer input:hover,
#questions .answer input:focus {
    background-position: right bottom;
}

#close-this-room { width: 340px; margin: 2em 0 0; }

#close-this-room label input { width: 305px; }
```

Reload your browser to see the properly styled presenter view (see Figure 7-26).

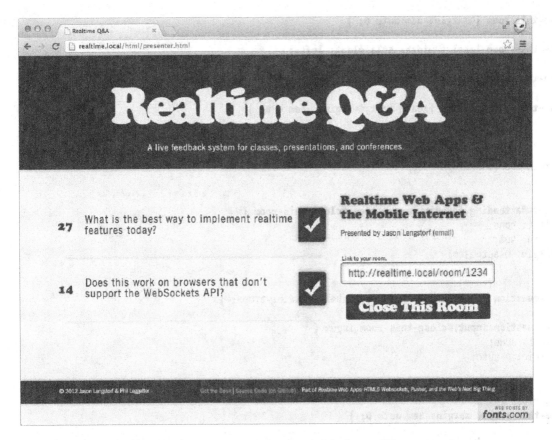

Figure 7-26. The styled presenter view with an active state for the "answer" button

Updating the Media Queries

The media queries for the presenter view follow suit with those from the attendee view, except instead of moving the vote count above the button on the left, it goes below the count on the right.

Other than that, the "close this room" form gets reflowed to fit with the single-column layout on tablets and handheld devices.

Update the existing rules and add the new rules to the "Media queries" section of main.css as shown here:

```
@media screen and (max-width: 960px)
{

    section header,#close-this-room {
        float: none;
        width: 680px;
        margin: 0 auto 1.5em;
        overflow: hidden;
    }
```

```
    #close-this-room { margin: 1em auto 0; }

    #close-this-room label { width: 59%; float: left;}

    #close-this-room label input { width: 88%; margin: 0; }

    #close-this-room input { float: left; margin: .6em 0 0; }

}

@media screen and (max-width: 768px)
{

    form,form#attending,form#ask-a-question,#close-this-room {
        float: none;
        width: 90%;
        margin: 0 auto 3em;
    }

    #ask-a-question label,#close-this-room label { width: 270px; }

    #ask-a-question input,#close-this-room input {
        float: none;
        margin: 0 auto;
    }

    /* New close rules */
    #close-this-room { margin: 1em auto 0; }

    #questions.presenter li:before {
        top: auto;
        right: 24px;
        bottom: 6px;
        left: auto;
        z-index: 10;
    }

}
```

Save and reload the page in your browser. You now have a responsive presenter view (see Figure 7-27).

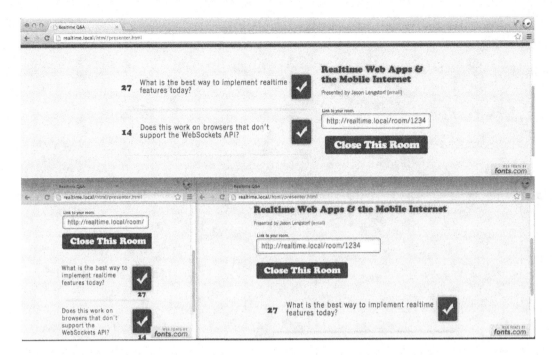

Figure 7-27. *The presenter view, complete with tablet and handheld layouts*

Summary

At this point, you have HTML and CSS templates for the app, and you're ready to start developing the back end with PHP and MySQL.

There are still a few things that will need CSS styles, such as the "vote" button after it has been clicked, or a question after it has been answered, but you'll add those styles in the next chapter when you develop that functionality.

In the next chapter, you'll build the server-side scripts and databases to make the app actually work.

CHAPTER 8

▪ ▪ ▪

Building the Back End: Part 1

So far in the app development process, most of the efforts have been targeted at the front end of the site. In this chapter, you'll be building the back-end scripts that will power the front end.

Rolling Your Own Simple MVC Framework

Before you can build the app, your first task is to build a framework for it. As we determined previously, a Model-View Controller (MVC) framework will be the best option in this particular build.

In this section, you'll build an MVC framework from scratch. This is a complex task, so we've built it across two chapters. In this first chapter you'll set up the framework for the home page and some of the logic behind it, and in Chapter 9 we'll fill out the MVC structure and complete the application.

Determining the Directory Structure

A good app starts with proper organization. In your web root folder, create two folders and add the subfolders as shown:

- assets
  - images
  - scripts
  - styles
- system
  - config
  - controllers
  - core
  - inc
  - lib
  - models
  - views

We'll cover what each of these folders is for as we build the app; for now, rest assured that this app will be well-organized.

Setting Up a Router for All Requests

The first thing that your framework needs is a script to route requests to the appropriate places. This script will initialize any necessary configuration variables, load any additional required scripts, and determine the user's intent (via the URL) to send requests through the proper controller.

Setting Configuration Variables

Because every installation of this app will likely have differences in configuration, you'll be setting up a configuration file. In /system/config, create a new file called config.inc.php and insert the following:

```php
<?php

/**
 * A sample configuration file
 *
 * The variables below need to be filled out with environment specific data.
 *
 * @author  Jason Lengstorf <jason@lengstorf.com>
 * @author  Phil Leggetter <phil@leggetter.co.uk>
 */

// Set up an array for constants
$_C = array();

//----------------------------------------------------------------------
// Converts the constants array into actual constants
//----------------------------------------------------------------------

foreach ($_C as $constant=>$value) {
    define($constant, $value);
}
```

So far, this doesn't actually create any configuration variables, but it sets up a structure to do so. All configuration variables will be added to the $_C array, which is run through a foreach loop at the bottom of the script to define each variable as a constant.

■ **Note** Configuration variables are defined as constants because 1) they are immutable, which means they cannot be altered during execution; and 2) they need to be in the global scope to be available to functions and classes.

With the structure in place, start adding configuration variables. In this chapter, we need the following bits of app-specific data to be stored:

- Time zone for the app
- Database configuration info
- Whether to show debugging info

In config.inc.php, add the code shown in bold to declare the configuration variables as constants:

```php
<?php

/**
 * A sample configuration file
 *
 * The variables below need to be filled out with environment specific data.
 *
 * @author  Jason Lengstorf <jason@lengstorf.com>
 * @author  Phil Leggetter <phil@leggetter.co.uk>
 */

// Set up an array for constants
$_C = array();

//-----------------------------------------------------------------------
// General configuration options
//-----------------------------------------------------------------------

$_C['APP_TIMEZONE'] = 'US/Pacific';

//-----------------------------------------------------------------------
// Database credentials
//-----------------------------------------------------------------------

$_C['DB_HOST'] = 'localhost';
$_C['DB_NAME'] = '';
$_C['DB_USER'] = '';
$_C['DB_PASS'] = '';

//-----------------------------------------------------------------------
// Enable debug mode (strict error reporting)
//-----------------------------------------------------------------------

$_C['DEBUG'] = TRUE;

//-----------------------------------------------------------------------
// Converts the constants array into actual constants
//-----------------------------------------------------------------------

foreach ($_C as $constant=>$value) {
    define($constant, $value);
}
```

Save this file after adding the correct values for each variable; you can close it in your editor afterward because you won't need to edit this file again during this chapter.

■ **Caution**　Don't forget to update the DB_HOST, DB_NAME, DB_USER, and DB_PASS values with your development database credentials. Without them, the app will throw a fatal error when you build the database connection scripts later in this chapter.

Initializing the App

The first order of business for an app is to set up the environmental variables and global settings. This will let the app know where files are located, how to connect to the database, whether to show debugging info, and other steps that keep things running smoothly and predictably under the hood.

In your web root folder, create a new file called index.php. Inside, start by setting up the basics of the app:

```php
<?php

/**
 * The initialization script for the app
 *
 * @author   Jason Lengstorf <jason@lengstorf.com>
 * @author   Phil Leggetter <phil@leggetter.co.uk>
 */


//-------------------------------------------------------------------------
// Initializes environment variables
//-------------------------------------------------------------------------


// Server path to this app (i.e. /var/www/vhosts/realtime/httpdocs/realtime)
define('APP_PATH',   dirname(__FILE__));

// App folder, relative from web root (i.e. /realtime)
define('APP_FOLDER', dirname($_SERVER['SCRIPT_NAME']));

// URL path to the app (i.e. http://example.org/realtime/)
define(
    'APP_URI',
    remove_unwanted_slashes('http://' . $_SERVER['SERVER_NAME'] . APP_FOLDER . '/')
);

// Server path to the system folder (for includes)
define('SYS_PATH',   APP_PATH . '/system');
```

APP_PATH is a constant that will store the absolute path to the app on your server. This is used for PHP includes.

APP_FOLDER, on the other hand, stores the relative path from web root. It would be used for relative links or CSS includes and asset paths. To avoid issues with the app running from a subdirectory, a trailing slash is included. We can do this comfortably because of the call to remove_unwanted_slashes().

APP_URI is the actual URI of the app. For example, if the app is at the web root of www.example.org, APP_URI would contain http://www.example.org/; if the app is in a subdirectory called realtime, APP_URI would store http://www.example.org/realtime/.

■ **Note** APP_URI is determined in part using a function called remove_unwanted_slashes(), which has not yet been defined. This will be added in the next section.

Finally, SYS_PATH contains the path to the system files (which is most of the MVC framework).

Below the app constants, you can now set up the session, include the configuration variables, set the appropriate level of error reporting for the app, and set the app time zone. Add the code shown in bold to index.php:

```php
<?php

/**
 * The initialization script for the app
 *
 * @author  Jason Lengstorf <jason@lengstorf.com>
 * @author  Phil Leggetter <phil@leggetter.co.uk>
 */

//-------------------------------------------------------------------------------
// Initializes environment variables
//-------------------------------------------------------------------------------

// Server path to this app (i.e. /var/www/vhosts/realtime/httpdocs/realtime)
define('APP_PATH',   dirname(__FILE__));

// App folder, relative from web root (i.e. /realtime)
define('APP_FOLDER', dirname($_SERVER['SCRIPT_NAME']));

// URL path to the app (i.e. http://example.org/realtime)
define(
    'APP_URI',
    remove_unwanted_slashes('http://' . $_SERVER['SERVER_NAME'] . APP_FOLDER)
);

// Server path to the system folder (for includes)
define('SYS_PATH',   APP_PATH . '/system');

// Relative path to the form processing script (i.e. /realtime/process.php)
define('FORM_ACTION', remove_unwanted_slashes(APP_FOLDER . '/process.php'));

//-------------------------------------------------------------------------------
// Initializes the app
//-------------------------------------------------------------------------------

// Starts the session
if (!isset($_SESSION)) {
    session_start();
}

// Loads the configuration variables
require_once SYS_PATH . '/config/config.inc.php';

// Turns on error reporting if in debug mode
if (DEBUG===TRUE) {
    ini_set('display_errors', 1);
    error_reporting(E_ALL^E_STRICT);
```

```
} else {
    ini_set('display_errors', 0);
    error_reporting(0);
}

// Sets the timezone to avoid a notice
date_default_timezone_set(APP_TIMEZONE);
```

Because this app will utilize sessions to pass data between page loads, the script calls session_start() if the $_SESSION superglobal isn't set.

Then, after loading the configuration variable, the script checks the DEBUG value and—if it's set to TRUE, which should always be the case during development—turns on strict error reporting; otherwise, errors are suppressed.

Finally, because PHP throws a notice without it, the time zone is set using the APP_TIMEZONE variable.

Setting Up Utility Functions

To avoid clouding up the router's logic, complicated operations should be encapsulated in functions. Fortunately, there aren't too many complicated operations in this section, so we'll need to create only four utility functions:

- A function to parse the URI and return its parts as an array

- A function to determine the controller name using the URI parts

- A function to prevent the occurrence of double slashes in any part of a URI except its protocol

- An autoloader that will check for classes within our app and include them (or provide a helpful error message if the requested class doesn't exist)

Parsing the URI

Because we want our app to have pretty URIs and not awkward query strings, we'll need a way to determine which parts of the URI are for configuration and which are simply part of the URI.

■ **Note**   Because this app may not always be installed at the root of a URI, the parsing script needs to compare the URI with the app's location and return *only* the parts of the URI that don't reference the app's location on the server.

For example, if the app is installed at http://www.example.org/, the URI for room ID 1234 would be http://www.example.org/room/1234. However, if the app is installed in a subdirectory called realtime, the URI for room ID 1234 would be http://www.example.org/realtime/room/1234.

In both cases, we only want "room" and "1234" to be returned by the parse_uri() function.

The parts of the URI that aren't location-related will then be split apart at the forward slashes and stored as an array for use with the app, which will use them to determine the view to be displayed (and a few other things that will be covered later).

At the bottom of index.php, add the URI parsing function using the code shown in bold:

```
//-------------------------------------------------------------------------
// Initializes the app
//-------------------------------------------------------------------------

// Starts the session
if (!isset($_SESSION)) {
    session_start();
}

// Loads the configuration variables
require_once SYS_PATH . '/config/config.inc.php';

// Turns on error reporting if in debug mode
if (DEBUG===TRUE) {
    ini_set('display_errors', 1);
    error_reporting(E_ALL^E_STRICT);
} else {
    ini_set('display_errors', 0);
    error_reporting(0);
}

// Sets the timezone to avoid a notice
date_default_timezone_set(APP_TIMEZONE);


//-------------------------------------------------------------------------
// Function declarations
//-------------------------------------------------------------------------

/**
 * Breaks the URI into an array at the slashes
 *
 * @return array   The broken up URI
 */
function parse_uri(  )
{
    // Removes any subfolders in which the app is installed
    $real_uri = preg_replace(
            '~^'.APP_FOLDER.'~',
            '',
            $_SERVER['REQUEST_URI'],
            1
        );

    $uri_array = explode('/', $real_uri);

    // If the first element is empty, get rid of it
    if (empty($uri_array[0])) {
        array_shift($uri_array);
    }
```

```
    // If the last element is empty, get rid of it
    if (empty($uri_array[count($uri_array)-1])) {
        array_pop($uri_array);
    }

    return $uri_array;
}
```

The parse_uri() function starts by removing the APP_FOLDER from the requested URI using preg_replace(), leaving only the bits that tell the app what the user is requesting. The function then uses explode() to split the URI up at the forward slashes, then checks for empty elements at the beginning and end of the array before returning it.

Getting the Controller Name

Next, you need to figure out the name of the appropriate controller to load given the URI parts. To do this, add the following bold code to index.php:

```
//--------------------------------------------------------------------------
// Function declarations
//--------------------------------------------------------------------------

/**
 * Breaks the URI into an array at the slashes
 *
 * @return array   The broken up URI
 */
function parse_uri(  )
{
    // Removes any subfolders in which the app is installed
    $real_uri = preg_replace(
            '~^'.APP_FOLDER.'~',
            '',
            $_SERVER['REQUEST_URI'],
            1
        );

    $uri_array = explode('/', $real_uri);

    // If the first element is empty, get rid of it
    if (empty($uri_array[0])) {
        array_shift($uri_array);
    }

    // If the last element is empty, get rid of it
    if (empty($uri_array[count($uri_array)-1])) {
        array_pop($uri_array);
    }

    return $uri_array;
}
```

```
/**
 * Determines the controller name using the first element of the URI array
 *
 * @param $uri_array array   The broken up URI
 * @return string            The controller classname
 */
function get_controller_classname( &$uri_array )
{
    $controller = array_shift($uri_array);
    return ucfirst($controller);
}
```

This function keeps it simple: the URI is passed *by reference* to the function, the first element is loaded into the $controller variable, and then the first letter is capitalized and that value is returned.

■ **Note**   Using the ampersand (&) to pass a variable by reference means that the actions performed inside the function affect the data passed to it not only within the function's scope but the scope from which the function is called as well.

What this means is that a URI of http://example.com/room/1234/ would be parsed as an array with the following structure:

```
array(2) {
  [0]=>
  string(4) "room"
  [1]=>
  string(4) "1234"
}
```

The first element of the array—"room"—would be isolated, capitalized, and then returned, giving us this return value of the get_controller_classname() function:

```
Room
```

■ **Note**   We'll go into how this return value will be used a little later in this chapter.

Avoiding Unwanted Slashes

Whenever you're dealing with URIs, there's always the possibility that URI parts will have leading or trailing slashes. When these parts are combined, it can cause problems.

For example, a site's URI might be stored in a variable like so:

```
$site_uri = 'http://www.example.org/';
```

And if a link is set up to be relative to web root, it might be declared like this:

```
$services_link = '/services/';
```

Now imagine that your app needs to provide a link to the services page that can be accessed from any web page. Your first instinct would probably be the following:

```
$services_uri = $site_uri . $services_link;
```

However, that variable would have the following value:

```
http://www.example.org//services/
```

That second double slash is a problem, and when your URI components are being grabbed from various locations (the $_SERVER superglobal, app-specific configuration, etc.) it's not unlikely that an unwanted double slash situation will occur.

Therefore, it's worth writing a function to detect and remove any unwanted double slashes in a given URI. However, because the protocol—meaning the "http://" part—has two slashes, special care needs to be taken not to break the URI.

To accomplish this, add the following bold code to index.php:

```php
//---------------------------------------------------------------------------
// Function declarations
//---------------------------------------------------------------------------

/**
 * Breaks the URI into an array at the slashes
 *
 * @return array  The broken up URI
 */
function parse_uri( )
{
    // Removes any subfolders in which the app is installed
    $real_uri = preg_replace(
            '~^'.APP_FOLDER.'~',
            '',
            $_SERVER['REQUEST_URI'],
            1
        );

    $uri_array = explode('/', $real_uri);

    // If the first element is empty, get rid of it
    if (empty($uri_array[0])) {
        array_shift($uri_array);
    }

    // If the last element is empty, get rid of it
    if (empty($uri_array[count($uri_array)-1])) {
        array_pop($uri_array);
    }

    return $uri_array;
}
```

```
/**
 * Determines the controller name using the first element of the URI array
 *
 * @param $uri_array array   The broken up URI
 * @return string           The controller classname
 */
function get_controller_classname( &$uri_array )
{
    $controller = array_shift($uri_array);
    return ucfirst($controller);
}


/**
 * Removes unwanted double slashes (except in the protocol)
 *
 * @param $dirty_path string    The path to check for unwanted slashes
 * @return string               The cleaned path
 */
function remove_unwanted_slashes( $dirty_path )
{
    return preg_replace('~(?<!:)//~', '/', $dirty_path);
}
```

Using preg_replace(), this function checks for any occurrences of a double slash (//) that isn't preceded by a colon (:) and replaces them with a single slash (/).

Because regular expressions can be a little hairy to look at[1], let's break this one down bit by bit:

- ~—The opening delimiter; this simply tells the function that a regex pattern is beginning

- (?<!:)—What's called a "negative lookbehind," which has three main components:

  - Enclosing parentheses—Define the lookbehind

  - ?<!—The actual lookbehind, which literally tells the regex, "look at the character right before the one being matched"

  - :—The expression or character that we *don't* want to match; in this case, it's the colon preceding the two slashes, which indicates that it's the protocol and should not be replaced

- //—The characters to look for; in this case, the double slashes

- ~—The closing delimiter; this tells the function that the regex pattern is ending

Continuing with the previous URI example, the double-slash problem is solved by running the combined URI parts through remove_unwanted_slashes():

```
$services_uri = remove_unwanted_slashes($site_uri . $services_link);
```

This stores a proper URI in $services_uri:

```
http://www.example.org/services/
```

---

[1]RegEx is complex enough to be worthy of its own book, which has conveniently been compiled online at http://www.regular-expressions.info/

Autoloading Classes

Finally, to avoid loading a large number of unused PHP classes, you'll need an autoloader to grab the required files only when they're being accessed.

This is accomplished by creating a function to search in all the places where classes will be stored; then registering that function as the autoloader using spl_autoload_register().

■ **Note** The __autoload() function used to be the standard, but PHP now recommends using spl_autoload_register() due to better flexibility and performance.

To start, let's refer to the app's folder structure and determine all the possible locations that may hold class files as the app is built out.

There will be three class types loaded by this function:

- Controllers will be stored in system/controllers/

- Models are stored in system/models/

- Core files will be stored in system/core/ (we'll talk more about these files later)

Armed with the list of possible locations, the function will loop through each one and see whether the class exists there; if so, it will load the class and return TRUE; if not, it throws an Exception stating the class doesn't exist.

Add the following bold code to make this happen. *Don't forget the call to* spl_autoload_register() *in the app initialization block!*

```php
<?php

/**
 * The initialization script for the app
 *
 * @author  Jason Lengstorf <jason@lengstorf.com>
 * @author  Phil Leggetter <phil@leggetter.co.uk>
 */

//-------------------------------------------------------------------------
// Initializes environment variables
//-------------------------------------------------------------------------

// Server path to this app (i.e. /var/www/vhosts/realtime/httpdocs/realtime)
define('APP_PATH',   dirname(__FILE__));

// App folder, relative from web root (i.e. /realtime)
define('APP_FOLDER', dirname($_SERVER['SCRIPT_NAME']));

// URI path to the app (i.e. http://example.org/realtime)
define(
    'APP_URI',
    remove_unwanted_slashes('http://' . $_SERVER['SERVER_NAME'] . APP_FOLDER)
);
```

```php
// Server path to the system folder (for includes)
define('SYS_PATH',   APP_PATH . '/system');

// Relative path to the form processing script (i.e. /realtime/process.php)
define('FORM_ACTION', remove_unwanted_slashes(APP_FOLDER . '/process.php'));

//---------------------------------------------------------------------------
// Initializes the app
//---------------------------------------------------------------------------

// Starts the session
if (!isset($_SESSION)) {
    session_start();
}

// Loads the configuration variables
require_once SYS_PATH . '/config/config.inc.php';

// Turns on error reporting if in debug mode
if (DEBUG===TRUE) {
    ini_set('display_errors', 1);
    error_reporting(E_ALL^E_STRICT);
} else {
    ini_set('display_errors', 0);
    error_reporting(0);
}

// Sets the timezone to avoid a notice
date_default_timezone_set(APP_TIMEZONE);

// Registers class_loader() as the autoload function
spl_autoload_register('class_autoloader');

//---------------------------------------------------------------------------
// Function declarations
//---------------------------------------------------------------------------

/**
 * Breaks the URI into an array at the slashes
 *
 * @return array  The broken up URI
 */
function parse_uri(  )
{
    // Removes any subfolders in which the app is installed
    $real_uri = preg_replace(
            '~^'.APP_FOLDER.'~',
            '',
            $_SERVER['REQUEST_URI'],
            1
        );
```

```php
    $uri_array = explode('/', $real_uri);

    // If the first element is empty, get rid of it
    if (empty($uri_array[0])) {
        array_shift($uri_array);
    }

    // If the last element is empty, get rid of it
    if (empty($uri_array[count($uri_array)-1])) {
        array_pop($uri_array);
    }

    return $uri_array;
}

/**
 * Determines the controller name using the first element of the URI array
 *
 * @param $uri_array array   The broken up URI
 * @return string            The controller classname
 */
function get_controller_classname( &$uri_array )
{
    $controller = array_shift($uri_array);
    return ucfirst($controller);
}

/**
 * Removes unwanted slashes (except in the protocol)
 *
 * @param $dirty_path string    The path to check for unwanted slashes
 * @return string               The cleaned path
 */
function remove_unwanted_slashes( $dirty_path )
{
    return preg_replace('~(?<!:)//~', '/', $dirty_path);
}

/**
 * Autoloads classes as they are instantiated
 *
 * @param $class_name string    The name of the class to be loaded
 * @return bool                 Returns TRUE on success (Exception on failure)
 */
function class_autoloader( $class_name )
{
    $fname = strtolower($class_name);
```

```php
// Defines all of the valid places a class file could be stored
$possible_locations = array(
    SYS_PATH . '/models/class.' . $fname . '.inc.php',
    SYS_PATH . '/controllers/class.' . $fname . '.inc.php',
    SYS_PATH . '/core/class.' . $fname . '.inc.php',
);

// Loops through the location array and checks for a file to load
foreach ($possible_locations as $loc) {
    if (file_exists($loc)) {
        require_once $loc;
        return TRUE;
    }
}

// Fails because a valid class wasn't found
throw new Exception("Class $class_name wasn't found.");
}
```

Finishing the Router

With the utility functions created and an autoloader in place to load the requested controller, the last step for the router script is to actually handle the URI components that request the controller and ultimately send the proper view to the user.

Loading the Controller

In index.php, add the following code between the initialization block and the function declarations:

```php
// Registers class_loader() as the autoload function
spl_autoload_register('class_autoloader');

//---------------------------------------------------------------------------
// Loads and processes view data
//---------------------------------------------------------------------------

// Parses the URI
$uri_array  = parse_uri();
$class_name = get_controller_classname($uri_array);
$options    = $uri_array;

// Sets a default view if nothing is passed in the URI (i.e. on the home page)
if (empty($class_name)) {
    $class_name = 'Home';
}
```

```
// Tries to initialize the requested view, or else throws a 404 error
try {
    $controller = new $class_name($options);
} catch (Exception $e) {
    $options[1] = $e->getMessage();
    $controller = new Error($options);
}

//--------------------------------------------------------------------------
// Function declarations
//--------------------------------------------------------------------------
```

Using the utility functions, the URI is broken apart and stored in $uri_array. It is then passed to get_controller_classname(), which stores the controller's class name in $class_name. The remaining URI components are stored in $options for later use.

Next, $class_name is checked to ensure it isn't empty; if it is, the default class name "Home" is supplied.

Finally, using a try...catch block, a new controller object of the requested type is instantiated, passing the $options as an argument to the constructor. If anything goes wrong, a new Error object is created to display an error message.

■ **Note** You will be building the Error class later in this chapter.

Outputting the View

With the controller loaded, there's nothing left to do but output the markup. In index.php, add the following bold code:

```
//--------------------------------------------------------------------------
// Loads and processes view data
//--------------------------------------------------------------------------

// Parses the URI
$uri_array  = parse_uri();
$class_name = get_controller_classname($uri_array);
$options    = $uri_array;

// Sets a default view if nothing is passed in the URI (i.e. on the home page)
if (empty($class_name)) {
    $class_name = 'Home';
}

// Tries to initialize the requested view, or else throws a 404 error
try {
    $controller = new $class_name($options);
} catch (Exception $e) {
    $options[1] = $e->getMessage();
    $controller = new Error($options);
}
```

```
//-----------------------------------------------------------------
// Outputs the view
//-----------------------------------------------------------------

// Includes the header, requested view, and footer markup
require_once SYS_PATH . '/inc/header.inc.php';

$controller->output_view();

require_once SYS_PATH . '/inc/footer.inc.php';

//-----------------------------------------------------------------
// Function declarations
//-----------------------------------------------------------------
```

The header and footer markup—which you'll be creating a little later in this chapter—are simple includes, and sandwiched between them is the call to the output_view() method of the controller object, which outputs the formatted markup for the requested view.

Adding a URI Rewrite

The final step for getting the router running is to add the .htaccess file that will direct all requests through the router (unless a file or subdirectory is directly requested).

In the root of your app, create a new file called .htaccess and insert the following code:

```
<IfModule mod_rewrite.c>
RewriteEngine On
RewriteBase /
RewriteRule ^index\.php$ - [L]
RewriteCond %{REQUEST_FILENAME} !-f
RewriteCond %{REQUEST_FILENAME} !-d
RewriteRule . index.php [L]
</IfModule>
```

You may need to update the value of RewriteBase to match the path to your app. Some server setups will run without the RewriteBase set, so if you get an error, try removing it first and then set it to your app's path.

■ **Note** If you're a WordPress developer, you might recognize this code. This is the same set of rewrite rules used on WordPress sites.

Setting Up the Core Classes

Because every controller, view, and model used in the app will have baseline functionality, before you build any of them you'll want to create *abstract classes* to house the common methods and declare any method and/or property stubs that need to be included in all classes that extend them.

WHAT ARE ABSTRACT CLASSES?

Classes defined as abstract may not be instantiated, and any class that contains at least one abstract method must also be abstract. Methods defined as abstract simply declare the method's signature— they cannot define the implementation.

When inheriting from an abstract class, all methods marked abstract in the parent's class declaration must be defined by the child[.]

—From the PHP manual entry on class abstraction[2]

What this means is that an abstract class allows developers to create classes that act as a kind of template for other classes while also providing common functionality. Because an abstract class can't be directly instantiated, method "stubs" can be created, which require child classes to declare those methods and provide functionality for them.

As a simple example, an abstract class might define a person. All people sleep and drink, so the abstract class should define those methods. Because sleeping is virtually the same for all people, that can be defined within the class. However, not all people drink the same things; that action should be defined as a stub to be declared in child classes.

Here's what that simple example might look like in real code:

```php
abstract class Person
{
    public $rest   = 0,
           $drinks = array();

    public function sleep(  )
    {
        ++$rest;
    }

    abstract public function drink(  );
}

class Jason extends Person
{
    private $_wishes = array(
        'a little bit taller',
        'a baller',
        'a girl who looks good',
        'a rabbit in a hat',
        'a bat',
        'a \'64 Impala',
    );
```

---

[2]http://us3.php.net/manual/en/language.oop5.abstract.php.

```php
    public function drink(  )
    {
        $this->drinks[] = 'coffee';
    }

    public function wish(  )
    {
        $wish_index = mt_rand(0, count($this->_wishes)-1);
        return $this->_wishes[$wish_index];
    }
}

class Phil extends Person
{
    public function drink(  )
    {
        $this->drinks[] = 'tea';
    }
}
```

The Person class sets up properties that are universal, as well as a sleep() method that all classes (people) extending the class will share.

It then defines an abstract method, drink(). Because all people drink, but not all people drink the same beverages, this method needs to be required, but not defined; that's where abstract classes are powerful.

Now when the Jason and Phil classes are defined, the groundwork is already laid—no extra code is required to allow for sleeping—so the code to finish these classes is extremely simple.

It's also worth noting that classes that extend an abstract class are not limited by the provided methods and method stubs; additional properties and methods can be declared as needed. For example, the Jason class includes a private property—$_wishes—and an additional method called wish().[3]

Creating the Abstract Controller Class

The Controller class is very straightforward: it needs to check that required data was passed in and define method stubs for generating a page title and parsing the view.

Create a new file called class.controller.inc.php and save it in the system/core/ subdirectory. Inside, paste the following code:

```php
<?php

/**
 * An abstract class that lays the groundwork for all controllers
 *
 * @author  Jason Lengstorf <jason@lengstorf.com>
 * @author  Phil Leggetter <phil@leggetter.co.uk>
 */
```

---

[3]Phil doesn't wish. He plans.

```php
abstract class Controller
{

    public $actions = array(),
           $model;

    protected static $nonce = NULL;

    /**
     * Initializes the view
     *
     * @param $options array    Options for the view
     * @return void
     */
    public function __construct( $options )
    {
        if (!is_array($options)) {
            throw new Exception("No options were supplied for the room.");
        }
    }

    /**
     * Generates a nonce that helps prevent XSS and duplicate submissions
     *
     * @return string    The generated nonce
     */
    protected function generate_nonce(  )
    {
        // TODO: Add the actual nonce generation script
        return "tempnonce";
    }

    /**
     * Performs basic input sanitization on a given string
     *
     * @param $dirty     string  The string to be sanitized
     * @return           string  The sanitized string
     */
    protected function sanitize( $dirty )
    {
        return htmlentities(strip_tags($dirty), ENT_QUOTES);
    }

    /**
     * Sets the title for the view
     *
     * @return string    The text to be used in the <title> tag
     */
    abstract public function get_title(  );
```

```
/**
 * Loads and outputs the view's markup
 *
 * @return void
 */
abstract public function output_view(  );

}
```

The __construct() method checks for an array of options (which will be the array extracted by parse_uri() in index.php) and throws an Exception if none was supplied.

For the moment, the generate_nonce() method simply returns a temporary string. You will revisit this method in the "Handling Form Submissions" section later in this chapter.

The sanitize() method does some very basic input sanitization, which should always be performed on user-supplied data.

Later in this chapter, you'll build a controller that extends this class, but first you'll need a way to handle views (or else the output_view() method will break).

Creating the View Class

In order to show output, you'll need a View class. This class will, in essence, load the views requested by the Controller class and return them. However, because the data being displayed will vary from room to room, the View class also needs to insert data into the views; this will require a simple *setter* implementation, which we'll discuss a bit later.

In the system/core/ subdirectory, create a new file called class.view.inc.php. Inside, add the following code:

```
<?php

/**
 * Parses template files with loaded data to output HTML markup
 *
 * @author  Jason Lengstorf <jason@lengstorf.com>
 * @author  Phil Leggetter <phil@leggetter.co.uk>
 */
class View
{

    protected $view,
              $vars = array();

    /**
     * Initializes the view
     *
     * @param $view array    The view slug
     * @return void
     */
    public function __construct( $view=NULL ) {
        if (!$view) {
            throw new Exception("No view slug was supplied.");
        }
```

```php
        $this->view = $view;
    }

    /**
     * Stores data for the view into an array
     *
     * @param $key string    The variable name
     * @param $var string    The variable value
     * @return void
     */
    public function __set( $key, $var ) {
        $this->vars[$key] = $var;
    }

    /**
     * Loads and parses the selected template using the provided data
     *
     * @param $print boolean    Whether the markup should be output directly
     * @return mixed            A string of markup if $print is TRUE or void
     */
    public function render( $print=TRUE ) {
        // Converts the array of view variables to individual variables
        extract($this->vars);

        // Checks to make sure the requested view exists
        $view_filepath = SYS_PATH . '/views/' . $this->view . '.inc.php';
        if (!file_exists($view_filepath)) {
            throw new Exception("That view file doesn't exist.");
        }

        // Turns on output buffering if markup should be returned, not printed
        if (!$print) {
            ob_start();
        }

        require $view_filepath;

        // Returns the markup if requested
        if (!$print) {
            return ob_get_clean();
        }
    }

}
```

■ **Note** You may have noticed that the View class isn't abstract. This is because its functionality doesn't need to be extended in this app.

Starting at the top, this class defines two properties: $view, which stores the name of the view to be loaded; and $vars, which is an array of view-specific key-value pairs to be used for customizing the output.

The __construct() method checks for a view slug or string identifying the view, and stores it in the object for later use, or it throws an Exception if none is supplied.

The __set() method is another magic method (which we'll talk more about in the next section) like __construct() that allows the storage of data in an object as properties, even when the properties are not explicitly defined. This creates a shortcut for adding variables for output in the views.

Finally, the render() function uses the extract() function to store all the custom properties into variables, checks for a valid view file, and either prints or returns the markup for the view based on the $print flag.

WHY SETTERS ARE USEFUL

Like all the other magic methods in PHP, the __set() method is not actually that magical; it simply provides a shortcut for doing something that would otherwise be cumbersome.

For example, our various views will not share the same variables for output: a room will have a title and presenter, whereas the question view will have the question text and number of votes.

While you *could* explicitly declare each property in their respective views, that adds a maintenance headache if additional properties are added in the future.

Alternatively, you might use a dedicated property to hold an array of custom variables for each view:

```php
<?php

class RWA_Example
{
    public $vars = array();
}

$test = new RWA_Example;

// Sets custom variables
$test->vars['foo'] = 'bar';
$test->vars['bat'] = 'baz';

// Gets custom variables
echo $test->vars['foo'];
echo $test->vars['bat'];
```

This is a perfectly acceptable solution, but it's a little unwieldy to type.

Using the magic setter method simplifies this process by providing a shortcut: simply set the properties as if they were explicitly declared, then use __set() to put them in an array.

To retrieve the custom variables, there's another magic method called __get().

Here's what the previous example would look like using getters and setters:

```php
<?php

class RWA_Example
{
    protected $magic = array();

    public function __set( $key, $val )
    {
        $this->magic[$key] = $val;
    }

    public function __get( $key )
    {
        return $this->magic[$key];
    }
}

$test = new RWA_Example;

// Sets custom properties
$test->foo = 'bar';
$test->bat = 'baz';

// Gets custom properties
echo $test->foo;
echo $test->bat;
```

This significantly improves the readability of the code and lowers the risk of typos, thus creating an effective shortcut for adding properties to an object on the fly.

Creating the Abstract Model Class

The last core class needed is the Model class, which is the simplest of the three. For this app, all the Model class needs to do is create a database connection.

In the system/core/ subdirectory, create a new file called class.model.inc.php and insert the following code:

```php
<?php

/**
 * Creates a set of generic database interaction methods
 *
 * @author  Jason Lengstorf <jason@lengstorf.com>
 * @author  Phil Leggetter <phil@leggetter.co.uk>
 */
```

```php
abstract class Model
{

    public static $db;

    /**
     * Creates a PDO connection to MySQL
     *
     * @return boolean  Returns TRUE on success (dies on failure)
     */
    public function __construct( ) {
        $dsn = 'mysql:dbname=' . DB_NAME . ';host=' . DB_HOST;
        try {
            self::$db = new PDO($dsn, DB_USER, DB_PASS);
        } catch (PDOException $e) {
            die("Couldn't connect to the database.");
        }

        return TRUE;
    }

}
```

The __construct() method attempts to create a new MySQL connection using the values you stored in system/config/config.inc.php and throws an Exception if the connection fails.

■ **Note**   We're using PHP Data Objects (PDO)[4] for database access because it provides an easy interface and makes SQL injection virtually impossible when used properly.

Adding the Header and Footer Markup

The last step before actually building one of the app's pages is to get the header and footer markup added to the app for common use.

Starting with the simplest file, create a new file in system/inc/ called footer.inc.php and insert the footer markup you built in Chapter 7:

```html
<footer>
    <ul>
        <li class="copyright">
            &copy; 2013 Jason Lengstorf &amp; Phil Leggetter
        </li><!--/.copyright-->
        <li>
            Part of <em>Realtime Web Apps: With HTML5 WebSocket, PHP,
                and jQuery</em>.
        </li>
```

---

[4]http://www.php.net/manual/en/intro.pdo.php

```
        <li>
            <a href="http://amzn.to/XKcBbG">Get the Book</a> |
            <a href="http://cptr.me/UkMSmn">Source Code (on GitHub)</a>
        </li>
    </ul>
</footer>

</body>

</html>
```

There's nothing of note in the footer markup; the header, however, introduces our first bit of markup that requires variable data. Let's start by creating the markup and then deal with setting the variables in the next section.

Create a new file called header.inc.php and save it in system/inc/ with the following markup inside (variables are in bold):

```
<!doctype html>
<html lang="en">

<head>

<meta charset="utf-8" />

<title><?php echo $title; ?></title>

<!-- Fonts via fonts.com -->
<script type="text/javascript"
        src="http://fast.fonts.com/jsapi/6a912a6e-163c-4c8b-afe0-e3d22ffab02e.js"></script>

<!-- Main site styles -->
<link rel="stylesheet" href="<?php echo $css_path; ?>" />

</head>

<body>

<header>
    <h1>Realtime Q&amp;A</h1>
    <p class="tagline">
        A live feedback system for classes, presentations, and conferences.
    </p><!--/.tagline-->
</header>
```

This markup sets the HTML5 doctype and basic metadata, uses a variable to set the title of the page, and then loads the font stylesheet (from Fonts.com). The site stylesheet location is stored in a variable because its location needs to be determined relative to the app's installation to avoid a broken URI.

Because the app shares common header markup at the top of every page, this is also included.

Setting Variables for the Header

In order to set the variables for the header, open index.php again and add the following code, shown in bold:

```
//----------------------------------------------------------------------
// Outputs the view
//----------------------------------------------------------------------

// Loads the <title> tag value for the header markup
$title = $controller->get_title();

// Sets the path to the app stylesheet for the header markup
$dirty_path = APP_URI . '/assets/styles/main.css';
$css_path = remove_unwanted_slashes($dirty_path);

// Includes the header, requested view, and footer markup
require_once SYS_PATH . '/inc/header.inc.php';

$controller->output_view();

require_once SYS_PATH . '/inc/footer.inc.php';

//----------------------------------------------------------------------
// Function declarations
//----------------------------------------------------------------------
```

The first variable—$title—is set using the get_title() method of the controller object.

Next, the stylesheet path is generated using the APP_URI constant and the path to the stylesheet, which is checked for double slashes before being stored in $css_path for output.

ISN'T THIS STYLESHEET PATH VARIABLE OVERKILL?

At first glance, it might seem like the steps taken to generate the $css_path variable are unnecessary and that the URI could easily be hard-coded into the header markup. After all, the file is always at assets/styles/main.css, right?

Because we're using URI-rewrites, we aren't able to use relative paths (i.e. href="./assets/styles/main.css").

Using an absolute URI, such as href="/assets/styles/main.css", is fine as long as the app is installed at the root of the server.

However, if the app is installed in a subdirectory, the absolute URI needs to be edited to include the subdirectory path, and we don't want to require editing of the header markup for every install.

As a result, putting together two lines of code to determine the absolute path of the stylesheet is a small effort to avoid a big headache.

Copying the Stylesheet and Assets to the Proper Directories

Now that the header markup is in place and referencing the stylesheet, you should copy main.css from Chapter 7 into the assets/styles/ folder. You should also copy the image sprite to assets/images/.

■ **Caution** The CSS markup and assets will not be mentioned again or printed in this chapter in the interest of keeping things moving forward. Don't forget to copy main.css from Chapter 7, or else the app will not match the screenshots to follow.

Building the Home Page

The router is created. The core classes are written. The common markup is ready to roll. All that's left to do is create the first actual page of the app.

Starting with the simplest page first, let's build the Home page.

Creating the Home Controller

To get started, create a new file in system/controllers/ called class.home.inc.php. Inside, add the following code:

```php
<?php

/**
 * Generates output for the Home view
 *
 * @author  Jason Lengstorf <jason@lengstorf.com>
 * @author  Phil Leggetter <phil@leggetter.co.uk>
 */
class Home extends Controller
{

    /**
     * Overrides the parent constructor to avoid an error
     *
     * @return bool TRUE
     */
    public function __construct( )
    {
        return TRUE;
    }

    /**
     * Generates the title of the page
     *
     * @return string   The title of the page
     */
```

```php
public function get_title(  )
{
    return 'Realtime Q&amp;A';
}

/**
 * Loads and outputs the view's markup
 *
 * @return void
 */
public function output_view(  )
{
    $view = new View('home');

    $view->render();
}

}
```

As we discussed when building the abstract `Controller` class, the `Home` class extends `Controller`. First—because the home page does not accept any arguments—the constructor is overridden to avoid an `Exception`. Then `get_title()` is declared, which simply returns the name of the app for use in the `<title>` tag.

Finally, the `output_view()` method creates a new instance of the `View` class and calls its `render()` method to output markup.

Next, let's create the home page markup and generate any necessary variables for output.

Creating the Home View

The markup for the home page will live in a file called `home.inc.php`, which should be created and saved in `system/views/`. Inside, add the home markup you created in Chapter 7 (the bits that need to be set by variables have been bolded):

```html
<section>

    <form id="attending" method="post"
        action="<?php echo $join_action; ?>">
        <h2>Attending?</h2>
        <p>Join a room using its ID.</p>
        <label>
            What is the room's ID?
            <input type="text" name="room_id" />
        </label>
        <input type="submit" value="Join This Room" />
        <input type="hidden" name="nonce"
                value="<?php echo $nonce; ?>" />
    </form><!--/#attending-->

    <form id="presenting" method="post"
        action="<?php echo $create_action; ?>">
        <h2>Presenting?</h2>
        <p>Create a room to start your Q&amp;A session.</p>
        <label>
```

```
                Tell us your name (so attendees know who you are).
                <input type="text" name="presenter-name" />
        </label>
        <label>
                Tell us your email (so attendees can get in touch with you).
                <input type="email" name="presenter-email" />
        </label>
        <label>
                What is your session called?
                <input type="text" name="session-name" />
        </label>
        <input type="submit" value="Create Your Room" />
        <input type="hidden" name="nonce"
                value="<?php echo $nonce; ?>" />
</form><!--/#presenting-->

</section>
```

This view requires three variables:

- $join_action: The form action that will allow a user to join an existing room

- $nonce: A security token that prevents the form from being submitted fraudulently or repeatedly

- $create_action: The form action that allows a user to create a new room

The $nonce is used in both forms because there's no way for both forms to be submitted simultaneously (and even if there were, that's not a behavior this app supports).

Generating Variables for Output

To create the variables for outputting the home view, go back into the Home controller (class.home.inc.php) and add the following bold code:

```
/**
 * Loads and outputs the view's markup
 *
 * @return void
 */
public function output_view(  )
{
    $view = new View('home');
    $view->nonce = $this->generate_nonce();

    // Action URIs for form submissions
    $view->join_action   = APP_URI . 'room/join';
    $view->create_action = APP_URI . 'room/create';

    $view->render();
}
```

Using the setter you created in the View class, adding variables is as simple as declaring new properties in the View object.

■ **Note**   Remember, these properties are converted to standalone variables by the View class' render() method, so whatever name you choose for the property is the variable name that will be available to the view (i.e., $view->nonce is available to the view as $nonce).

Giving the App its First Spin

With the completion of the home view, your app is finally in a state where you can actually load it in a browser. Navigate to the app in your browser—this book assumes that the app is installed at http://rwa.local/—and you'll see the home page designed in Chapter 7 (see Figure 8-1).

Figure 8-1. The home view, generated by the app

Adding an Error Handler

Next, the app needs an error handler. Currently, if a non-working URI is visited (such as `http://rwa.loca/not-real/`) there is an ugly "uncaught exception" error message displayed (see Figure 8-2).

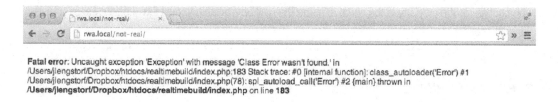

Figure 8-2. *Non-working URIs cause ugly errors to be displayed*

The app is already attempting to load the Error class if something goes wrong, so all you need to do is build that controller and view to catch the errors and display them in an easy-to-read manner.

Creating the Error Controller

To begin, create a new file called `class.error.inc.php` and save it in `system/controllers/`. Inside, place the following code:

```php
<?php

/**
 * Processes output for the Room view
 *
 * @author  Jason Lengstorf <jason@lengstorf.com>
 * @author  Phil Leggetter <phil@leggetter.co.uk>
 */
class Error extends Controller
{
    private $_message = NULL;

    /**
     * Initializes the view
     *
     * @param $options array    Options for the view
     * @return void
     */
    public function __construct( $options )
    {
        if (isset($options[1])) {
            $this->_message = $options[1];
        }
    }

    /**
     * Generates the title of the page
     *
     * @return string    The title of the page
     */
```

```php
public function get_title(  )
{
    return 'Something went wrong.';
}

/**
 * Loads and outputs the view's markup
 *
 * @return void
 */
public function output_view(  )
{
    $view = new View('error');
    $view->message = $this->_message;
    $view->home_link = APP_URI;

    $view->render();
}

}
```

The Error class is a little different in that it declares a private property $_message that will store the Exception class' error message.

The constructor stores the supplied error message in $_message if one is supplied, and get_title() returns a generic error message for the <title> tag.

The view() method simply adds the error message and home page URI to the view object for use in the markup; then renders the output.

Creating the Error View

To display the results of the Error controller, create a new file in system/views/ called error.inc.php and add the following markup:

```html
<section id="error">

    <h2>
        I&rsquo;m sorry, Dave.<br />
        I&rsquo;m afraid I can&rsquo;t do that.
    </h2>

    <p>
        Sorry, but something went wrong. Maybe the error message below
        will help.
    </p>

    <p><code><?php echo $message; ?></code></p>

    <p>
        <a href="<?php echo $home_link; ?>">&larr; go back to the home page</a>
    </p>

</section>
```

The $message variable outputs the actual message supplied to the Exception. The "back to home" link uses $home_link to link to the home page.

Adding Error-Specific Styles

The error page requires a few small adjustments to the stylesheet in order to display things properly, so open up assets/styles/main.css and add the following just above the media queries:

```
/* Error Styling
 -------------------------------------------------------------------------*/

section#error { text-align: center; }

section#error p { margin: 0 auto 2em; }
```

Testing the Error Page

To verify that everything is working, visit the broken link (http://rwa.local/not-real/) in your browser to see the error page (see Figure 8-3).

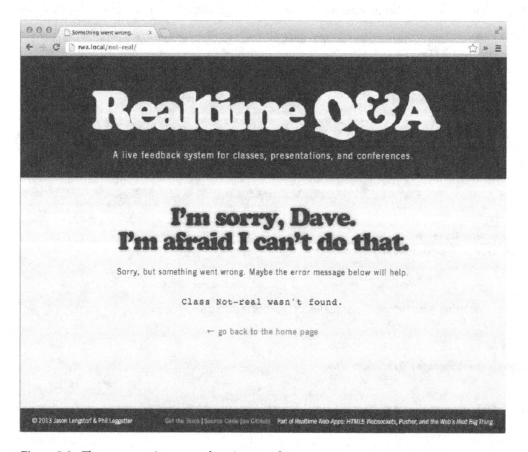

Figure 8-3. *The error page is now much easier to read*

Building the Database

Before we can go any farther in the app, the database needs to be built. The two remaining controllers—Question and Room—both store data and will thus need models.

We already discussed how the database would be structured back in Chapter 5, so we'll jump right into the code here. In phpMyAdmin, the terminal, or whatever your preferred method of executing MySQL queries happens to be, run the following commands:

```
CREATE TABLE IF NOT EXISTS 'presenters' (
  'id' int(11) NOT NULL AUTO_INCREMENT,
  'name' varchar(255) COLLATE utf8_unicode_ci NOT NULL,
  'email' varchar(255) COLLATE utf8_unicode_ci NOT NULL,
  PRIMARY KEY ('id'),
  UNIQUE KEY 'email' ('email')
) ENGINE=MyISAM  DEFAULT CHARSET=utf8 COLLATE=utf8_unicode_ci;

CREATE TABLE IF NOT EXISTS 'questions' (
  'id' int(11) NOT NULL AUTO_INCREMENT,
  'room_id' int(11) NOT NULL,
  'question' text COLLATE utf8_unicode_ci NOT NULL,
  'is_answered' tinyint(1) NOT NULL DEFAULT '0',
  PRIMARY KEY ('id'),
  KEY 'room_id' ('room_id')
) ENGINE=MyISAM  DEFAULT CHARSET=utf8 COLLATE=utf8_unicode_ci;

CREATE TABLE IF NOT EXISTS 'question_votes' (
  'question_id' int(11) NOT NULL,
  'vote_count' int(11) NOT NULL,
  PRIMARY KEY ('question_id')
) ENGINE=MyISAM DEFAULT CHARSET=utf8 COLLATE=utf8_unicode_ci;

CREATE TABLE IF NOT EXISTS 'rooms' (
  'id' int(11) NOT NULL AUTO_INCREMENT,
  'name' varchar(255) COLLATE utf8_unicode_ci NOT NULL,
  'is_active' tinyint(1) NOT NULL DEFAULT '1',
  PRIMARY KEY ('id')
) ENGINE=MyISAM  DEFAULT CHARSET=utf8 COLLATE=utf8_unicode_ci;

CREATE TABLE IF NOT EXISTS 'room_owners' (
  'room_id' int(11) NOT NULL,
  'presenter_id' int(11) NOT NULL,
  KEY 'room_id' ('room_id','presenter_id')
) ENGINE=MyISAM DEFAULT CHARSET=utf8 COLLATE=utf8_unicode_ci;
```

This code creates the database tables necessary for the app to run. If you view the database in phpMyAdmin, you'll see the newly created tables (see Figure 8-4).

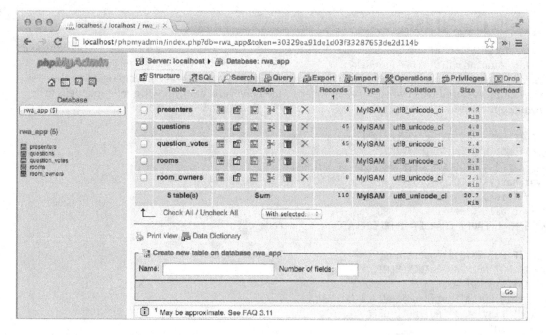

Figure 8-4. *The database tables viewed in phpMyAdmin*

Handling Form Submissions

One of the major components of any app is the manner in which it accepts form submissions. In order to maximize the efficiency of your app, it's worth taking some time to plan how all form submissions should be structured, sanitized, processed, and stored.

Planning the Form Submission Workflow

First, we need to establish the form submission workflow:

1. The user submits a form to the appropriate controller, which is determined by the form's `action` attribute.

2. The controller recognizes a form submission and checks for a valid action.

3. If a valid action is found, the submission is checked for legitimacy using a nonce.

4. Valid submissions are sent to the method specified by the action.

5. The handler method processes data, hands it to the model for storage, and returns a Boolean flag to indicate success or failure.

6. The user is redirected to the proper page (or, in many cases, the page simply updates with the new data).

Given this workflow, you can now start to flesh out the different steps of the form submission process.

Setting Up and Checking for Valid Actions

Earlier in this chapter you set up the abstract Controller class, which has a property called $actions. This property will be used by both the Room and Question controllers to define an array of actions and their corresponding methods.

Each controller will have its own distinct actions, so the array will need to be declared in the constructor of the Controller class. A sample controller with an action might look like this:

```
class Example extends Controller
{

    public function __construct( $options )
    {
        parent::__construct($options);

        $this->model = new Example_Model;

        $this->actions = array(
            'action-one' => 'say_foo',
        );

        if (array_key_exists($options[0], $this->actions)) {
            $this->handle_form_submission($options[0]);
            exit;
        } else {
            // If we get here, no valid form was submitted...
        }
    }

    /* get_title() and output_view() would go here */

}
```

The important bits above have been bolded. For now, ignore the new Example_Model bit; we'll go over that in a few pages.

The $actions array is set up as a key-value pair, where the key is the name of the action (which is triggered by virtue of the submission URI), and the value is the name of the method that will process the form.

The constructor adds an if...else check to see whether a valid form submission URI was reached. If so, it triggers the as-yet unwritten handle_form_submission() method.

To trigger an action, the form would need to submit to a URI that had the class name, a forward slash, and then the action:

```
<form action="http://rwa.local/example/action-one">...</form>
```

The method to process the action needs to be added to this class as well, but we'll cover that a little later in this section.

Preventing Duplicate or Fraudulent Submissions

To prevent erroneous, duplicate, or fraudulent form submissions, you need to implement a *nonce*—or *n*umber used *once*—to make sure that every form submission is both from a valid form and being submitted for the first time.

Creating Nonces

To create a nonce, all you need to do is generate a random string once per page load for each user. This nonce is then added as a hidden form field for any forms loaded in the current view, and it's stored in the user's session.

Open system/core/class.controller.inc.php and add the following bold code to the generate_nonce() method:

```php
protected function generate_nonce(  )
{
    // Checks for an existing nonce before creating a new one
    if (empty(self::$nonce)) {
        self::$nonce = base64_encode(uniqid(NULL, TRUE));
        $_SESSION['nonce'] = self::$nonce;
    }

    return self::$nonce;
}
```

This method checks to see whether $nonce is empty first because there are often multiple forms displayed in the app; if the first form's nonce were overwritten, it could not successfully be submitted, which would break the app.

If the nonce isn't set, a new one is generated by generating a uniqid() and then encoding it with base64_encode(). This is stored both in the object as a static property (so all Controller-based classes use the same nonce in their views) and in the $_SESSION superglobal to allow the nonce to be verified after submission.

Checking Nonces

When a form is submitted, the first thing that needs to be checked is that the nonce submitted through the form matches the one stored in the session. If they don't match, something is fishy and the submission should not be processed.

To check the nonce, add a new method to system/core/class.controller.inc.php called check_nonce() with the following bold code:

```php
protected function generate_nonce(  )
{
    // Checks for an existing nonce before creating a new one
    if (empty(self::$nonce)) {
        self::$nonce = base64_encode(uniqid(NULL, TRUE));
        $_SESSION['nonce'] = self::$nonce;
    }

    return self::$nonce;
}

/**
* Checks for a valid nonce
*
* @return bool      TRUE if the nonce is valid; otherwise FALSE
*/
```

```php
protected function check_nonce(  )
{
    if (
        isset($_SESSION['nonce']) && !empty($_SESSION['nonce'])
        && isset($_POST['nonce']) && !empty($_POST['nonce'])
        && $_SESSION['nonce']===$_POST['nonce']
    ) {
        $_SESSION['nonce'] = NULL;
        return TRUE;
    } else {
        return FALSE;
    }
}

/**
 * Performs basic input sanitization on a given string
 *
 * @param $dirty    string  The string to be sanitized
 * @return          string  The sanitized string
 */
protected function sanitize( $dirty )
{
    return htmlentities(strip_tags($dirty), ENT_QUOTES);
}
```

This method checks three criteria:

- That the nonce was stored in the session

- That the nonce was submitted with the form

- That the nonces in the session and form are identical

If all three conditions are met, the nonce is removed from the session (so the form cannot be submitted again successfully) and Boolean TRUE is returned to signify a successful nonce check.

Writing the Form Handling Methods

To actually process the form submissions, you need three methods:

- The first will check the nonce, execute the action handler method, and redirect the user to the proper location, pending success or failure.

- The second is the aforementioned action handler, which actually processes the submitted form data.

- The third is the model method, which takes the processed data from the action handler and manipulates the database accordingly.

Adding the Main Form Handling Method

The first method, which will reside in system/core/class.controller.inc.php, will be called handle_form_submission(). It accepts one parameter: the action.

Add the following bold code to the Controller class:

```php
protected function check_nonce(  )
{
    if (
        isset($_SESSION['nonce']) && !empty($_SESSION['nonce'])
        && isset($_POST['nonce']) && !empty($_POST['nonce'])
        && $_SESSION['nonce']===$_POST['nonce']
    ) {
        $_SESSION['nonce'] = NULL;
        return TRUE;
    } else {
        return FALSE;
    }
}

/**
 * Handles form submissions
 *
 * @param    $action string  The form action being performed
 * @return            void
 */
protected function handle_form_submission( $action )
{
    if ($this->check_nonce()) {

        // Calls the method specified by the action
        $output = $this->{$this->actions[$action]}();

        if (is_array($output) && isset($output['room_id'])) {
            $room_id = $output['room_id'];
        } else {
            throw new Exception('Form submission failed.');
        }

        header('Location: ' . APP_URI . 'room/' . $room_id);
        exit;
    } else {
        throw new Exception('Invalid nonce.');
    }
}

/**
 * Performs basic input sanitization on a given string
 *
 * @param $dirty    string  The string to be sanitized
 * @return          string  The sanitized string
 */
protected function sanitize( $dirty )
{
    return htmlentities(strip_tags($dirty), ENT_QUOTES);
}
```

This method starts by validating the nonce; it then calls the action handler method and stores the output in a variable. For this app, every action will return a room ID, so the method checks to make sure one was returned. Using the room ID, the user is then redirected to the room in which she should be viewing.

Adding an Action Method to the Controller

To actually process the submitted form data, a new method needs to be added to the Controller class that outputs the form. Using our previous Example class, the two actions defined would require that methods called say_foo() and say_bar() were added to the Example class, which is shown here in bold:

```
class Example extends Controller
{

    public function __construct( $options )
    {
        parent::__construct($options);

        $this->actions = array(
            'action-one' => 'say_foo',
        );

        if (array_key_exists($options[0], $this->actions)) {
            $this->handle_form_submission($options[0]);
            exit;
        } else {
            // If we get here, no form was submitted...
        }
    }

    /* get_title() and output_view() would go here */

    protected function say_foo(  )
    {
        $room_id  = $this->sanitize($_POST['room_id']);
        $sayer_id = $this->sanitize($_POST['sayer_id']);

        echo 'Foo!';

        return $this->model->update_foo_count($room_id, $sayer_id);
    }

}
```

First, this method grabs any data that was passed from the submitted form, sanitizes it, and stores it in a variable. Even though this method is just an example, the $room_id is being passed to follow suit with the action handlers that will exist in the app.

Next, the action handler performs the requested action: in this case, outputting the string, "Foo!" to the screen. Finally, it executes the model method and returns the result.

Adding a Method to the Model Class

The last step in the form-handling chain is to add a model method. But first, we need a model class.

Fortunately, this app will keep things simple, so the model classes simply extend the Model class, which gives them access to the PDO-powered database connection, and then declare the required methods. No additional setup is required.

Continuing with our Example class, we need to create the Example_Model class that was instantiated earlier. The only method this class needs is the update_foo_count() method called by the action handler method, and the method simply needs to increment the count of "foos" that have occurred and return an array of data.

Here's what that would look like:

```
class Example_Model extends Model
{
    public function vote_question( $room_id, $sayer_id )
    {
        // Increments the vote count for the question
        $sql = "UPDATE sayings
                    SET foo_count = foo_count+1
                    WHERE sayer_id = :sayer_id";
        $stmt = self::$db->prepare($sql);
        $stmt->bindParam(':sayer_id', $sayer_id, PDO::PARAM_INT);
        $stmt->execute();
        $stmt->closeCursor();

        return array(
            'room_id'  => $room_id,
            'sayer_id' => $sayer_id,
        );
    }
}
```

This is the basic pattern of all the models that will be built in this app. This method creates an SQL statement, prepares it using PDO, and then performs whatever database manipulation is required (an UPDATE in this case).

Once the query is executed, an array with relevant data is returned.

■ **Note** The models in this app rely heavily on prepared statements, which are much more secure than standard SQL queries. You won't need to know much more than what's displayed in the previous example to complete the models in this book, but if you need a refresher on PDO, visit the PHP manual at http://php.net/pdo.

Summary

This chapter was a dense one. At this point, you've successfully built a framework for your app based on the principles of MVC.

However, you've still got a little ways to go before the back end is complete. In the next chapter, you'll build the controllers, views, and models for the Room and Question data types.

■ ■ ■

CHAPTER 9

Building the Back-End: Part 2

In the last chapter, you built a working MVC framework and put together the Home controller and view. In this chapter, you'll complete the back end of the app by building the Question and Room components. This chapter puts the Model class to work, as well as the form submission handling that you built in the previous chapter.

Building the Questions

It might seem backward to build the Question controller before the Room controller, but because the Room controller needs several snippets of markup from the Question controller to output its view, let's start here and work to the Room controller.

Building the Question Controller

To begin, create a new file called class.question.inc.php in system/controllers/ and add the following code:

```php
<?php

/**
 * Processes output for the Question view
 *
 * @author  Jason Lengstorf <jason@lengstorf.com>
 * @author  Phil Leggetter <phil@leggetter.co.uk>
 */
class Question extends Controller
{

    public $room_id,
           $is_presenter = FALSE;

    /**
     * Initializes the class
     *
     * @param $options  array    Options for the controller
     * @return          void
     */
```

```php
    public function __construct( $options )
    {
        parent::__construct($options);

        $this->room_id = isset($options[0]) ? (int) $options[0] : 0;
        if ($this->room_id===0) {
            throw new Exception("Invalid room ID supplied");
        }
    }

    /**
     * Generates the title of the page
     *
     * @return string   The title of the page
     */
    public function get_title( )
    {
        // Questions can't be called directly, so this is unused
        return NULL;
    }

    /**
     * Loads and outputs the view's markup
     *
     * @return string   The HTML markup to display the view
     */
    public function output_view( )
    {
        $questions = $this->get_questions();

        $output = NULL;
        foreach ($questions as $question) {

            /*
             * Questions have their own view type, so this section initializes
             * and sets up variables for the question view
             */
            $view = new View('question');
            $view->question      = $question->question;
            $view->room_id       = $this->room_id;
            $view->question_id   = $question->question_id;
            $view->vote_count    = $question->vote_count;

            if ($question->is_answered==1) {
                $view->answered_class = 'answered';
            } else {
                $view->answered_class = NULL;
            }
```

```php
        // TODO: Check if the user has already voted up the question
        $view->voted_class = NULL;

        // TODO: Load the vote up form for attendees, but not presenters
        $view->vote_link = '';

        // TODO: Load the answer form for presenters, but not attendees
        $view->answer_link = '';

        // Returns the output of render() instead of printing it
        $output .= $view->render(FALSE);
      }

    return $output;
  }

}
```

This method isn't complete yet, but the building blocks are in place to start looking at how the view will shape up.

The constructor fires the main `Controller` constructor and then checks for a valid room ID, throwing an error if none was passed in the URI.

Because a question will never be displayed on its own—meaning outside the context of a room—the `get_title()` method simply returns NULL. Remember that it *does* need to be declared because it's part of the abstract parent class.

The `output_view()` method loads all questions for the room using the `get_questions()` method, which you'll define a bit later. It then loops through each question, loading the question view and populating it with the individual question's data. Some of the variables need to be updated; each of them has been marked with a TODO comment, so it'll be easy to spot them later, when it's time to come back and write those bits.

Adding the Question View

The view for the question app doesn't look like much; it's just a snippet of the HTML you wrote back in chapter 7. However, it's got a lot of variables.

Create a new file called `question.inc.php` and store it in `system/views/`. Inside, add the following:

```php
<li id="question-<?php echo $question_id; ?>"
    data-count="<?php echo $vote_count; ?>"
    class="<?php echo $voted_class, ' ', $answered_class; ?>">
    <?php echo $answer_link; ?>
    <p>
        <?php echo $question; ?>
    </p>
    <?php echo $vote_link; ?>
</li><!--/#question-<?php echo $question_id; ?>-->
```

This markup spits out the variables set in `output_view()`, shown previously. At the moment, this view wouldn't look like much because `$voted_class`, `$voted_link`, and `$answer_link` are all NULL or empty.

Finishing the View

Several of the variables being declared are NULL or empty because the methods to retrieve the needed data don't exist yet. According to the TODOs in the comments, the loop still needs to:

- Check to see whether the user has already voted up the question

- Load the vote up form for attendees, but not presenters

- Load the answer form for presenters, but not attendees

Checking to See Whether the User Has Already Voted Up a Question

In order to determine whether or not a user has voted up a question, you'll be using a simple cookie. When a user votes for a question, a cookie named voted_for_n (where n is the ID of the question) will be stored. This will allow the app to prevent multiple votes from being submitted by a single user.

To check the cookie, add the following bold code to output_view():

```
public function output_view(  )
{
    $questions = $this->get_questions();

    $output = NULL;
    foreach ($questions as $question) {

        /*
         * Questions have their own view type, so this section initializes
         * and sets up variables for the question view
         */
        $view = new View('question');
        $view->question      = $question->question;
        $view->room_id       = $this->room_id;
        $view->question_id   = $question->question_id;
        $view->vote_count    = $question->vote_count;

        if ($question->is_answered==1) {
            $view->answered_class = 'answered';
        } else {
            $view->answered_class = NULL;
        }

        // Checks if the user has already voted up this question
        $cookie = 'voted_for_' . $question->question_id;
        if (isset($_COOKIE[$cookie]) && $_COOKIE[$cookie]==1) {
            $view->voted_class = 'voted';
        } else {
            $view->voted_class = NULL;
        }

        // TODO: Load the vote up form for attendees, but not presenters
        $view->vote_link = '';
```

```
        // TODO: Load the answer form for presenters, but not attendees
        $view->answer_link = '';

        // Returns the output of render() instead of printing it
        $output .= $view->render(FALSE);
    }

    return $output;
}
```

This code checks for a cookie signaling the question has been voted for already, setting a class name to alter the styling if so.

■ **Caution** In a production environment, the app would need to either add a failsafe for users who have cookies turned off or simply disallow use of the app without first enabling cookies. Fully locking down form submissions is outside the scope of this book, but there are many great resources available online if you want to learn more.

Loading the Vote Up Form

In order to display the vote up form for attendees, but not to presenters, a new method needs to be created that will conditionally generate a view that can be used for output within the question view.

In system/controllers/class.question.inc.php, add the following bold code:

```
public function output_view(  )
{
    $questions = $this->get_questions();

    $output = NULL;
    foreach ($questions as $question) {

        /*
         * Questions have their own view type, so this section initializes
         * and sets up variables for the question view
         */
        $view = new View('question');
        $view->question     = $question->question;
        $view->room_id      = $this->room_id;
        $view->question_id  = $question->question_id;
        $view->vote_count   = $question->vote_count;

        if ($question->is_answered==1) {
            $view->answered_class = 'answered';
        } else {
            $view->answered_class = NULL;
        }

        // Checks if the user has already voted up this question
        $cookie = 'voted_for_' . $question->question_id;
```

```
        if (isset($_COOKIE[$cookie]) && $_COOKIE[$cookie]==1) {
            $view->voted_class = 'voted';
        } else {
            $view->voted_class = NULL;
        }

        $view->vote_link = $this->output_vote_form(
            $this->room_id,
            $question->question_id,
            $question->is_answered
        );

            // TODO: Load the answer form for presenters, but not attendees
            $view->answer_link = '';

        // Returns the output of render() instead of printing it
        $output .= $view->render(FALSE);
    }

    return $output;
}

/**
 * Generates the voting form for attendees
 *
 * @param $question_id  int     The ID of the question
 * @param $answered     int     1 if answered, 0 if unanswered
 * @return              mixed   Markup if attendee, NULL if presenter
 */
protected function output_vote_form( $room_id, $question_id, $answered )
{
    $view = new View('question-vote');
    $view->room_id     = $room_id;
    $view->question_id = $question_id;
    $view->form_action = APP_URI . 'question/vote';
    $view->nonce       = $this->generate_nonce();
    $view->disabled    = $answered==1 ? 'disabled' : NULL;

    return $view->render(FALSE);
}
```

The output_vote_form() method accepts three parameters: the ID of the current room, the ID of the current question, and whether or not that question has been answered.

It then loads a new view—question-vote—and sets up variables for output. The room ID, question ID, form action, and nonce are stored, as well as $disabled, which prevents the form from being submitted if the question is already marked as answered.

This method returns its output to be stored in the $vote_link variable, where it becomes part of the question view.

Adding the Vote Up Form View

The view for the vote up form keeps it pretty simple. Create a new file in system/views/ called question-vote.inc.php and add the following markup:

```
<form method="post" class="vote"
      action="<?php echo $form_action; ?>">
    <input value="I also have this question."
           type="submit" <?php echo $disabled; ?> />
    <input type="hidden" name="question_id"
           value="<?php echo $question_id; ?>" />
    <input type="hidden" name="room_id"
           value="<?php echo $room_id; ?>" />
    <input type="hidden" name="nonce"
           value="<?php echo $nonce; ?>" />
</form>
```

This markup uses the variables set in output_vote_form() to dynamically generate the button that allows attendees to submit a vote for a question.

Loading the Answer Form

Very similar to the vote up form, you now need to add a method to load the answer form, which allows the presenter to mark a question answered. Add the following code to the Question class:

```
public function output_view(  )
{
    $questions = $this->get_questions();

    $output = NULL;
    foreach ($questions as $question) {

        /*
         * Questions have their own view type, so this section initializes
         * and sets up variables for the question view
         */
        $view = new View('question');
        $view->question      = $question->question;
        $view->room_id       = $this->room_id;
        $view->question_id   = $question->question_id;
        $view->vote_count    = $question->vote_count;

        if ($question->is_answered==1) {
            $view->answered_class = 'answered';
        } else {
            $view->answered_class = NULL;
        }

        // Checks if the user has already voted up this question
        $cookie = 'voted_for_' . $question->question_id;
        if (isset($_COOKIE[$cookie]) && $_COOKIE[$cookie]==1) {
            $view->voted_class = 'voted';
```

```
        } else {
            $view->voted_class = NULL;
        }

        $view->vote_link = $this->output_vote_form(
            $this->room_id,
            $question->question_id,
            $question->is_answered
        );

        $view->answer_link = $this->output_answer_form(
            $this->room_id,
            $question->question_id
        );

        // Returns the output of render() instead of printing it
        $output .= $view->render(FALSE);
    }

    return $output;
}

protected function output_vote_form( $room_id, $question_id, $answered )
{
    $view = new View('question-vote');
    $view->room_id     = $room_id;
    $view->question_id = $question_id;
    $view->form_action = APP_URI . 'question/vote';
    $view->nonce       = $this->generate_nonce();
    $view->disabled    = $answered==1 ? 'disabled' : NULL;

    return $view->render(FALSE);
}

/**
 * Generates the answering form for presenter
 *
 * @param $room_id       int      The ID of the room
 * @param $question_id   int      The ID of the question
 * @return               mixed    Markup if presenter, NULL if attendee
 */
protected function output_answer_form( $room_id, $question_id )
{
    $view = new View('question-answer');
    $view->room_id     = $room_id;
    $view->question_id = $question_id;
    $view->form_action = APP_URI . 'question/answer';
    $view->nonce       = $this->generate_nonce();

    return $view->render(FALSE);
}
```

This method follows the same pattern as output_vote_form(): it creates a new view using question-answer and sets variables with which to generate the markup.

Adding the Answer Form View

Create a new file called `question-answer.inc.php` and save it in `system/views/` with the following markup inside:

```
<form method="post" class="answer"
      action="<?php echo $form_action; ?>">
    <input type="submit" value="Answer this question." />
    <input type="hidden" name="question_id"
           value="<?php echo $question_id; ?>" />
    <input type="hidden" name="room_id"
           value="<?php echo $room_id; ?>" />
    <input type="hidden" name="nonce"
           value="<?php echo $nonce; ?>" />
</form>
```

This markup uses the variables set in `output_answer_form()` to generate the markup for presenters to mark a question as answered.

Adding Styles for Voted and Answered Questions

Because a question that has been voted up or answered is no longer interactive, the buttons should no longer appear clickable. Open `assets/styles/main.css` and insert the following CSS just above the media queries:

```css
/* Voted and answered styles
 --------------------------------------------------------------------------*/

#questions .voted .vote input {
    background-position: left bottom;
    width: 78px;
    cursor: initial;
}

#questions .answered .answer input:active,
#questions .answered .answer input:hover,
#questions .answered .answer input:focus {
    background-position: right top;
    cursor: initial;
}

#questions .answered .vote input:active,
#questions .answered .vote input:hover,
#questions .answered .vote input:focus {
    background-position: left bottom;
    cursor: initial;
}

/* Transition effects
 --------------------------------------------------------------------------*/

#questions li,#questions .vote {
    -webkit-transition: opacity 1s ease-in-out;
```

```
    -moz-transition: opacity 1s ease-in-out;
     -ms-transition: opacity 1s ease-in-out;
      -o-transition: opacity 1s ease-in-out;
         transition: opacity 1s ease-in-out;
}


#questions.closed,#questions li.answered { opacity: .4; }


#questions.closed .vote,#questions .answered .vote { opacity: .2; }
```

These styles prevent the button from highlighting when hovered, as well as preventing the mouse cursor from turning into a pointer, which is a standard indication that an element is clickable.

The transition effects are in place to create an animated fade when questions are voted or answered. In order to trigger a CSS transition in this case, the element needs to have a class added, so keep in mind that the transitions won't be visible until we implement realtime and jQuery effects in the next chapter.

Loading All Questions for the Room

The last piece of the output_view() method is the currently nonexistent method get_questions(). The actual database query will be added to the question model a little later in this chapter, but for now, let's declare the method in the controller.

Add the following bold code to the Question class:

```
public function output_ask_form( $is_active, $email )
{
    if ($is_active) {
        $view = new View('ask-form');
        $view->room_id     = $this->room_id;
        $view->form_action = APP_URI . 'question/ask';
        $view->nonce       = $this->generate_nonce();

        return $view->render(FALSE);
    } else {
        $view = new View('room-closed');
        $view->email = $email;

        return $view->render(FALSE);
    }
}

/**
 * Loads questions for the room
 *
 * @return array    The question data as an array of objects
 */
protected function get_questions(  )
{
    return $this->model->get_room_questions($this->room_id);
}
```

This method simply calls a method from the Question_Model class, which has not yet been defined. Once the model is built, this method will return all the questions for a given room ID.

Adding the Ask a Question Form

In addition to the vote up and answer forms, there is one additional form that needs to be added to the Question class: the form for asking new questions.

Adding the Ask a Question Method

In the Question class, add the new method using the following bold code:

```
protected function output_answer_form( $room_id, $question_id )
{
    $view = new View('question-answer');
    $view->room_id     = $room_id;
    $view->question_id = $question_id;
    $view->form_action = APP_URI . 'question/answer';
    $view->nonce       = $this->generate_nonce();

    return $view->render(FALSE);
}

/**
 * Generates the form to ask a new question
 *
 * @param   $is_active    bool     Whether or not the room is active
 * @param   $email        string   The email address of the presenter
 * @return                string   The markup to display the form
 */
public function output_ask_form( $is_active, $email )
{
    if ($is_active) {
        $view = new View('ask-form');
        $view->room_id     = $this->room_id;
        $view->form_action = APP_URI . 'question/ask';
        $view->nonce       = $this->generate_nonce();

        return $view->render(FALSE);
    } else {
        $view = new View('room-closed');
        $view->email = $email;

        return $view->render(FALSE);
    }
}
```

This method is very similar to the other two form methods, but there's one important difference: there are two views that can be returned from this method depending on whether the room is active or not.

The `ask-form` view outputs the form that allows an attendee to ask a new question.

The `room-closed` view uses the presenter's e-mail address to allow anyone landing on a closed room to follow up with additional questions if they have any.

Adding the Ask a Question View

Create a new file called ask-form.inc.php in system/views/ and insert the following markup:

```php
<form id="ask-a-question" method="post"
      action="<?php echo $form_action; ?>">
    <label>
        If you have a question and you don't see it below, ask it here.
        <input type="text" name="new-question" tabindex="1" />
    </label>
    <input type="submit" value="Ask" tabindex="2" />
    <input type="hidden" name="room_id"
           value="<?php echo $room_id; ?>" />
    <input type="hidden" name="nonce"
           value="<?php echo $nonce; ?>" />
</form><!--/#ask-a-question-->
```

This markup creates the form for asking new questions.

Adding the Room Closed View

In system/views/, add a new file called room-closed.inc.php with the following markup:

```php
<h3>This session has ended.</h3>
<p>
    If you have a question that wasn't answered, please
    <a href="mailto:<?php echo $email; ?>">email the presenter</a>.
</p>
```

This markup lets the attendee know that the room is closed, but offers him an e-mail address to get in touch with the presenter so he's not totally out of luck.

Building the Question Model

To store data about questions and their votes, you now need to create a model class that will house all the question-related database manipulation methods.

Start by creating a new file in system/models/ called class.question_model.inc.php with the following class definition:

```php
<?php

/**
 * Creates database interaction methods for questions
 *
 * @author  Jason Lengstorf <jason@lengstorf.com>
```

```
 * @author  Phil Leggetter <phil@leggetter.co.uk>
 */
class Question_Model extends Model
{

}
```

Loading All Questions for a Room

To load all the questions for a room, the room ID is passed to the get_room_questions() method. The results are loaded as an object, which is then passed back to the controller for processing.

In order to retrieve the questions in a logical order (i.e., the highest-voted, unanswered questions showing at the top of the list), a LEFT JOIN is used to leverage the vote count from question_votes for ordering.

Add the following bold code to Question_Model:

```
class Question_Model extends Model
{

    /**
     * Loads all questions for a given room
     *
     * @param    $room_id    int      The ID of the room
     * @return               array    The questions attached to the room
     */
    public function get_room_questions( $room_id )
    {
        $sql = "SELECT
                    id AS question_id,
                    room_id,
                    question,
                    is_answered,
                    vote_count
                FROM questions
                    LEFT JOIN question_votes
                        ON( questions.id = question_votes.question_id )
                WHERE room_id = :room_id
                ORDER BY is_answered, vote_count DESC";
        $stmt = self::$db->prepare($sql);
        $stmt->bindParam(':room_id', $room_id, PDO::PARAM_INT);
        $stmt->execute();
        $questions = $stmt->fetchAll(PDO::FETCH_OBJ);
        $stmt->closeCursor();

        return $questions;
    }

}
```

Saving New Questions

In order to save a new question to the database, both the room ID and the new question text (as a string) are passed to the create_question() method. The first query inserts the question into the questions table and then stores the ID of the newly saved question in $question_id.

Next, the first vote for the question—because the user who asked it counts as the first vote—is added to the question_votes table using the newly created question ID.

Implement this method by adding the following bold code to Question_Model:

```php
public function get_room_questions( $room_id )
{
    $sql = "SELECT
                id AS question_id,
                room_id,
                question,
                is_answered,
                vote_count
            FROM questions
                LEFT JOIN question_votes
                    ON( questions.id = question_votes.question_id )
            WHERE room_id = :room_id
            ORDER BY is_answered, vote_count DESC";
    $stmt = self::$db->prepare($sql);
    $stmt->bindParam(':room_id', $room_id, PDO::PARAM_INT);
    $stmt->execute();
    $questions = $stmt->fetchAll(PDO::FETCH_OBJ);
    $stmt->closeCursor();

    return $questions;
}

/**
 * Stores a new question with all the proper associations
 *
 * @param    $room_id    int     The ID of the room
 * @param    $question   string  The question text
 * @return               array   The IDs of the room and the question
 */
public function create_question( $room_id, $question )
{
    // Stores the new question in the database
    $sql = "INSERT INTO questions (room_id, question)
            VALUES (:room_id, :question)";
    $stmt = self::$db->prepare($sql);
    $stmt->bindParam(':room_id', $room_id);
    $stmt->bindParam(':question', $question);
    $stmt->execute();
    $stmt->closeCursor();

    // Stores the ID of the new question
    $question_id = self::$db->lastInsertId();
```

```
/*
 * Because creating a question counts as its first vote, this adds a
 * vote for the question to the database
 */
$sql = "INSERT INTO question_votes
        VALUES (:question_id, 1)";
$stmt = self::$db->prepare($sql);
$stmt->bindParam(":question_id", $question_id, PDO::PARAM_INT);
$stmt->execute();
$stmt->closeCursor();

return array(
    'room_id'     => $room_id,
    'question_id' => $question_id,
);
}
```

Adding Votes to a Question

Updating the vote count keeps it simple: the vote_question() method increments the vote count by 1 for the given question ID. Add this method (in bold) to the Question_Model class:

```
    return array(
        'room_id'     => $room_id,
        'question_id' => $question_id,
    );
}

/**
 * Increases the vote count of a given question
 *
 * @param    $room_id       int     The ID of the room
 * @param    $question_id   int     The ID of the question
 * @return                  array   The IDs of the room and the question
 */
public function vote_question( $room_id, $question_id )
{
    // Increments the vote count for the question
    $sql = "UPDATE question_votes
            SET vote_count = vote_count+1
            WHERE question_id = :question_id";
    $stmt = self::$db->prepare($sql);
    $stmt->bindParam(':question_id', $question_id, PDO::PARAM_INT);
    $stmt->execute();
    $stmt->closeCursor();
```

```
    return array(
        'room_id'     => $room_id,
        'question_id' => $question_id,
    );
    }

}
```

The database query increments the vote count by 1 for the question with the given ID by adding 1 to its current value—vote_count = vote_count+1—and then returns the room and question IDs.

Marking a Question as Answered

Finally, to mark a question as answered, the is_answered column for the question with the given ID is updated to 1. Add the following bold code to Question_Model:

```
    $stmt->closeCursor();

    return array(
        'room_id'     => $room_id,
        'question_id' => $question_id,
    );
    }

/**
 * Marks a given question as answered
 *
 * @param    $room_id       int      The ID of the room
 * @param    $question_id   int      The ID of the question
 * @return                  array    The IDs of the room and question
 */
public function answer_question( $room_id, $question_id )
{
    $sql = "UPDATE questions
            SET is_answered = 1
            WHERE id = :question_id";
    $stmt = self::$db->prepare($sql);
    $stmt->bindParam(':question_id', $question_id, PDO::PARAM_INT);
    $stmt->execute();
    $stmt->closeCursor();

    return array(
        'room_id'     => $room_id,
        'question_id' => $question_id,
    );
    }

}
```

Adding Form Handlers and Data Access Methods to the Controller

The last bit of the question segment of the app is to add the action array, model, and action handler classes to the Question controller.

Start by updating the constructor with the model declaration and action array. Add the following to system/controllers/class.question.inc.php:

```php
public function __construct( $options )
{
    parent::__construct($options);

    $this->model = new Question_Model;

    // Checks for a form submission
    $this->actions = array(
        'ask'    => 'create_question',
        'vote'   => 'vote_question',
        'answer' => 'answer_question',
    );

    if (array_key_exists($options[0], $this->actions)) {
        $this->handle_form_submission($options[0]);
        exit;
    } else {
        $this->room_id = isset($options[0]) ? (int) $options[0] : 0;
        if ($this->room_id===0) {
            throw new Exception("Invalid room ID supplied");
        }
    }
}
```

This loads the Question_Model class for data access and then declares three possible form actions and their required action handler methods.

Saving New Questions

The action handler for saving new questions is rather complex because it's built with the next chapter—in which we start adding realtime functionality—in mind. As a result, it not only stores the new question but also generates a new question view for return so that the markup doesn't need to be rendered client-side later. It also adds a cookie for users to indicate that they've already voted for the question.

Add the following bold code to the Question class:

```php
protected function get_questions(  )
{
    return $this->model->get_room_questions($this->room_id);
}

/**
 * Adds a new question to the database
 *
 * @return array    Information about the updated question
 */
```

```php
    protected function create_question(  )
    {
        $room_id  = $this->sanitize($_POST['room_id']);
        $question = $this->sanitize($_POST['new-question']);

        $output = $this->model->create_question($room_id, $question);

        // Make sure valid output was returned
        if (is_array($output) && isset($output['question_id'])) {
            $room_id      = $output['room_id'];
            $question_id = $output['question_id'];

            // Generates markup for the question (for realtime addition)
            $view = new View('question');
            $view->question        = $question;
            $view->room_id         = $room_id;
            $view->question_id     = $question_id;
            $view->vote_count      = 1;
            $view->answered_class = NULL;
            $view->voted_class    = NULL;

            $view->vote_link = $this->output_vote_form(
                $room_id,
                $question_id,
                FALSE
            );

            $view->answer_link = $this->output_answer_form(
                $room_id,
                $question_id
            );

            $output['markup'] = $view->render(FALSE);
        } else {
            throw new Exception('Error creating the room.');
        }

        // Stores a cookie so the attendee can only vote once
        setcookie('voted_for_' . $question_id, 1, time() + 2592000, '/');

        return $output;
    }

}
```

This method starts by sanitizing the data that was submitted, storing it in the database using the model's create_question() method, and checking for valid return values. It then creates a new question view and stores all the variables to generate markup for a new question. A cookie is stored, indicating that the attendee posted the question's first upvote; then the markup is returned.

Adding Votes to a Question

Adding a new vote to a question executes the vote_question() method to store the new vote in the database and then sets a cookie for the voter to prevent multiple votes for the same question. Add the following bold code to the Question controller:

```
    // Stores a cookie so the attendee can only vote once
    setcookie('voted_for_' . $question_id, 1, time() + 2592000, '/');

    return $output;
}

/**
 * Increments the vote count for a given question
 *
 * @return array    Information about the updated question
 */
protected function vote_question(  )
{
    $room_id     = $this->sanitize($_POST['room_id']);
    $question_id = $this->sanitize($_POST['question_id']);

    // Makes sure the attendee hasn't already voted for this question
    $cookie_id = 'voted_for_' . $question_id;
    if (!isset($_COOKIE[$cookie_id]) || $_COOKIE[$cookie_id]!=1) {
        $output = $this->model->vote_question($room_id, $question_id);

        // Sets a cookie to make it harder to post multiple votes
        setcookie($cookie_id, 1, time() + 2592000, '/');
    } else {
        $output = array('room_id'=>$room_id);
    }

    return $output;
}

}
```

Marking a Question as Answered

In order to mark a question as answered, the user submitting the form must be the presenter. This, like voting, will be cookie-based. This method checks the presenter's cookie before executing the answer_question() method.

Add the following code shown in bold to the Question controller:

```
    // Stores a cookie so the attendee can only vote once
    setcookie('voted_for_' . $question_id, 1, time() + 2592000, '/');

    return $output;
}
```

```php
/**
 * Marks a given question as answered
 *
 * @return array    Information about the updated question
 */
protected function answer_question(  )
{
    $room_id     = $this->sanitize($_POST['room_id']);
    $question_id = $this->sanitize($_POST['question_id']);

    // Makes sure the person answering the question is the presenter
    $cookie_id = 'presenter_room_' . $room_id;
    if (isset($_COOKIE[$cookie_id]) && $_COOKIE[$cookie_id]==1) {
        return $this->model->answer_question($room_id, $question_id);
    }

    return array('room_id'=>$room_id);
}

}
```

This method sanitizes the posted form values and then checks for a presenter's cookie to verify that the current user has permission to mark a question as answered. If the cookie is valid, the model's answer_question() method is fired, and its returned data is passed through; an invalid or missing cookie simply loops the user back to the room without processing anything by returning the room ID.

Building the Rooms

The final piece of this app is to add the controller, model, and view for the rooms. This is very similar to the functionality of the questions, except it actually loads the Question controller to load those views and leverage its methods.

Adding the Room Controller

The first step is to create the Room controller. In system/controllers/, add a new file called class.room.inc.php and start with the following code:

```php
<?php

/**
 * Processes output for the Room view
 *
 * @author  Jason Lengstorf <jason@lengstorf.com>
 * @author  Phil Leggetter <phil@leggetter.co.uk>
 */
class Room extends Controller
{

    public $room_id,
            $is_presenter,
            $is_active;
```

```php
/**
 * Initializes the view
 *
 * @param $options array     Options for the view
 * @return void
 */
public function __construct( $options )
{
    parent::__construct($options);

    $this->model = new Room_Model;

    $this->room_id = isset($options[0]) ? (int) $options[0] : 0;
    if ($this->room_id===0) {
        throw new Exception("Invalid room ID supplied");
    }

    $this->room          = $this->model->get_room_data($this->room_id);
    $this->is_presenter = $this->is_presenter();
    $this->is_active     = (boolean) $this->room->is_active;
}

/**
 * Generates the title of the page
 *
 * @return string    The title of the page
 */
public function get_title(  )
{
    return $this->room->room_name . ' by ' . $this->room->presenter_name;
}

/**
 * Loads and outputs the view's markup
 *
 * @return void
 */
public function output_view(  )
{
    $view = new View('room');
    $view->room_id   = $this->room->room_id;
    $view->room_name = $this->room->room_name;
    $view->presenter = $this->room->presenter_name;
    $view->email     = $this->room->email;

    if (!$this->is_presenter) {
        $view->ask_form = $this->output_ask_form();
        $view->questions_class = NULL;
    } else {
        $view->ask_form = NULL;
        $view->questions_class = 'presenter';
    }
```

```
    if (!$this->is_active) {
        $view->questions_class = 'closed';
    }

    $view->controls  = $this->output_presenter_controls();
    $view->questions = $this->output_questions();

    $view->render();
    }

}
```

In addition to the standard constructor stuff—calling the parent constructor, setting the model, and ensuring that valid options were supplied—the Room constructor also sets some room-specific properties.

The $room property will hold basic information about the room, which is returned from the get_room_data() method as an object. The model will be set up to retrieve this data later in this chapter.

To handle the differences in the room markup for presenters versus attendees, $is_presenter holds a Boolean value that is determined by the is_presenter() method, which will be written shortly.

Finally, the $is_active property acts as a shortcut to the active state of the room. Because it is stored in the database as a 1 or 0, it is cast as a Boolean to allow for strict Boolean comparisons within the controller's methods.

The get_title() method uses the room's and presenter's names to generate a meaningful title for the room.

In output_view(), the room view is loaded, and a handful of variables are set, which will be gone over a bit later in this chapter.

Determining Whether the User Is the Presenter

Because different markup is shown to the presenter than to the attendees, the app needs a method to determine whether the user is the presenter for the current room. This will be stored as a cookie.

Add the following bold code to the Room controller:

```
    $view->controls  = $this->output_presenter_controls();
    $view->questions = $this->output_questions();

    $view->render();
    }

/**
 * Determines whether or not the current user is the presenter
 *
 * @return boolean  TRUE if it's the presenter, otherwise FALSE
 */
protected function is_presenter(  )
{
    $cookie = 'presenter_room_' . $this->room->room_id;
    return (isset($_COOKIE[$cookie]) && $_COOKIE[$cookie]==1);
}

}
```

This method figures out the cookie name using the current room's ID and then returns TRUE if the cookie is both set and equal to 1.

Adding the Room View

Using the room markup from Chapter 7, create the room view by adding the following code to a new file located at system/views/room.inc.php:

```
<section>

    <header>
        <h2><?php echo $room_name; ?></h2>
        <p>
            Presented by <?php echo $presenter; ?>
            (<a href="mailto:<?php echo $email; ?>">email</a>)
        </p>
        <?php echo $controls; ?>
    </header>

    <?php echo $ask_form; ?>

    <ul id="questions" class="<?php echo $questions_class; ?>">
        <?php echo $questions; ?>
    </ul><!--/#questions-->

</section>
```

This markup generates everything needed to show a room and its questions for both attendees and presenters.

Showing the Ask Form

The ask form requires a new view, which will be loaded by a new method in the Room class. If you remember, the ask form generation was already handled by the Question controller, so the new method will simply invoke the output_ask_form() method on the Question controller.

Add the following bold code to the Room controller:

```
    $view->controls  = $this->output_presenter_controls();
    $view->questions = $this->output_questions();

    $view->render();
}

/**
 * Shows the "ask a question" form or a notice that the room has ended
 *
 * @param $email string The presenter's email address
 * @return string       Markup for the form or notice
 */
protected function output_ask_form(  )
{
    $controller = new Question(array($this->room_id));
    return $controller->output_ask_form(
        $this->is_active,
        $this->room->email
    );
}
```

```
/**
 * Determines whether or not the current user is the presenter
 *
 * @return boolean   TRUE if it's the presenter, otherwise FALSE
 */
protected function is_presenter(  )
{
```

Showing the Presenter Controls

For the presenter of a room, we need to provide the room's direct link and an option to close the room (or to reopen the room if it's already closed). To do this, add a new method to the Room controller that checks whether the user is the presenter; then checks whether the room is active.

For inactive rooms, the reopening controls are loaded and returned for use in the main room view.

Active rooms load the standard controls and return them.

Add the following bold code to class.room.inc.php:

```
    return $controller->output_ask_form(
        $this->is_active,
        $this->room->email
    );
}


/**
 * Shows the presenter his controls (or nothing, if not the presenter)
 *
 * @return mixed     Markup for the controls (or NULL)
 */
protected function output_presenter_controls(  )
{
    if ($this->is_presenter) {
        if (!$this->is_active) {
            $view_class  = 'presenter-reopen';
            $form_action = APP_URI . 'room/open';
        } else {
            $view_class  = 'presenter-controls';
            $form_action = APP_URI . 'room/close';
        }

        $view = new View($view_class);
        $view->room_id     = $this->room->room_id;
        $view->room_uri    = APP_URI . 'room/' . $this->room_id;
        $view->form_action = $form_action;
        $view->nonce       = $this->generate_nonce();

        return $view->render(FALSE);
    }

    return NULL;
}
```

```
/**
 * Determines whether or not the current user is the presenter
 *
 * @return boolean  TRUE if it's the presenter, otherwise FALSE
 */
protected function is_presenter(  )
{
```

Adding the Inactive Room Presenter Controls View

The view for the inactive room is a simple form with an input reading "Open This Room".

Create a file called `presenter-reopen.inc.php` in `system/views/` with the following markup:

```
<form id="close-this-room" method="post"
     action="<?php echo $form_action; ?>">
    <input type="submit" value="Open This Room" />
    <input type="hidden" name="room_id"
          value="<?php echo $room_id; ?>" />
    <input type="hidden" name="nonce"
          value="<?php echo $nonce; ?>" />
</form><!--/#close-this-room-->
```

Adding the Active Room Presenter Controls View

For active rooms, a disabled input with the room's URI is displayed, as well as a button reading "Close This Room".

Add the following markup to a new file called `presenter-controls.inc.php` in `system/views/`:

```
<form id="close-this-room" method="post"
     action="<?php echo $form_action; ?>">
    <label>
        Link to your room.
        <input type="text" name="room-uri"
              value="<?php echo $room_uri; ?>"
              disabled />
    </label>
    <input type="submit" value="Close This Room" />
    <input type="hidden" name="room_id"
          value="<?php echo $room_id; ?>" />
    <input type="hidden" name="nonce"
          value="<?php echo $nonce; ?>" />
</form><!--/#close-this-room-->
```

Showing the Questions

In order to show the questions for the room, the `output_questions()` method will leverage the `Question` controller to loop through the existing questions and return markup.

Before generating the markup, it sets the `$is_presenter` property so the proper markup is returned for the user type.

Add the following bold code to the Room controller:

```
        return $view->render(FALSE);
    }

    return NULL;
}

/**
 * Loads and formats the questions for this room
 *
 * @return string    The marked up questions
 */
protected function output_questions(  )
{
    $controller = new Question(array($this->room_id));

    // Allows for different output for presenters vs. attendees
    $controller->is_presenter = $this->is_presenter;

    return $controller->output_view();
}

/**
 * Determines whether or not the current user is the presenter
 *
 * @return boolean  TRUE if it's the presenter, otherwise FALSE
 */
protected function is_presenter(  )
{
```

Building the Room Model

Because the app needs to store and manipulate room data, you'll need to create a model for rooms, called Room_Model. This will be stored in the system/models/ subdirectory in a file called class.room_model.inc.php.

Create the file and start it out with this basic class definition:

```
<?php

/**
 * Creates database interaction methods for rooms
 *
 * @author   Jason Lengstorf <jason@lengstorf.com>
 * @author   Phil Leggetter <phil@leggetter.co.uk>
 */
class Room_Model extends Model
{

}
```

Creating a Room

The first method for the model will save new rooms to the database.

This is a multistep process; this method needs to do the following:

- Create the new room in the rooms table

- Retrieve the new room's ID

- Add the presenter to the presenters table (or update the presenter's display name in the case of a duplicate email)

- Retrieve the presenter's ID from the presenters table

- Map the room's ID to the presenter's ID in the room_owners table.

Add the following bold code to the room model:

```php
class Room_Model extends Model
{

    /**
     * Saves a new room to the database
     *
     * @param   $presenter  string  The name of the presenter
     * @param   $email      string  The presenter's email address
     * @param   $name       string  The name of the room
     * @return              array   An array of data about the room
     */
    public function create_room( $presenter, $email, $name )
    {
        // Creates a new room
        $sql = 'INSERT INTO rooms (name) VALUES (:name)';
        $stmt = self::$db->prepare($sql);
        $stmt->bindParam(':name', $name, PDO::PARAM_STR, 255);
        $stmt->execute();
        $stmt->closeCursor();

        // Gets the generated room ID
        $room_id = self::$db->lastInsertId();

        // Creates (or updates) the presenter
        $sql = "INSERT INTO presenters (name, email)
                VALUES (:name, :email)
                ON DUPLICATE KEY UPDATE name=:name";
        $stmt = self::$db->prepare($sql);
        $stmt->bindParam(':name', $presenter, PDO::PARAM_STR, 255);
        $stmt->bindParam(':email', $email, PDO::PARAM_STR, 255);
        $stmt->execute();
        $stmt->closeCursor();

        // Gets the generated presenter ID
        $sql = "SELECT id
                FROM presenters
                WHERE email=:email";
```

```
$stmt = self::$db->prepare($sql);
$stmt->bindParam(':email', $email, PDO::PARAM_STR, 255);
$stmt->execute();
$pres_id = $stmt->fetch(PDO::FETCH_OBJ)->id;
$stmt->closeCursor();

// Stores the room:presenter relationship
$sql = 'INSERT INTO room_owners (room_id, presenter_id)
        VALUES (:room_id, :pres_id)';
$stmt = self::$db->prepare($sql);
$stmt->bindParam(":room_id", $room_id, PDO::PARAM_INT);
$stmt->bindParam(":pres_id", $pres_id, PDO::PARAM_INT);
$stmt->execute();
$stmt->closeCursor();

return array(
    'room_id' => $room_id,
);
}

}
```

Checking to See Whether a Room Exists

As part of the process of joining a room, the Room controller needs to be able to verify that a room exists. This method simply selects the COUNT() of rooms in the rooms table matching the given ID; a count of 1 means the room exists, and 0 means it does not.

Add the following bold code to Room_Model:

```
// Stores the room:presenter relationship
$sql = 'INSERT INTO room_owners (room_id, presenter_id)
        VALUES (:room_id, :pres_id)';
$stmt = self::$db->prepare($sql);
$stmt->bindParam(":room_id", $room_id, PDO::PARAM_INT);
$stmt->bindParam(":pres_id", $pres_id, PDO::PARAM_INT);
$stmt->execute();
$stmt->closeCursor();

return array(
    'room_id' => $room_id,
);
}

/**
 * Checks if a given room exists
 *
 * @param   $room_id    int     The ID of the room being checked
 * @return              bool    Whether or not the room exists
 */
public function room_exists( $room_id )
{
    // Loads the number of rooms matching the provided room ID
```

```
$sql = "SELECT COUNT(id) AS the_count FROM rooms WHERE id = :room_id";
$stmt = self::$db->prepare($sql);
$stmt->bindParam(':room_id', $room_id, PDO::PARAM_INT);
$stmt->execute();
$room_exists = (bool) $stmt->fetch(PDO::FETCH_OBJ)->the_count;
$stmt->closeCursor();

        return $room_exists;
    }

}
```

Using (bool) to explicitly cast the count as a Boolean value means that this method will always return TRUE or FALSE, which is helpful for a method whose sole purpose is to check if something exists.

Opening a Room

For a room that has been closed, opening it again is as simple as setting the is_active column to 1 in the rooms table for the room with the given ID.

Add the code shown in bold to class.room_model.inc.php:

```
$room_exists = (bool) $stmt->fetch(PDO::FETCH_OBJ)->the_count;
$stmt->closeCursor();

        return $room_exists;
    }

/**
 * Sets a given room's status to "open"
 *
 * @param    $room_id      int      The ID of the room being checked
 * @return                 array    An array of data about the room
 */
public function open_room( $room_id )
{
    $sql = "UPDATE rooms SET is_active=1 WHERE id = :room_id";
    $stmt = self::$db->prepare($sql);
    $stmt->bindParam(':room_id', $room_id, PDO::PARAM_INT);
    $stmt->execute();
    $stmt->closeCursor();

    return array(
        'room_id' => $room_id,
    );
}

}
```

Closing a Room

Closing a room is the same process as opening one, except that the is_active column is set to 0 in the rooms table. Insert the following bold code into Room_Model:

```
public function open_room( $room_id )
{
    $sql = "UPDATE rooms SET is_active=1 WHERE id = :room_id";
    $stmt = self::$db->prepare($sql);
    $stmt->bindParam(':room_id', $room_id, PDO::PARAM_INT);
    $stmt->execute();
    $stmt->closeCursor();

    return array(
        'room_id' => $room_id,
    );
}

/**
 * Sets a given room's status to "closed"
 *
 * @param    $room_id    int     The ID of the room being checked
 * @return               array   An array of data about the room
 */
public function close_room( $room_id )
{
    $sql = "UPDATE rooms SET is_active=0 WHERE id = :room_id";
    $stmt = self::$db->prepare($sql);
    $stmt->bindParam(':room_id', $room_id, PDO::PARAM_INT);
    $stmt->execute();
    $stmt->closeCursor();

    return array(
        'room_id' => $room_id,
    );
}

}
```

Loading Room Information

To load a room's information is arguably the most complex query in the app. It requires the following:

- Joining the room_owners table to the rooms table; then joining the presenters table to that to make a complete dataset

- Loading the id, name, and is_active columns from the rooms table

- Renaming id to room_id and name to room_name

- Loading the id, name, and email columns from the presenters table

- Renaming id to presenter_id and name to presenter_name

Complete the preceding steps with the query shown in the following bold code, which is added to class.room_model.inc.php:

```php
public function close_room( $room_id )
{
    $sql = "UPDATE rooms SET is_active=0 WHERE id = :room_id";
    $stmt = self::$db->prepare($sql);
    $stmt->bindParam(':room_id', $room_id, PDO::PARAM_INT);
    $stmt->execute();
    $stmt->closeCursor();

    return array(
        'room_id' => $room_id,
    );
}

/**
 * Retrieves details about a given room
 *
 * @param    $room_id    int     The ID of the room being checked
 * @return               array   An array of data about the room
 */
public function get_room_data( $room_id )
{
    $sql = "SELECT
                rooms.id AS room_id,
                presenters.id AS presenter_id,
                rooms.name AS room_name,
                presenters.name AS presenter_name,
                email, is_active
            FROM rooms
            LEFT JOIN room_owners
                ON( rooms.id = room_owners.room_id )
            LEFT JOIN presenters
                ON( room_owners.presenter_id = presenters.id )
            WHERE rooms.id = :room_id
            LIMIT 1";
    $stmt = self::$db->prepare($sql);
    $stmt->bindParam(':room_id', $room_id, PDO::PARAM_INT);
    $stmt->execute();
    $room_data = $stmt->fetch(PDO::FETCH_OBJ);
    $stmt->closeCursor();

    return $room_data;
}

}
```

Adding Form Handlers to the Room Controller

The final step in the back end of the app is to add the form actions and action handlers to the Room controller.

Adding Form Actions to the Room Controller

The Room controller supports four actions:

- Joining a room

- Creating a room

- Opening a room

- Closing a room

Add the following bold code to the constructor of the Room class to add support for these four actions:

```
public function __construct( $options )
{
    parent::__construct($options);

    $this->model = new Room_Model;

    // Checks for a form submission
    $this->actions = array(
        'join'   => 'join_room',
        'create' => 'create_room',
        'open'   => 'open_room',
        'close'  => 'close_room',
    );

    if (array_key_exists($options[0], $this->actions)) {
        $this->handle_form_submission($options[0]);
        exit;
    } else {
        $this->room_id = isset($options[0]) ? (int) $options[0] : 0;
        if ($this->room_id===0) {
            throw new Exception("Invalid room ID supplied");
        }
    }

    $this->room          = $this->model->get_room_data($this->room_id);
    $this->is_presenter  = $this->is_presenter();
    $this->is_active     = (boolean) $this->room->is_active;
}
```

The array creates a map of actions to the methods that should be called. Next, the if...else statement checks for a valid action and, if one was passed, it calls handle_form_submission() to process it.

Joining a Room

When a user attempts to join a room, the controller needs to first check to see whether it exists using the room_exists() method from Room_Model. If so, the user should be redirected to the requested room; if not, they should receive an error message.

Add the following bold code to the Room controller:

```php
protected function output_questions(  )
{
    $controller = new Question(array($this->room_id));

    // Allows for different output for presenters vs. attendees
    $controller->is_presenter = $this->is_presenter;

    return $controller->output_view();
}

/**
 * Checks if a room exists and redirects the user appropriately
 *
 * @return void
 */
protected function join_room(  )
{
    $room_id = $this->sanitize($_POST['room_id']);

    // If the room exists, creates the URL; otherwise, sends to a 404
    if ($this->model->room_exists($room_id)) {
        $header = APP_URI . 'room/' . $room_id;
    } else {
        $header = APP_URI . 'no-room';
    }

    header("Location: " . $header);
    exit;
}

/**
 * Determines whether or not the current user is the presenter
 *
 * @return boolean  TRUE if it's the presenter, otherwise FALSE
 */
protected function is_presenter(  )
{
```

Creating New Rooms

To create a new room, the controller needs to sanitize the presenter's name, e-mail, and room name; store them using the room model's create_room() method; and then check that the room was created successfully. It should also set a cookie identifying the room's creator as the presenter.

In class.room.inc.php, add the following bold code:

```php
if ($this->model->room_exists($room_id)) {
    $header = APP_URI . 'room/' . $room_id;
} else {
```

```
        $header = APP_URI . 'no-room';
    }

    header("Location: " . $header);
    exit;
}

/**
 * Creates a new room and sets the creator as the presenter
 *
 * @return array Information about the updated room
 */
protected function create_room(  )
{
    $presenter = $this->sanitize($_POST['presenter-name']);
    $email     = $this->sanitize($_POST['presenter-email']);
    $name      = $this->sanitize($_POST['session-name']);

    // Store the new room and its various associations in the database
    $output = $this->model->create_room($presenter, $email, $name);

    // Make sure valid output was returned
    if (is_array($output) && isset($output['room_id'])) {
        $room_id = $output['room_id'];
    } else {
        throw new Exception('Error creating the room.');
    }

    // Makes the creator of this room its presenter
    setcookie('presenter_room_' . $room_id, 1, time() + 2592000, '/');

    return $output;
}

/**
 * Determines whether or not the current user is the presenter
 *
 * @return boolean  TRUE if it's the presenter, otherwise FALSE
 */
protected function is_presenter(  )
{
```

Reopening a Closed Room

To reopen a room that has been closed, the sanitized room ID is passed to the model's open_room( ) method.

```
    // Makes the creator of this room its presenter
    setcookie('presenter_room_' . $room_id, 1, time() + 2592000, '/');

    return $output;
}
```

```
/**
 * Marks a given room as active
 *
 * @return array Information about the updated room
 */
protected function open_room(  )
{
    $room_id = $this->sanitize($_POST['room_id']);
    return $this->model->open_room($room_id);
}

/**
 * Determines whether or not the current user is the presenter
 *
 * @return boolean  TRUE if it's the presenter, otherwise FALSE
 */
protected function is_presenter(  )
{
```

Closing a Room

Closing a room is nearly identical to opening one, except that the close_room() method is called instead.

```
protected function open_room(  )
{
    $room_id = $this->sanitize($_POST['room_id']);
    return $this->model->open_room($room_id);
}

/**
 * Marks a given room as closed
 *
 * @return array Information about the updated room
 */
protected function close_room(  )
{
    $room_id = $this->sanitize($_POST['room_id']);
    return $this->model->close_room($room_id);
}

/**
 * Determines whether or not the current user is the presenter
 *
 * @return boolean  TRUE if it's the presenter, otherwise FALSE
 */
protected function is_presenter(  )
{
```

Testing it All Out

At this point, your app is code complete and ready for testing. Let's run through each of the available actions to verify that everything is working according to plan.

Creating Your First Room

To begin, load up the app in your browser of choice and enter the details for a new room (see Figure 9-1).

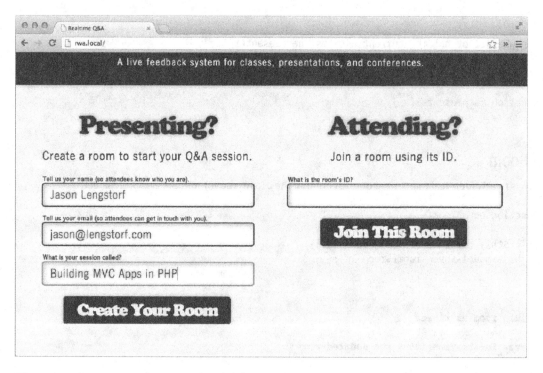

Figure 9-1. *Creating a new room on the app's home page*

Click Create Your Room and you'll be taken to the new empty room (see Figure 9-2).

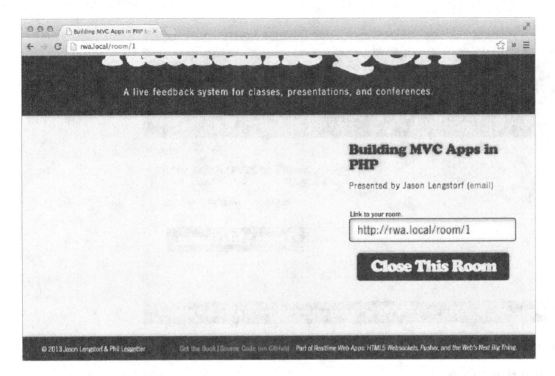

Figure 9-2. *The newly created room*

■ **Note**   In some server configurations, you might get MySQL errors when running PDO::__construct(). This typically means that you need to point your php.ini file to the correct location of mysql.sock. There's a simple walkthrough at https://gist.github.com/jlengstorf/5184301, and there are several walkthroughs available if you do a Google search for the error message.

Closing the Room

Test out that the presenter controls work by closing the room. Click the Close This Room button and the room becomes inactive (see Figure 9-3).

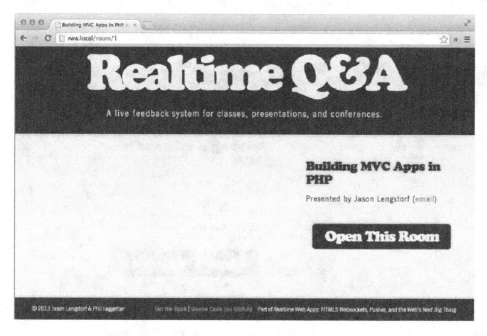

Figure 9-3. The closed room

Reopening the Room

Make sure the room can be reopened by clicking the Open This Room button, which brings the room back to its original active state (see Figure 9-4).

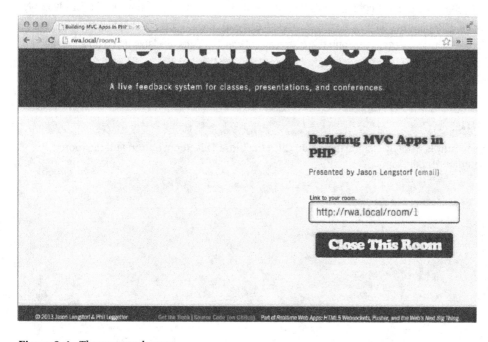

Figure 9-4. The reopened room

Joining a Room

Next, open a different browser (meaning an entirely different application: Firefox, Safari, Opera, or Internet Explorer if you started out using Google Chrome) and navigate to `http://rwa.local/`.

Enter 1 for the room's ID, according to the figures in this section,—and click the Join This Room button (see Figure 9-5).

Figure 9-5. *Joining a room (using a different browser) from the home page*

The room opens, and you can now see the "ask a question" form (see Figure 9-6).

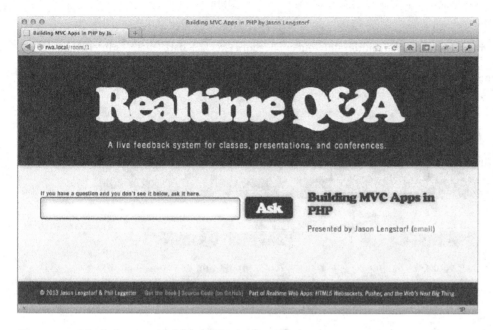

Figure 9-6. *The "ask a question" form is shown you view the room as an attendee*

Asking Your First Question

Test that attendees can ask new questions by typing a new question into the form field (see Figure 9-7).

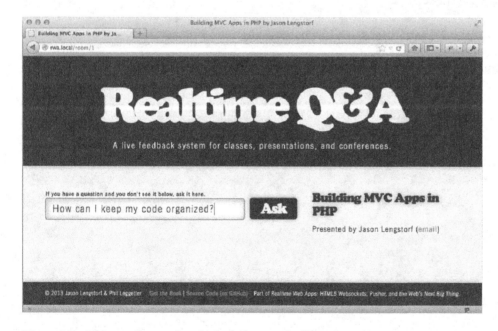

Figure 9-7. *Asking a new question via the "ask a question" form*

After you click the Ask button, the new question is created and displayed as having already been voted up by you (see Figure 9-8).

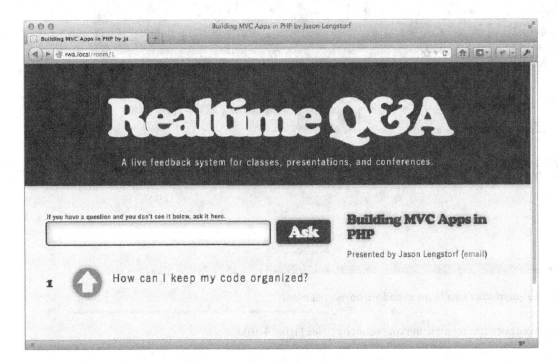

Figure 9-8. *The question is created; the creator's vote is already counted*

Voting Up the Question

To test voting up the question, you'll need to open a third browser so you can join the room as an attendee who has not yet voted for the new question (see Figure 9-9).

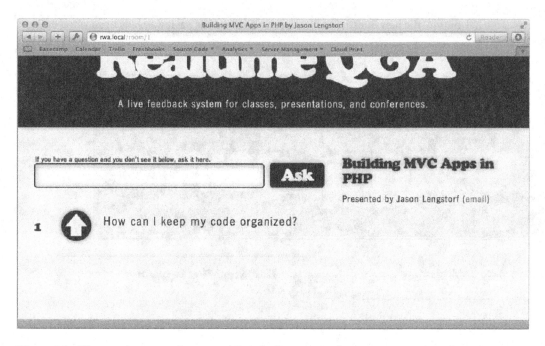

Figure 9-9. *The question as seen by an attendee who has not voted*

Click the vote button to increase the vote count by 1 (see Figure 9-10).

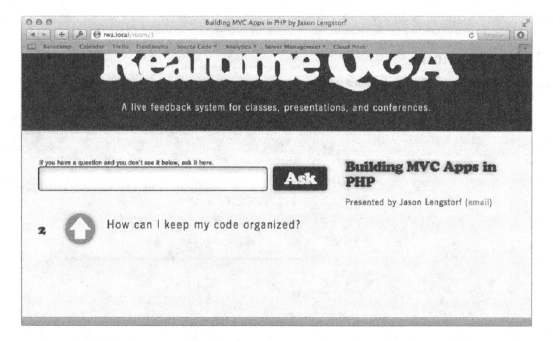

Figure 9-10. *The question after receiving its second vote*

Answering the Question

Back in the first browser—the one in which your user is the presenter—reload to see the new question (see Figure 9-11).

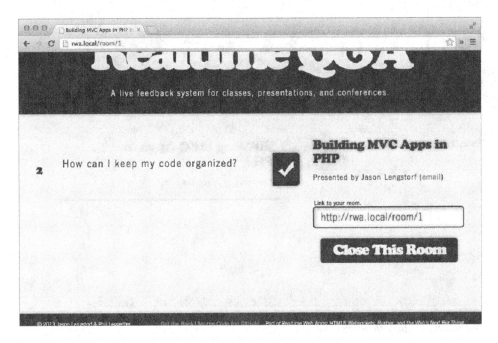

Figure 9-11. *The question on the presenter's dashboard, complete with vote count*

Now click the answer button to mark the question as answered (see Figure 9-12).

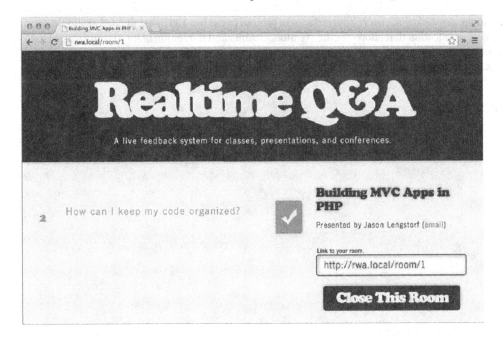

Figure 9-12. *The answered question in the presenter's view*

Verify that this also displays correctly for attendees by checking either of the other two browsers (see Figure 9-13).

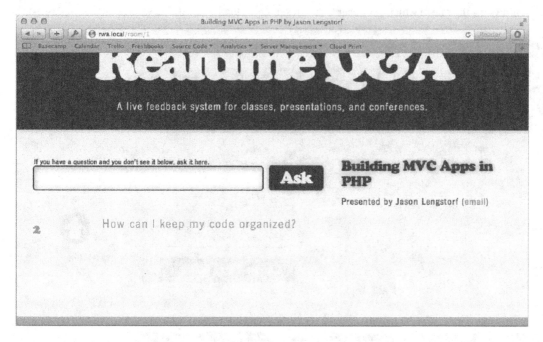

Figure 9-13. *The answered question in the attendee's view*

Summary

Between this chapter and the one before it, you've covered a lot of ground in the last 100 pages or so. You should now have a fully functional MVC application that allows for the creation, closing, and reopening of rooms; and the asking, voting, and answering of questions.

In the next chapter, you'll add realtime event notifications to the app and implement JavaScript effects to animate those events.

■ ■ ■

CHAPTER 10

Implementing Realtime Events and jQuery Effects

At this point, you have a fully functional app. However, in order for this particular app to be useful, it needs to implement realtime functionality so its users aren't forced to constantly reload to get new data.

In this chapter, you'll hook the app up to Pusher and add code to the back end that will create realtime events. You'll also use Pusher's JavaScript application programming interface (API) to subscribe to those events and jQuery to animate the app so the new data can be manipulated onscreen in a non-jarring way.

Which events need realtime enhancement?

- Closing a Room

- Opening a Room

- Asking a Question

- Voting a Question

- Answering a Question

Adding the Required Credentials and Libraries

Before you can start adding realtime, you'll need to make sure you have all the proper credentials and libraries on hand to configure the app.

Obtaining Your Pusher API Credentials

The Pusher API requires your app to authenticate using an app key, an app secret, and an app ID.

To obtain them, log in to your account at `http://pusher.com` and select "Add new app" from the top left of your dashboard. Name your new app "Realtime Web Apps" and leave the two boxes below unchecked (see Figure 10-1).

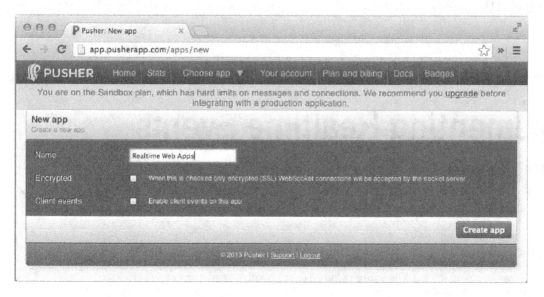

Figure 10-1. *Creating a new app in Pusher*

Click "Create app" and then click "API access" on the next screen to bring up your API credentials (see Figure 10-2).

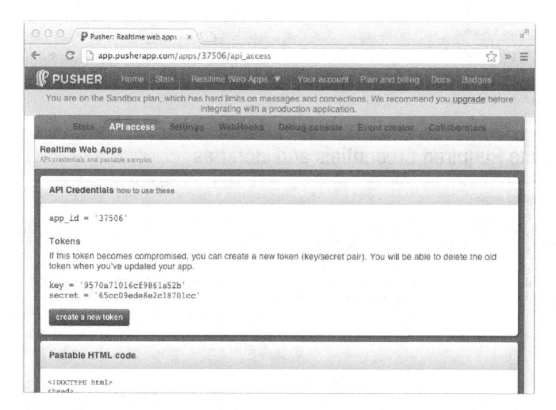

Figure 10-2. *Viewing the app's API credentials on the Pusher dashboard*

Adding the Pusher API Credentials to the Config File

Now that you have the API credentials, they need to be included in the app. To do this, add three new constants—shown in bold—to system/config/config.inc.php:

```
//-----------------------------------------------------------------------
// Database credentials
//-----------------------------------------------------------------------

$_C['DB_HOST'] = 'localhost';
$_C['DB_NAME'] = 'rwa_app';
$_C['DB_USER'] = 'root';
$_C['DB_PASS'] = '';

//-----------------------------------------------------------------------
// Pusher credentials
//-----------------------------------------------------------------------

$_C['PUSHER_KEY']    = '9570a71016cf9861a52b';
$_C['PUSHER_SECRET'] = '65cc09ede8e2c18701cc';
$_C['PUSHER_APPID']  = '37506';

//-----------------------------------------------------------------------
// Enable debug mode (strict error reporting)
//-----------------------------------------------------------------------

$_C['DEBUG'] = TRUE;
```

Downloading the PHP API Wrapper for Pusher

For the back-end portion of the app, we need to use an API wrapper to make accessing Pusher a breeze.

Download the API wrapper from https://github.com/pusher/pusher-php-server. The ZIP will contain several files and directories, but the only one you need to grab is at lib/Pusher.php, which you should now copy to system/lib/ in your app.

Including the PHP API Wrapper in the App

Now that the Pusher API wrapper is in the app's directory structure, it needs to be included for use. In index.php, add the following bold code to the initialization block:

```
// Starts the session
if (!isset($_SESSION)) {
    session_start();
}

// Loads the configuration variables
require_once SYS_PATH . '/config/config.inc.php';
```

```
// Loads Pusher
require_once SYS_PATH . '/lib/Pusher.php';

// Turns on error reporting if in debug mode
if (DEBUG===TRUE) {
    ini_set('display_errors', 1);
    error_reporting(E_ALL^E_STRICT);
} else {
    ini_set('display_errors', 0);
    error_reporting(0);
}
```

Loading Pusher's JavaScript API Wrapper

For the front-end portion of your realtime implementation, the app needs to include Pusher's JavaScript API wrapper. In system/inc/footer.inc.php, add the following bold code:

```
    </ul>
</footer>

<script src="http://js.pusher.com/1.12/pusher.min.js"></script>

</body>

</html>
```

Loading jQuery

For the effects, your app will need the jQuery library. Add it right after the Pusher JS in the footer:

```
    </ul>
</footer>

<script src="http://js.pusher.com/1.12/pusher.min.js"></script>
<script src="http://code.jquery.com/jquery-1.8.2.min.js"></script>

</body>

</html>
```

■ **Note** The code in this app has been tested only up to version 1.8.2 of jQuery. Newer versions may introduce issues and should be used only after thorough testing.

Implementing Realtime on the Back End

To get the ball rolling with realtime, the events need to be created and triggered on the back end of the app.

Creating the Event

Because of the way the app handles form submissions—all of them are passed through a single form handler method—sending realtime event notifications takes only a few lines of code, which will be added to the handle_form_submission() method in the abstract Controller class.

Open system/core/class.controller.inc.php and insert the following bold code:

```
protected function handle_form_submission( $action )
{
    if ($this->check_nonce()) {

        // Calls the method specified by the action
        $output = $this->{$this->actions[$action]}();

        if (is_array($output) && isset($output['room_id'])) {
            $room_id = $output['room_id'];
        } else {
            throw new Exception('Form submission failed.');
        }

        // Realtime stuff happens here
        $pusher  = new Pusher(PUSHER_KEY, PUSHER_SECRET, PUSHER_APPID);
        $channel = 'room_' . $room_id;
        $pusher->trigger($channel, $action, $output);

        header('Location: ' . APP_URI . 'room/' . $room_id);
        exit;
    } else {
        throw new Exception('Invalid nonce.');
    }
}
```

A new Pusher object is created and stored in the $pusher variable, then a channel for the room is created using its ID. Using the action name as the event name, a new event is triggered on the room's channel using the trigger() method that sends the output array for client-side use.

Testing Out Realtime Events

To make sure your realtime events are being triggered on the back end, head back to your Pusher dashboard and open the Debug console for your app. With this page open, navigate to `http://rwa.local` in a new tab or browser and then create a new room.

After the room is created, look at the Debug console and you'll see something similar to Figure 10-3.

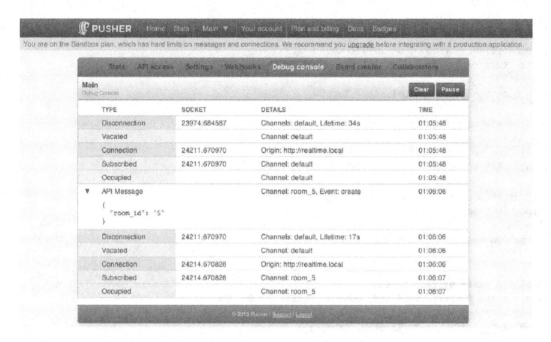

Figure 10-3. *The Pusher Debug console shows the creation of a room in realtime*

Next, close the room; then reopen it. Check the console again and you'll see that the `close` and `open` events were triggered (see Figure 10-4).

▼ API Message		Channel: room_5, Event: create	01:06:06

`{`
   `"room_id": "5"`
`}`			

Disconnection	24211.670970	Channels: default, Lifetime: 17s	01:06:06
Vacated		Channel: default	01:06:06
Connection	24214.670828	Origin: http://realtime.local	01:06:06
Subscribed	24214.670828	Channel: room_5	01:06:07
Occupied		Channel: room_5	01:06:07
▼ API Message		Channel: room_5, Event: close	01:12:41

`{`
   `"room_id": "5"`
`}`			

Disconnection	24214.670828	Channels: room_5, Lifetime: 394s	01:12:41
Vacated		Channel: room_5	01:12:41
Connection	24224.669701	Origin: http://realtime.local	01:12:41
Subscribed	24224.669701	Channel: room_5	01:12:41
Occupied		Channel: room_5	01:12:41
▼ API Message		Channel: room_5, Event: open	01:12:43

`{`
   `"room_id": "5"`
`}`			

Disconnection	24224.669701	Channels: room_5, Lifetime: 1s	01:12:43
Vacated		Channel: room_5	01:12:43
Connection	24059.679687	Origin: http://realtime.local	01:12:43
Subscribed	24059.679687	Channel: room_5	01:12:43
Occupied		Channel: room_5	01:12:43

Figure 10-4. The Pusher console shows events for closing and reopening the room

From a second browser, join the room (ID 5 in this example) and ask a question. The new connection shows up on the console as well as the triggered ask event (see Figure 10-5).

Occupied		Channel: room_5	01:16:45
Connection	24230.671187	Origin: http://realtime.local	01:16:23
Subscribed	24230.671187	Channel: room_5	01:16:23
▼ API Message		Channel: room_5, Event: ask	01:16:44

```
{
  "room_id": "5",
  "question_id": "10",
  "markup": "\n          <li id=\"question-10\" \n                    data-count=\"1\"\n
class=\" \">\n              \n          <form method=\"post\" class=\"answer\"\n
action=\"http://realtime.local/question/answer\">\n                      <input type=\"submit\"
value=\"Answer this question.\" />\n          <input type=\"hidden\"
name=\"question_id\" \n                    value=\"10\" />\n                    <input
type=\"hidden\" name=\"room_id\" \n                    value=\"5\" />\n
<input type=\"hidden\" name=\"nonce\" \n
value=\"NTE0NjZhZmMyYTk4MTEuMTg2OTExOTY=\" />\n          </form> \n \n          <p>\n
How cool are realtime events? \n          </p>\n          \n          <form
method=\"post\" class=\"vote\"\n
action=\"http://realtime.local/question/vote\">\n          <input value=\"I also have
this question.\" \n          type=\"submit\" />\n          <input
type=\"hidden\" name=\"question_id\" \n          value=\"10\" />\n
<input type=\"hidden\" name=\"room_id\" \n          value=\"5\" />\n
<input type=\"hidden\" name=\"nonce\" \n
value=\"NTE0NjZhZmMyYTk4MTEuMTg2OTExOTY=\" />\n          </form> \n \n          </li><!--
/#question-10-->\n"
}
```

Disconnection	24230.671187	Channels: room_5, Lifetime: 21s	01:16:44
Connection	24313.662864	Origin: http://realtime.local	01:16:44
Subscribed	24313.662864	Channel: room_5	01:16:45

Figure 10-5. *The console shows the new question markup, which is sent by the ask event*

In a third browser, vote up the question to see the vote event triggered (see Figure 10-6).

Disconnection	24230.671187	Channels: room_5, Lifetime: 21s	01:16:44
Connection	24313.662864	Origin: http://realtime.local	01:16:44
Subscribed	24313.662864	Channel: room_5	01:16:45
▼ API Message		Channel: room_5, Event: vote	01:21:41

```
{
  "room_id": "5",
  "question_id": "9"
}
```

Disconnection	24313.662864	Channels: room_5, Lifetime: 297s	01:21:42
Connection	24101.679169	Origin: http://realtime.local	01:21:42
Subscribed	24101.679169	Channel: room_5	01:21:42

Figure 10-6. *The console shows the vote event as it occurs*

Finally, go back to the browser in which you created the room and mark the question as answered. This triggers the answer event in the console (see Figure 10-7).

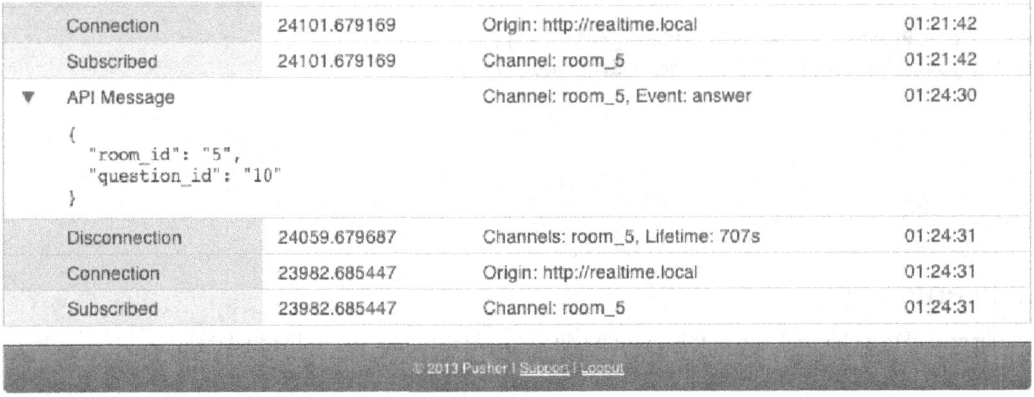

Connection	24101.679169	Origin: http://realtime.local	01:21:42
Subscribed	24101.679169	Channel: room_5	01:21:42
▼ API Message		Channel: room_5, Event: answer	01:24:30

```
{
    "room_id": "5",
    "question_id": "10"
}
```

Disconnection	24059.679687	Channels: room_5, Lifetime: 707s	01:24:31
Connection	23982.685447	Origin: http://realtime.local	01:24:31
Subscribed	23982.685447	Channel: room_5	01:24:31

© 2013 Pusher | Support | Logout

Figure 10-7. The answer event in the console

Implementing Realtime on the Front End

Now that the back end of the app is triggering events, the front end needs to listen for them.

Subscribing to the Channel

The first step is to create a JavaScript Pusher object and use it to subscribe to the room's channel.

Determining the Channel Name

Before subscribing to the channel, you first need to create a new template variable that holds the proper channel name. In index.php, add the following bold code to generate the channel name:

```
require_once SYS_PATH . '/inc/header.inc.php';

$controller->output_view();

// Configures the Pusher channel if we're in a room
$channel = !empty($uri_array[0]) ? 'room_' . $uri_array[0] : 'default';

require_once SYS_PATH . '/inc/footer.inc.php';
```

Adding the Channel Subscription JavaScript

Now that the channel name is determined, create a new Pusher object and subscribe to the channel by adding the following bold code in system/inc/footer.inc.php:

```
</footer>

<script src="http://js.pusher.com/1.12/pusher.min.js"></script>
<script src="http://code.jquery.com/jquery-1.8.2.min.js"></script>
```

```
<script>
    var pusher  = new Pusher('<?php echo PUSHER_KEY; ?>'),
        channel = pusher.subscribe('<?php echo $channel; ?>');
</script>

</body>

</html>
```

Binding to Events

The app is now subscribed to a channel, but at this point it still needs to listen for the individual events.

Create an Initialization JavaScript File

In an effort to keep the footer clean, create a new file in `assets/scripts/` called `init.js` and initialize it with the following:

```
/**
 * Initialization script for Realtime Web Apps
 */
(function($) {


})(jQuery);
```

This file will contain the rest of the app's JavaScript.

■ **Tip** Wrapping your app scripts in a closure[footnote] prevents conflicts with other libraries that use the dollar sign ($) shortcut, such as Prototype and MooTools.

Load this file in your app by inserting the following bold code into the footer:

```
<script src="http://js.pusher.com/1.12/pusher.min.js"></script>
<script src="http://code.jquery.com/jquery-1.8.2.min.js"></script>
<script>
    var pusher  = new Pusher('<?php echo PUSHER_KEY; ?>'),
        channel = pusher.subscribe('<?php echo $channel; ?>');
</script>
<script src="<?php echo APP_URI; ?>assets/scripts/init.js"></script>

</body>

</html>
```

■ **Note** The Pusher object initialization and channel subscription are placed directly in the footer to take advantage of PHP-powered templating.

Add Event Binding for Each Supported Action

For every action that needs a realtime response, an event will be fired that needs to be "listened" for by our app. Pusher makes this extremely easy with the bind() method, which should be familiar to any developer who has used JavaScript in previous projects.

The bind() method takes the name of the event to be listened for as its first argument and the function to be executed when that event occurs as its second.

Bind a function for each event in the app using the following bold code:

```
(function($) {

    channel.bind('close',  function(data){ });
    channel.bind('open',   function(data){ });
    channel.bind('ask',    function(data){ });
    channel.bind('vote',   function(data){ });
    channel.bind('answer', function(data){ });

})(jQuery);
```

These bindings add virtually no overhead to the app, so binding to all five at once will not add a performance hit.

■ **Note** These methods don't do anything just yet; you'll add that functionality in the next section.

Adding Effects

The app is now sending and receiving realtime events, so all that's left to do is add the effects that do something with the new data.

Handling Room Events

When the presenter closes a room, it needs to be made known to the attendees immediately so they don't try to ask any new questions or cast new votes.

Similarly, if a presenter reopens a room, all attendees should immediately be made aware that the room is now open again.

Since the markup varies significantly from a closed room to an open one, the most straightforward and least error-prone method of alerting attendees of changes to a room's open state is to simply refresh the page.

In init.js, create a new object called room that has two methods: open() and close(). Both should simply reload the page when called.

The corresponding events should trigger these methods as well. To accomplish this, add the following bold code to init.js:

```
(function($) {

    channel.bind('close',  function(data){ room.close(data); });
    channel.bind('open',   function(data){ room.open(data); });
    channel.bind('ask',    function(data){  });
    channel.bind('vote',   function(data){  });
    channel.bind('answer', function(data){  });


    var room = {
            open: function(data){
                location.reload();
            },
            close: function(data){
                location.reload();
            }
        };

})(jQuery);
```

Note that we have chosen to have the page reload automatically when a room is closed by the presenter. Normally, you would not want to reload a page without the user's input because it can be confusing, but we have good reason to here. In this particular case, as already mentioned, a lot of markup changes on the page when a room closes. In addition, the user cannot submit a new question to a closed room, so the presenter closing the room should be disruptive; otherwise, an attendee could spend extra time working on a question that can't be submitted anyway, which could be more frustrating than simply realizing that the room is now closed and they should email the presenter instead.

Adding New Questions with Animation

When a new question is asked, it should be made available for everyone viewing the room immediately. To make the introduction of new data less jarring, it should be added with an animation.

In Chapter 8, when the action handler method create_question() was added to the Question controller for asking new questions, you already did the view generation for this event, so formatted HTML will be sent in the data object.

However, because the back end can't possibly know the nonce currently being used for your view, we need to read the nonce and insert it into the value attribute of all newly generated nonce fields before animating the question's addition to the top of the list with slideDown():

```
(function($) {

    channel.bind('close',  function(data){ room.close(data); });
    channel.bind('open',   function(data){ room.open(data); });
    channel.bind('ask',    function(data){ question.ask(data); });
    channel.bind('vote',   function(data){  });
    channel.bind('answer', function(data){  });

    var nonce = $('input[name=nonce]:eq(0)').val(),
        room = {
```

```
            open: function(data){
                location.reload();
            },
            close: function(data){
                location.reload();
            }
        },
        question = {
            ask: function(data){
                $(data.markup)
                    .find('input[name=nonce]').val(nonce).end()
                    .hide().prependTo('#questions').slideDown('slow');
            }
        };

})(jQuery);
```

■ **Note** To keep the JavaScript concise, we're using the var declaration only once for all three variables in this script. This is mostly a stylistic choice, but there are also arguments out there claiming a miniscule performance improvement using this approach.

Adding Votes to a Question

When an attendee votes up a question, the count should update next to the vote button. However, we want to draw just a bit more attention to the event than that, so let's add a subtle animation as well.

Adding the Animation to the Stylesheet

Because CSS3 introduced animation, and because most modern browsers support hardware acceleration for CSS3 animations, your app will use a keyframed CSS animation in favor of a jQuery animation.

To accomplish this, you first have to determine which class (.new-vote in this case) will trigger the animation and then set it up. For this animation, called vote, we're going to quickly fade the question out and then back in again by adjusting opacity. This will be done—or iterated—twice.

Unfortunately, you'll need vendor-specific prefixes to ensure that the animation works in all browsers, so what should be a quick addition turns into a fairly large amount of CSS.

Add the following code to the bottom of assets/styles/main.css:

```
/*
 * ANIMATION
 ***********************************************************************/

#questions li.new-vote {
    -webkit-animation-name: vote;
    -webkit-animation-duration: 0.5s;
    -webkit-animation-timing-function: ease-in-out;
    -webkit-animation-iteration-count: 2;
```

```
    -moz-animation-name: vote;
    -moz-animation-duration: 0.5s;
    -moz-animation-timing-function: ease-in-out;
    -moz-animation-iteration-count:2;

    -ms-animation-name: vote;
    -ms-animation-duration: 0.5s;
    -ms-animation-timing-function: ease-in-out;
    -ms-animation-iteration-count: 2;

    animation-name: vote;
    animation-duration: 0.5s;
    animation-timing-function: ease-in-out;
    animation-iteration-count: 2;
}

@-webkit-keyframes vote {
    0% { opacity: 1; }
    50% { opacity: .4; }
    100% { opacity: 1; }
}

@-moz-keyframes vote {
    0% { opacity: 1; }
    50% { opacity: .4; }
    100% { opacity: 1; }
}

@-ms-keyframes vote {
    0% { opacity: 1; }
    50% { opacity: .4; }
    100% { opacity: 1; }
}

@keyframes vote {
    0% { opacity: 1; }
    50% { opacity: .4; }
    100% { opacity: 1; }
}
```

Triggering the Animation with a Class

Now that the animation is in place, all that the JavaScript needs to do is add a class to trigger it.

In addition to the animation, the script also needs to update the vote count and because there might be multiple people voting for a question, remove the class after the animation is completed so that it can be triggered multiple times.

Add the following bold code to init.js to complete the voting effects:

```
(function($) {
```

```
channel.bind('close',  function(data){ room.close(data); });
channel.bind('open',   function(data){ room.open(data); });
channel.bind('ask',    function(data){ question.ask(data); });
channel.bind('vote',   function(data){ question.vote(data); });
channel.bind('answer', function(data){  });

var nonce = $('input[name=nonce]:eq(0)').val(),
    room = {
        open: function(data){
            location.reload();
        },
        close: function(data){
            location.reload();
        }
    },
    question = {
        ask: function(data){
            $(data.markup)
                .find('input[name=nonce]').val(nonce).end()
                .hide().prependTo('#questions').slideDown('slow');
        },
        vote: function(data){
            var question  = $('#question-'+data.question_id),
                cur_count = question.data('count'),
                new_count = cur_count+1;

            // Updates the count
            question
                .attr('data-count', new_count)
                .data('count', new_count)
                .addClass('new-vote');

            setTimeout(1000, function(){
                question.removeClass('new-vote');
            });
        }
    };

})(jQuery);
```

Testing Out the Animation

To see this in action, use two browsers to join a room—make sure neither browser is the presenter—and place them side-by-side so you can see both at once.

In one browser, ask a new question; it will be dynamically added to the other browser window when the ask event is triggered.

In the other browser, vote up the new question. Watch the first browser as you submit the vote: it will run through the animation before returning to its normal state. It's difficult to demonstrate this in a still image, but Figure 10-8 shows the animation in progress.

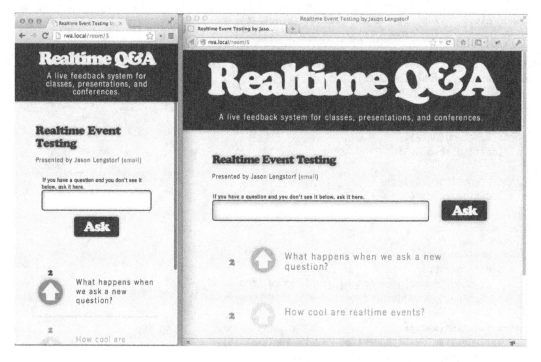

Figure 10-8. *When voting for the top question using the browser on the left, the animation is triggered in the browser to the right*

Answering a Question with Animation and Reordering

When a question is marked as answered, it should fade out and then be removed from the list (by an animated slide up) and reattached to the bottom (also by an animated slide) to make room for the unanswered questions.

Add the following code shown in bold to init.js to make it happen:

```
(function($) {

    channel.bind('close',  function(data){ room.close(data); });
    channel.bind('open',   function(data){ room.open(data); });
    channel.bind('ask',    function(data){ question.ask(data); });
    channel.bind('vote',   function(data){ question.vote(data); });
    channel.bind('answer', function(data){ question.answer(data); });

    var nonce = $('input[name=nonce]:eq(0)').val(),
        room = {
            open: function(data){
                location.reload();
            },
            close: function(data){
                location.reload();
            }
        },
```

```
question = {
    ask: function(data){
        $(data.markup)
            .find('input[name=nonce]').val(nonce).end()
            .hide().prependTo('#questions').slideDown('slow');
    },
    vote: function(data){
        var question   = $('#question-'+data.question_id),
            cur_count = question.data('count'),
            new_count = cur_count+1;

        // Updates the count
        question
            .attr('data-count', new_count)
            .data('count', new_count)
            .addClass('new-vote');

        setTimeout(1000, function(){
            question.removeClass('new-vote');
        });
    },
    answer: function(data){
        var question = $("#question-"+data.question_id),
            detach_me = function() {
                question
                    .detach()
                    .appendTo('#questions')
                    .slideDown(500);
            }

        question
            .addClass('answered')
            .delay(1000)
            .slideUp(500, detach_me);
    }
};

})(jQuery);
```

Testing Out Answering Questions

To see how a question marked as answered looks to an attendee, open two browsers and place the windows side-by-side so you can see both at once. In one browser, create a new room; in the other, join that room and ask a question.

The question will show up on the browser that created the room, at which point you can mark the question answered. In the attendee view, the question will fade, disappear, and then be reattached in its "answered" state (see Figure 10-9). Because there is only one question in the room, it won't demonstrate moving the question to the bottom of the list, but you can perform your own experiments to see that in action if you so choose.

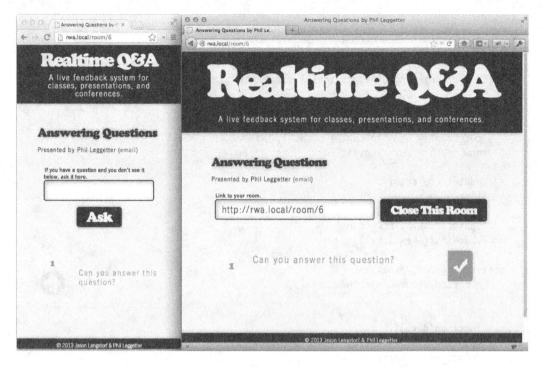

Figure 10-9. A question that has been marked as answered in both attendee and presenter views

Summary

In this chapter, you learned exactly how quick and easy it is to implement realtime events and the effects to integrate them into your applications.

At this point, the application is complete, and you're ready to start building your own amazing realtime applications. Please find your authors on Twitter—@jlengstorf and @leggetter—and share your creations.

Welcome to the future of web design, friend.

APPENDIX A

OAuth

In this appendix, we'll walk through the process of authenticating users within your web app using their existing social media accounts, thus eliminating the need for *yet another* username-password combo on *yet another* site.

To accomplish this, we'll be using the OAuth protocol.

What Is OAuth?

According to the OAuth home page, *OAuth* is "an open protocol to allow secure API authorization in a simple and standard method from desktop and web applications."[1]

What that means at a high level is that OAuth provides a way for your app to access a user's other accounts, such as Facebook, without requiring the user's Facebook password to be entered into your app.

To get a little more in depth, OAuth provides a standardized protocol for developers to register with a service provider, obtain credentials, and use those credentials to let their app request permissions from the service provider on a user's behalf.

The History of OAuth

OAuth 1.0 was finalized in 2007 as the answer to a problem that had been plaguing developers as sites like Facebook and Twitter exploded in popularity. How can these sites interact with each other without requiring users to give their passwords to the other apps?

Early adopters of Twitter were inundated with new apps, tools, and services that augmented Twitter, automated tweets, connected people with similar interests, and showed myriad other interesting ways to use the Twitter platform. Unfortunately, to use one of these apps, users were originally required to enter their Twitter username and password to grant the app access to the account. This access was unrestricted, so users simply trusted that these app developers would be responsible and hoping for the best.

Obviously, this was not a sustainable model.

OAuth emerged as an alternative authentication protocol after the team behind it studied many of the proprietary solutions that existed—services such as Google AuthSub, AOL OpenAuth, and the Amazon Web Services API—and combined the best practices into an open protocol that would be easy for any service to use and any developer to implement.

OAuth is currently working on the OAuth 2.0 draft, which has been implemented by several service providers, including Facebook.

---

[1]http://oauth.net/

How OAuth Works

Before we talk about what's happening, let's look at a real-world OAuth workflow: social photo-sharing site Flickr is part of the Yahoo! family of companies, but it also allows users to log in to the service using its Facebook or Google accounts.

Most likely, this workflow is something you've seen before and possibly even something you've used on multiple occasions. On the user side, it's extremely simple, which is part of its appeal. A user clicks the sign in button and chooses to log in with one of the existing accounts that supports OAuth (see Figure A-1), then confirms with the selected service—Facebook, in this example—that the requesting app has permission to access the requested data (Figure A-2). After that, the user is logged in.

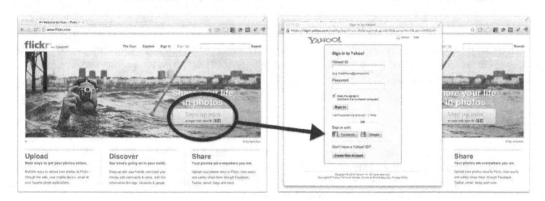

Figure A-1. *The Flickr home page allows login with Google or Facebook in addition to its Yahoo–based account system*

Figure A-2. *After clicking to sign in with Facebook, Yahoo! requests permissions from Facebook, which you are given the option to approve or cancel*

■ **Note** If you look at the lower right of the Facebook login dialog, the requested permissions are listed for the user to review before approving.

From a user's perspective, this is three quick clicks. On the developer side, it's a little more complex (though it's still considerably easier to implement than a custom account registration and login system).

OAuth Developer Workflow

The developer workflow for implementing OAuth in an app is fairly straightforward:

1. Your app sends the user to the authorization *endpoint*, or uniform resource indicator (URI), through which the API exposes an action, along with its credentials, its own authorization endpoint, what permissions it requires, and a security token.

2. The authorization endpoint for the service asks the user to confirm that your app is allowed to access the API on the user's behalf.

3. Assuming the user grants access, the service redirects the user back to your app's authorization endpoint, along with authorization code and the security token from step 1.

4. Your app requests an access token from the service's token endpoint by sending the authorization code received in step 3, plus its credentials and your app's authorization endpoint again.

5. The service authenticates your app, checks the authorization code, and sends back an access token that can be used to access the user's data via the service's API.

Using a real service as an example, let's look at the actual endpoints used by Facebook's OAuth 2.0[2] implementation.

Building the Login Link

The first step for an app requesting access to a user's data is to direct the user to the service provider's authorization endpoint. The endpoint URI to do this for Facebook is https://www.facebook.com/dialog/oauth, and the app has to send its client_id, redirect_uri, scope, and state along with the request.

Assuming that users should be redirected to http://app.example.org/login.php after granting access to the app, a login link for the app might look like this:

https://www.facebook.com/dialog/oauth?**client_id**=YOUR_APP_ID&**redirect_uri**=
http%3a%2f%2fapp.example.org%2flogin.php&**scope**=email&**state**=73ef0836082f31

■ **Note**   The value of client_id is a unique value provided by Facebook once you have registered your app. The current value, YOUR_APP_ID, is a placeholder and should be replaced with your own app's credentials. Don't worry about registering your app just yet; we'll walk through that process later in this chapter during Exercise A-1.

This example uses the GET method to send parameters to the endpoint. To make them easier to spot, they're shown in bold.

*   client_id is the public identifier Facebook generates for the app after it is registered. It lets Facebook know who requests access.

*   redirect_uri is the URI to which the user should be redirected after authorizing the app. This URI is your app's authorization endpoint, where the app will process the data sent by Facebook.

---

[2]https://developers.facebook.com/docs/authentication/server-side/

- scope is a comma-separated list of permissions that are being requested from Facebook. There is a full list in Facebook's developer docs, referenced earlier, but the only one used in this book is email.[3]

- state is an arbitrary string generated to guard against cross-site request forgery. This is technically optional, but it should be used.

Obtaining Authorization from the User

After the user clicks the login link generated in the previous section, she will see Facebook's authorization dialog. This shows her what permissions were requested and gives her the option to confirm or deny that she wishes to grant these permissions to your app.

Assuming that she approves the authorization request, Facebook will redirect her back to your app's authorization endpoint, which was passed in the redirect_uri parameter of the login link. Facebook will send back a code and the value of state from the login link, which will look something like this:

```
http://app.example.org/login.php?code=CODE_GENERATED_BY_FACEBOOK&state=73ef0836082f31
```

Note The value of code will be a long string generated by Facebook that is unique to each request. CODE_GENERATED_BY_FACEBOOK is a placeholder.

Requesting an Access Token

Armed with the value of code, your app can request an access token from Facebook. This is accomplished by sending the code, your app's credentials in client_id and client_secret, and your app's authorization endpoint in redirect_uri.

The URL will look something like this:

```
https://graph.facebook.com/oauth/access_token?client_id=YOUR_APP_ID&redirect_uri=http%3a%2f%2fapp.example.org%2flogin.php&client_secret=YOUR_APP_SECRET&code=CODE_GENERATED_BY_FACEBOOK
```

Note The value of client_secret is the other part of the credentials provided for your app by Facebook after it's registered. The value YOUR_APP_SECRET is a placeholder and should be replaced with your app's credentials.

Assuming that all the required parameters are correct and valid, Facebook will return an access token in access_token, along with an indication of how long the token is valid (in seconds) in expires.

```
access_token=USER_ACCESS_TOKEN&expires=NUMBER_OF_SECONDS_UNTIL_TOKEN_EXPIRES
```

Note The value of access_token is a unique value generated by Facebook. The value of expires will be an integer. The current values USER_ACCESS_TOKEN and NUMBER_OF_SECONDS_UNTIL_TOKEN_EXPIRES are placeholders.

---

[3]https://developers.facebook.com/docs/concepts/login/permissions-login-dialog/

What to Do with the Access Token

With the access token, your app can now make requests for the user's info from the Facebook API. Because it only requested e-mail in additional to basic user info, your app will not be able to look at the users' stream, make posts on their behalf, or do anything advanced. It provides your app with everything it needs for authentication and a bit of profile personalization.

To load the user's info, simply use one of Facebook's API endpoints (in this example, we load the basic user info from the Graph API) and pass along the access token in access_token:

```
https://graph.facebook.com/me?access_token=USER_ACCESS_TOKEN
```

Loading this with a valid access token will generate a JSON-encoded output something like this:

```
{
    "id": "1468448880",
    "name": "Jason Lengstorf",
    "first_name": "Jason",
    "last_name": "Lengstorf",
    "link": "https://www.facebook.com/jlengstorf",
    "username": "jlengstorf",
    "hometown": {
        "id": "109281049091287",
        "name": "Whitefish, Montana"
    },
    "location": {
        "id": "112548152092705",
        "name": "Portland, Oregon"
    },
    "bio": " I\u2019m a turbogeek from Portland. I design and develop websites, and sometimes I draw
pictures of stuff.\n\nI\u2019ve written two books (check 'em out here: http://cptr.me/LP9YAm), and
I\u2019ve written articles on development and design for Nettuts, CSS Tricks, and Smashing Magazine,
among others.",
    "quotes": "That dog'll hunt.",
    "work": [
        {
            "employer": {
                "id": "169249483097082",
                "name": "Copter Labs"
            },
            "position": {
                "id": "137221592980321",
                "name": "Developer"
            },
            "description": "Making the web a better-looking place.",
            "start_date": "2010-12"
        }

    ],
```

```
   "education": [
      {
         "school": {
            "id": "107993102567513",
            "name": "Whitefish High School"
         },
         "year": {
            "id": "194603703904595",
            "name": "2003"
         },
         "type": "High School"
      }
   ],
   "gender": "male",
   "email": "jason\u0040lengstorf.com",
   "timezone": -7,
   "locale": "en_US",
   "languages": [
      {
         "id": "113301478683221",
         "name": "American English"
      }
   ],
   "verified": true,
   "updated_time": "2012-06-29T21:53:51+0000"
}
```

This data can be used within your app to customize the user's experience, identify any actions they make, and other functions that would require information about the user.

Why OAuth Is Better Than Building a Login System

Using OAuth to authenticate users is, in many cases, a better solution to the "user account" problem. Creating new accounts is a pain for both developers and users, so when the app doesn't have an explicit need to closely control its own registration process, there are a lot of good reasons to use OAuth rather than implementing something specific to your application. Some of the benefits include these:

- One fewer account registration and password for users to deal with, which lowers the barrier to entry for potential new users: getting started means three clicks versus filling out a form, checking their confirmation e-mail, and then logging in.

- The app has access to basic user info without asking for any additional input or actions from the user beyond authorization.

- The app has access to the service provider's API and its benefits (such as sharing a user's app activity on Facebook, if the permissions allow it).

- It eliminates the need to build a complex and customized login system, which saves hours of maintenance and development.

EXERCISE A-1: BUILD A SIMPLE LOGIN SYSTEM USING OAUTH AND FACEBOOK

Let's get our hands dirty with OAuth by building a very simple app that will just allow a user to log in using their Facebook account.

This app will forego CSS styling and any non-essential markup because a reasonable amount of PHP is required to achieve the desired functionality. You will be building an abstract PHP class to define basic OAuth 2.0 workflow and then extending that class with a Facebook-specific class that defines endpoints, credentials, and API interaction methods.

This app will consist of five files: two PHP classes, a configuration file, a login file, and the app's home page.

Step 1: Register Your App with Facebook

To register your app with Facebook, start by navigating to `https://developers.facebook.com/apps`. Once there, click the Create New App button at the top right of the screen. A modal window will appear asking you to name your app (see Figure A-3).

Figure A-3. *The modal dialog to register a new app with Facebook*

Next, you'll be taken to the app's home screen. Inside, check the boxes to indicate that the app will allow login on a website and that it will also be a mobile app (see Figure A-4).

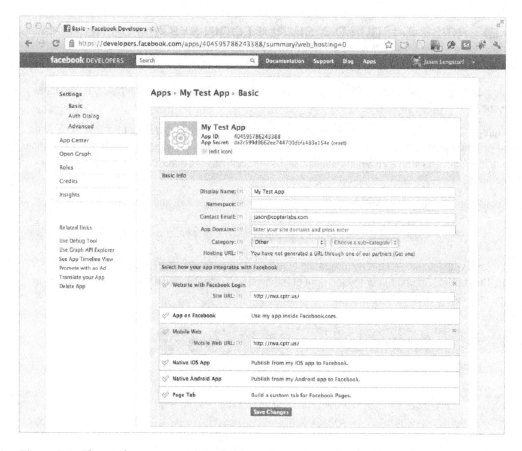

Figure A-4. *The app home screen on Facebook*

Save those changes, and the app is registered. Make a note of the App ID and App Secret at the top of the page; they will be used to obtain authorization later on.

Step 2: Create a Base OAuth Class

The first step is to create the abstract class that will handle all general OAuth 2.0 workflow. The reason for making this class abstract is that it can't work without first having a service provider to whom requests should be made. The reason for separating this class from the Facebook-specific class is that it will prevent duplicate code if this app were to add a second service provider as an option for login.

In web root, create a folder called `includes`, and inside create a new file named `class.rwa_oauth.inc.php`. To start, add some basic checks and declare this class:

```php
<?php

// Makes sure cURL is loaded
if (!extension_loaded('curl')) {
    throw new Exception('OAuth requires the cURL PHP extension.');
}
```

```
// Makes sure the session is started
if (!session_id()) {
    session_start();
}

/**
 * An abstract class for handling the basics of OAuth 2.0 authorization
 *
 * @author Jason Lengstorf
 * @copyright 2012 Jason Lengstorf
 */
abstract class RWA_OAuth
{

}
```

Because using OAuth requires the app to request external URIs to function properly, the cURL extension is required. This script uses `extension_loaded()` to verify that cURL support is available, or throws an Exception if not.

■ **Note**   It's possible to work around lack of cURL support,[4] but that's outside the scope of this exercise.

Next, it checks for an active session ID and starts a session if none is found.

The class is called RWA_OAuth (there may be other classes that are called "OAuth" so the RWA_ prefix is used to prevent class naming conflicts). It's abstract, which means that it cannot be instantiated directly; in other words, another class must extend RWA_OAuth before its methods and properties can be accessed.

Class Properties

With the class declared, we can now define all the class properties:

```
abstract class RWA_OAuth
{

  /**
   * The service's auth endpoint
   * @var string
   */
  public $service_auth_endpoint,
```

---

[4]https://gist.github.com/4359352

```php
/**
 * The service's token endpoint
 * @var string
 */
    $service_token_endpoint,

/**
 * The scope, or permissions, required for the app to work properly
 * @var string
 */
    $scope,

/**
 * The service-generated client ID
 * @var string
 */
    $client_id,

/**
 * The service-generated client secret
 * @var string
 */
    $client_secret,

/**
 * The app's authorization endpoint
 * @var string
 */
    $client_auth_endpoint,

/**
 * The user's account ID as loaded from the service
 * @var string
 */
    $id,

/**
 * The user's username as loaded from the service
 * @var string
 */
    $username,

/**
 * The user's name as loaded from the service
 * @var string
 */
    $name,

/**
 * The user's email as loaded from the service
 * @var string
```

```
      */
            $email,
      /**
       * Generated HTML markup to display the user's profile image
       * @var string
       */
            $profile_image;

      /**
       * The current logged in state
       * @var bool
       */
      protected $logged_in      = FALSE,

      /**
       * The user access token or FALSE if none is set
       * @var mixed
       */
              $access_token = FALSE;

}
```

■ **Note**   In order to save space and focus only on the relevant code, code outside the class definition will be omitted, and code within the class not relevant to the current example will be folded with comments omitted. New code will be shown in bold.

- $service_auth_endpoint, $service_token_endpoint, and $client_auth_endpoint will store URIs pointing to each endpoint required for user authorization.

- $scope stores the permissions requested by the app.

- $client_id and $client_secret store your app's credentials (obtained by registering your app with the service provider).

- $id, $username, $name, and $email store data about the user.

- $profile_image stores HTML markup to display the user's profile image.

- $logged_in stores a Boolean value indicating whether the user is currently logged in.

- $access_token stores the access token acquired from the service provider after successful authorization.

Next, lay out the skeleton of the class by defining all the method names:

```php
abstract class RWA_OAuth
{

    public $service_auth_endpoint, $service_token_endpoint, $scope,
            $client_id, $client_secret, $client_auth_endpoint,
            $id, $username, $name, $email, $profile_image;

    protected $logged_in    = FALSE,
              $access_token = FALSE;

    /**
     * Checks for a login or logout attempt
     *
     * @return void
     */
    public function __construct(  )
    {

    }

    /**
     * Checks a login attempt for validity
     *
     * @return void
     */
    public function check_login(  )
    {

    }

    /**
     * Returns the current logged in state
     *
     * @return bool The current logged in state
     */
    public function is_logged_in(  )
    {

    }

    /**
     * Processes a logout attempt
     *
     * @return void
     */
    public function logout(  )
    {

    }
```

```php
/**
 * Returns the URI with which a authorization can be requested
 *
 * @return string    The authorization endpoint URI with params
 */
public function get_login_uri(   )
{

}


/**
 * Returns the URI with which an access token can be generated
 *
 * @return string    The access token endpoint URI with params
 */
protected function get_access_token_uri(   )
{

}


/**
 * Saves the access token in the session and as a class property
 *
 * @return bool TRUE on success, FALSE on failure
 */
protected function save_access_token(   )
{

}


/**
 * Makes a request using cURL and returns the resulting data
 *
 * @param string $uri    The URI to be requested
 * @return string        The data returned by the requested URI
 */
protected function request_uri(   )
{

}

/**
 * Loads the basic user data, including name and email
 *
 * This method will be different for each OAuth authorized service,
 * so it will need to be defined in the child class for the service.
 */
abstract protected function load_user_data();

/**
 * Generates markup to display the user's profile image
 *
```

```
 * This method will be different for each OAuth authorized service,
 * so it will need to be defined in the child class for the service.
 */
abstract protected function load_user_profile_image();

}
```

Each of these methods will be covered in detail as they're defined. In a nutshell, these are all the methods required to complete the OAuth workflow described in the section "OAuth Developer Workflow" earlier in this chapter.

get_login_uri() & get_access_token_uri()

With the class skeleton defined, let's start with the required endpoints for authorization and token generation, and define get_login_uri() and get_access_token_uri():

```
abstract class RWA_OAuth
{

    public $service_auth_endpoint, $service_token_endpoint, $scope,
            $client_id, $client_secret, $client_auth_endpoint,
            $id, $username, $name, $email, $profile_image;

    protected $logged_in     = FALSE,
                $access_token = FALSE;

    public function __construct(  ) {...}

    public function check_login(  ) {...}

    public function is_logged_in(  ) {...}

    public function logout(  ) {...}

    public function get_login_uri(  )
    {
        $state = uniqid(mt_rand(10000,99999), TRUE);
        $_SESSION['state'] = $state;
        return $this->service_auth_endpoint
            . '?client_id='     . $this->client_id
            . '&redirect_uri=' . urlencode($this->client_auth_endpoint)
            . '&scope='         . $this->scope
            . '&state='         . $state;
    }

    protected function get_access_token_uri( $code=NULL )
    {
        return $this->service_token_endpoint
            . '?client_id='     . $this->client_id
```

```
              . '&redirect_uri='  . urlencode($this->client_auth_endpoint)
              . '&client_secret=' . $this->client_secret
              . '&code='          . $code;
      }

      protected function save_access_token(  ) {...}

      protected function request_uri(  ) {...}

      abstract protected function load_user_data();

      abstract protected function load_user_profile_image();

}
```

The first thing the get_login_uri() method does is generate a unique string to be passed as the state parameter, which will be used to verify that the authorization request is genuine. This is stored in the session as well for later reference.

After that, we concatenate the $service_auth_endpoint with the required parameters. In order to avoid encoding issues, the $client_auth_endpoint value is run through urlencode() first.

Once assembled, the authorization request, or login, URI is returned.

This same process is followed for get_access_token_uri(), with two small differences: 1) the state parameter is not used, and 2) the client_secret parameter is added. It also accepts a parameter, $code, which is sent back from the service provider. We'll cover how we're obtaining that value in the next section.

save_access_token() and request_uri()

In order to load and save the generated token, let's define save_access_token() and request_uri():

```
abstract class RWA_OAuth
{
    public $service_auth_endpoint, $service_token_endpoint, $scope,
           $client_id, $client_secret, $client_auth_endpoint,
           $id, $username, $name, $email, $profile_image;

    protected $logged_in    = FALSE,
              $access_token = FALSE;

    public function __construct(  ) {...}

    public function check_login(  ) {...}

    public function is_logged_in(  ) {...}

    public function logout(  ) {...}

    public function get_login_uri(  ) {...}

    protected function get_access_token_uri(  ) {...}
```

```php
    protected function save_access_token(  )
    {
        $token_uri = $this->get_access_token_uri($_GET['code']);
        $response = $this->request_uri($token_uri);

        // Parse the response
        $params = array();
        parse_str($response, $params);
        if (isset($params['access_token'])) {
            $_SESSION['access_token'] = $params['access_token'];
            $this->access_token       = $params['access_token'];
            $this->logged_in          = TRUE;
            return TRUE;
        }

        return FALSE;
    }

    protected function request_uri( $uri )
    {
        $ch = curl_init();
        curl_setopt($ch, CURLOPT_URL, $uri);
        curl_setopt($ch, CURLOPT_RETURNTRANSFER, 1);
        curl_setopt($ch, CURLOPT_CONNECTTIMEOUT, 4);

        return curl_exec($ch);
    }

    abstract protected function load_user_data();

    abstract protected function load_user_profile_image();

}
```

First, let's look at request_uri(). This method accepts one parameter, $uri, which is the URI to be requested. It then initializes cURL, sets the URI to request to $uri, tells cURL to return the output of the request, and sets the timeout to an arbitrary, but reasonable, value of four seconds.

Next, in save_access_token(), the token request URI is loaded into $token_uri using get_access_token_uri() and the value of code (that is presumed to have been passed in the query string). Then the response from $token_uri is stored in $response after loading it with request_uri().

The value in $response, unless there has been an error, will contain the access token in query string format. Using the $params array and parse_str(), the query string is broken into an associative array, in which we check for access_token. If it's set, it's stored in both the object's properties and the session, $logged_in is set to TRUE, and the method returns TRUE; if not, the method returns FALSE to indicate failure.

The Rest of the Class Methods

Let's wrap up the RWA_OAuth class by defining the remaining four methods:

```php
abstract class RWA_OAuth
{

    public $service_auth_endpoint, $service_token_endpoint, $scope,
        $client_id, $client_secret, $client_auth_endpoint,
        $id, $username, $name, $email, $profile_image;

    protected $logged_in    = FALSE,
            $access_token = FALSE;

    public function __construct(  )
    {
        if (isset($_GET['logout']) && $_GET['logout']==1) {
            $this->logout();
            header('Location: ' . $this->client_auth_endpoint);
            exit;
        }

        $this->check_login();
    }

    public function check_login(  )
    {
        if (isset($_GET['state']) && isset($_GET['code'])) {
            if ($_GET['state']===$_SESSION['state']) {
                $this->save_access_token();
                $this->load_user_data();
                $this->load_user_profile_image();
            } else {
                throw new Exception("States don't match.");
            }
        } elseif (!$this->logged_in && !$this->access_token) {
            if (isset($_SESSION['access_token'])) {
                $this->access_token = $_SESSION['access_token'];
                $this->logged_in = TRUE;
                $this->load_user_data();
                $this->load_user_profile_image();
            }
        }
    }

    public function is_logged_in(  )
    {
        return $this->logged_in;
    }
```

```php
        public function logout(  )
        {
            $this->logged_in = FALSE;
            $this->access_token = FALSE;
            unset($_SESSION['access_token']);
            session_regenerate_id();
            session_destroy();
        }

        public function get_login_uri(  ) {...}

        protected function get_access_token_uri(  ) {...}

        protected function save_access_token(  ) {...}

        protected function request_uri(  ) {...}

        abstract protected function load_user_data();

        abstract protected function load_user_profile_image();

}
```

The is_logged_in() method is the simplest of the bunch, simply returning the value of $logged_in.

logout() is also pretty simple: it sets $logged_in and $access_token to FALSE, makes sure the access token is removed from the session, and then destroys the session altogether.

check_login() looks for state and code in the query string, and if they're present it checks that the state matches the one stored in the session. If they match, the save_access_token() method is run; then the two abstract methods from the class are called (load_user_data() and load_user_profile_image(), which will be defined in a child class). If they don't match, an Exception is thrown.

If the user is not logged in, but an access token is present in the session, the script will save the access token in the object, set $logged_in to TRUE, and load the user data and profile image.

The constructor for the object checks first for a logout attempt, which is sent via the query string ($_GET['logout']). Barring that, it runs check_login().

Step 3: Build the Facebook OAuth Child Class

With the RWA_OAuth class in place, we can work on a service-specific OAuth implementation. For this example, we'll use Facebook.

In the includes folder, create a new file called class.rwa_facebook.inc.php. Inside, place the following code:

```php
<?php

// Makes sure JSON can be parsed
if (!extension_loaded('json')) {
    throw new Exception('OAuth requires the JSON PHP extension.');
}
```

```php
/**
 * An RWA_OAuth extension for Facebook's OAuth 2.0 implementation
 *
 * @author Jason Lengstorf
 * @copyright 2012 Jason Lengstorf
 */
class RWA_Facebook extends RWA_OAuth
{

    public $service_auth_endpoint
                = 'https://www.facebook.com/dialog/oauth',
           $service_token_endpoint
                = 'https://graph.facebook.com/oauth/access_token';

    /**
     * Sets defaults, calls the parent constructor to check login/logout
     *
     * @param array $config Configuration parameters for Facebook OAuth
     * @return void
     */
    public function __construct( $config=array() )
    {
        /*
         * In order to use OAuth, the client_id, client_secret, and
         * client_auth_endpoint must be set, so execution fails here if
         * they aren't provided in the config array
         */
        if (   !isset($config['client_id'])
            || !isset($config['client_secret'])
            || !isset($config['client_auth_endpoint'])
        ) {
            throw new Exception('Required config data was not set.');
        }

        $this->client_id            = $config['client_id'];
        $this->client_secret        = $config['client_secret'];
        $this->client_auth_endpoint = $config['client_auth_endpoint'];
        /*
         * Adding scope is optional, so if it's in the config, this sets
         * the class property for authorization requests
         */
        if (isset($config['scope'])) {
            $this->scope = $config['scope'];
        }

        // Calls the OAuth constructor to check login/logout
        parent::__construct();
    }
```

```php
/**
 * Loads the user's data from the Facebook Graph API
 *
 * @return void
 */
protected function load_user_data(  )
{
    $graph_uri = 'https://graph.facebook.com/me?'
               . 'access_token=' . $this->access_token;
    $response = $this->request_uri($graph_uri);

    // Decode the response and store the values in the object
    $user = json_decode($response);
    $this->id       = $user->id;
    $this->name     = $user->name;
    $this->username = $user->username;
    $this->email    = $user->email;
}

/**
 * Generates HTML markup to display the user's Facebook profile image
 *
 * @return void
 */
protected function load_user_profile_image(  )
{
    $image_path = 'https://graph.facebook.com/' . $this->id
                . '/picture';
    $this->profile_image = '<img src="' . $image_path . '" '
                         . 'alt="' . $this->name . '" />';
}

}
```

First, because Facebook sends back data in JSON-encoded format, the script will throw an Exception if the json extension isn't loaded in PHP.

After that, the RWA_Facebook class is declared to extend RWA_OAuth. Inside, two properties are redeclared—$service_auth_endpoint and $service_token_endpoint—the constructor is redefined, and the two abstract methods from RWA_OAuth are declared.

$service_auth_endpoint and $service_token_endpoint are Facebook-specific, and as such they can be hard-coded into the class.

Other property values—namely, $client_auth_endpoint, $client_id, $client_secret, and, optionally, $scope (if we require more than basic application, which we don't)—are set via the constructor. The endpoint and app credentials are required, throwing an Exception if they're not set, and after that the method checks for scope in the $config array. Then the parent constructor is run to check for login and logout attempts.

Step 4: Create a Facebook Config File

The `RWA_Facebook` class will be loaded on both the app's home page and the app's auth endpoint, so the Facebook configuration details will be abstracted to a separate file. In the `includes` folder, create a new file named `fb_config.inc.php` and put the following inside:

```php
<?php

$fb_config = array(
    'client_id' => '404595786243388',
    'client_secret' => 'da2c599d9662ee744700dbfa483a154e',
    'client_auth_endpoint'
            => 'http://rwa.cptr.us/exercises/05/01/login.php',
    'scope' => 'email',
);
```

This file is extremely simple: it defines an array, stored in `$fb_config`, that will be passed to the constructor of the `RWA_Facebook` class when it is instantiated.

▦ **Note**   Make sure to replace `client_id` and `client_secret` with your app's credentials, because they are domain-specific and *will not work* on domains for which they are not set up.

Step 5: Create the App's Auth Endpoint

Now that all the classes and config files are in place, you can start building the actual pages for the app. Start by creating the file `login.php` in web root. Inside, place the following:

```php
<?php

// Set error reporting to keep the code clean
error_reporting(E_ALL^E_STRICT);
ini_set('display_errors', 1);

// Loads the Facebook class
require_once 'includes/class.rwa_oauth.inc.php';
require_once 'includes/class.rwa_facebook.inc.php';

// Loads the $fb_config array
require_once 'includes/fb_config.inc.php';

$facebook = new RWA_Facebook($fb_config);

// If the user is logged in, send them to the home page
if ($facebook->is_logged_in()) {
```

```php
        header("Location: ./");
        exit;
    }

?>
<!doctype html>
<html lang="en">
    <head>
        <meta charset="utf8" />
        <title>Please Log In</title>
    </head>
    <body>
        <h2>Please Log In</h2>
        <p>
            Before you can use this sweet app, you have to log in.
        </p>
        <p>
            <a href="<?php echo $facebook->get_login_uri(); ?>">
                Log In with Facebook
            </a>
        </p>
    </body>
</html>
```

This file starts by setting error reporting as high as possible to make sure the code is squeaky clean and then includes both OAuth classes and the Facebook config file.

With the necessary files loaded, a new `RWA_Facebook` object is instantiated and stored in `$facebook`. The script then checks if the user is logged in by running the `is_logged_in()` method and redirects to the home page if so.

For a logged-out user, a simple HTML page is displayed asking the user to log in. A login URI is generated using the `get_login_uri()` method.

Step 6: Create the App's Home Page

The last file to create is the app's home page. Create a file called index.php in web root and then add the following code:

```php
<?php

// Set error reporting to keep the code clean
error_reporting(E_ALL^E_STRICT);
ini_set('display_errors', 1);

// Loads the Facebook class
require_once 'includes/class.rwa_oauth.inc.php';
require_once 'includes/class.rwa_facebook.inc.php';

// Loads the $fb_config array
require_once 'includes/fb_config.inc.php';
```

```php
$facebook = new RWA_Facebook($fb_config);

// If the user is not logged in, send them to the login page
if (!$facebook->is_logged_in()) {
    header('Location: login.php');
    exit;
}

?>
<!doctype html>
<html lang="en">
    <head>
        <meta charset="utf8" />
        <title>Logged In!</title>
    </head>
    <body>
        <h2>You're Logged In</h2>
        <p>
            Welcome to our super-sweet app!
        </p>
        <h3>Your Info</h3>
        <ul>
            <li>
                <?php echo $facebook->profile_image; ?>
            </li>
            <li>
                <strong>Name:</strong>
                <?php echo $facebook->name; ?>
            </li>
            <li>
                <strong>Email:</strong>
                <?php echo $facebook->email; ?>
            </li>
            <li>
                <strong>Username:</strong>
                <?php echo $facebook->username; ?>
            </li>
        </ul>
        <p>

            <a href="?logout=1">Log out</a>
        </p>
    </body>
</html>
```

Like login.php, this file starts by turning on error reporting, including necessary files, and instantiating the RWA_Facebook object in $facebook. It checks if the user is logged in and, if not, sends him to the login page.

For a logged-in user, a simple HTML page is displayed with a quick welcome message, their info, and their profile picture, as well as a logout button.

Step 7: Test the App

The app is now ready for testing. Load it in a browser and you should see the login screen (see Figure A-5).

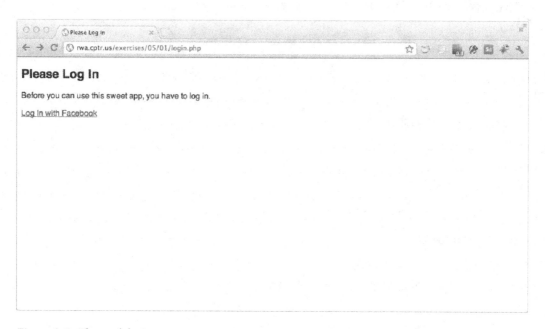

Figure A-5. *The app's login screen*

Click the login button and you'll be taken to Facebook's authorization endpoint, which asks you to confirm that the app is authorized to access your information (see Figure A-6).

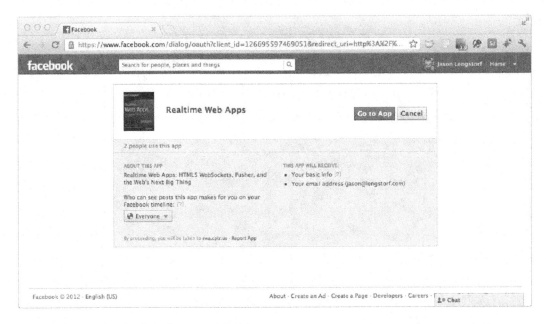

Figure A-6. *The Facebook authorization dialog*

Confirm the authorization by clicking the Go to App button and you will be redirected to your app, where you will see your information on the home page (see Figure A-7).

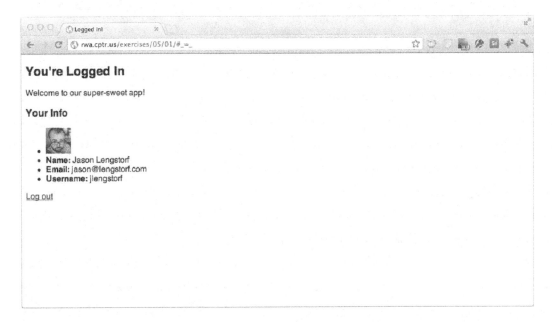

Figure A-7. *After logging in, the app will display a welcome message and your info*

Index

■ C